EXODUS:
A Teacher's Guide

THE MELTON GRADED CURRICULUM SERIES

BIBLE   LEVEL ה   שמות

EXODUS:
A Teacher's Guide

by Ruth Zielenziger

Edited by Marcia Lapidus Kaunfer and Barry W. Holtz

SECOND EDITION

Edited by Miles B. Cohen

Seymour Fox, *Curriculum Supervisor*

The Melton Research Center for Jewish Education
of The Jewish Theological Seminary of America

Copyright © 1994 by The Melton Research Center for Jewish Education
of The Jewish Theological Seminary of America
3080 Broadway, New York, NY 10027

All rights reserved

First edition, 1984

5 4 3 2 1

Manufactured in the United States of America
Design and composition by Bet Sha'ar Press, Inc.

CONTENTS

ACKNOWLEDGMENTS	vii
INTRODUCTION Teaching Bible	ix
UNIT ONE Enslavement Exod. 1:1–6:1	1
UNIT TWO The Ten Plagues Exod. 6:2–11:10	45
UNIT THREE The Exodus Exod. 12:1–15:21	79
UNIT FOUR Revelation at Sinai Exod. 15:22–20:23	115
UNIT FIVE The Book of the Covenant Exod. 21:1–24:18	157
UNIT SIX The Mishkan Exod. 25:1–31:17	203
UNIT SEVEN Rebellion and Reconciliation Exod. 31:18–34:35	253
APPENDIX Understanding the Sinai Revelation Edward L. Greenstein	273

ACKNOWLEDGMENTS

Exodus: A Teacher's Guide largely depends on the scholarship of Professor Moshe Greenberg's *Lessons on Exodus* (Melton Research Center, 1974), a transcription of classes he taught to a group of Melton teachers in the mid-1960s. It also relies on Greenberg's *Understanding Exodus* (Behrman House, 1969). Much of the introduction is based on Professor Fritz Rothschild's essay, "The Concept of God in Jewish Education" (*Genesis: A New Teacher's Guide*, 3rd ed. (Melton Research Center, 1991), pp. 357–378).

We also made extensive use of the fine lesson plans for Exodus developed by Shirley Newman and of unpublished materials by Dr. Leonard Gardner, Dr. Jeffrey Tigay, Nehama Hameiri, and many others. We thank these people for their contributions. We are deeply grateful to Louis Newman, our teacher, who influenced and guided our efforts during his years as Director of the Center.

Dr. Edward L. Greenstein has given us a great deal of time and useful criticism throughout the writing of the book. We thank him and also Dr. Avraham Holtz, who read the manuscript and gave us his very helpful observations.

Our thanks are extended to others who inspired, challenged, and encouraged us: Dr. Seymour Fox, the initiator of the Melton Bible Program; Sylvia Ettenberg, who has always been our staunch supporter; Dr. Elaine Morris, who as Director of the Center supervised the preparation of the first edition; and Dr. Barry Holtz and Dr. Eduardo Rauch, Co-directors of the Center, who gave us of their best.

INTRODUCTION

Teaching Bible

Exodus: A Teacher's Guide has been prepared specifically for teaching a class of twelve- or thirteen-year-olds in an afternoon school. The Melton Research Center's approach to the teaching of Bible can, however, be used for students of all ages, including adults. (With modification it can also be used for students too young to analyze a text.)

Two considerations underlie our approach to teaching Bible. These must be mentioned at the outset:

(a) Do not teach students anything that they will eventually have to *unlearn*. Do not teach false information which will have to be discarded at some later date.

(b) Do not present students with information that they can discover for themselves when directed to the proper texts. Information which is discovered firsthand by the student will be more meaningful and better remembered than information presented by the teacher.

In our experience, the most effective way of learning Bible is through a careful analysis of a text, taught by means of a guided discussion, or *inquiry*.

❐ BIBLICAL INQUIRY: A METHODOLOGY

Students attending a Jewish religious school must, of course, be able to read and know the biblical narrative. Superficial knowledge of the biblical stories, however, is only the first step in teaching a biblical passage. The teacher must next determine what *ideas* can be learned by studying that passage and then decide which of those ideas will be discussed in class.

Biblical inquiry is a method of studying Bible which uses the biblical text itself as data. In conducting an inquiry, one directs questions to specific places in the biblical text, drawing the reader's attention to significant aspects of the text. This inquiry takes place on three different levels:

1. What does the text say?
2. What does the text mean?
3. What does the text mean to me?

1. WHAT DOES THE TEXT SAY?

At this point we are only interested in *objective statements*. Opinions or underlying meanings do not belong at this stage. A teacher may want to ask students to restate the story, explaining difficult words and clarifying possible confusions and misunderstandings. For example: "How are the Israelites to prepare for the Exodus?" (Exodus 11).

A word of warning: Many teachers consider this first level of text analysis too "simple" or "obvious" and thus skip it altogether. However, not all students are careful readers.

Students should have their copies of the biblical text open throughout the inquiry. The goal is to achieve understanding, not memorization.

2. WHAT DOES THE TEXT MEAN?

This level of inquiry is much more difficult than the first. Progress initially may be slow. Textual analysis is a skill which must be learned; once learned, the skill can be applied to other texts as well.

Shadings and Nuances of Words

At first students may feel that there is little difference between one word or expression and the next. A teacher will have to sensitize students to the different shadings and nuances of words and expressions.

For example: When Moses and Aaron first appear before Pharaoh, they declare, "Thus says the Lord, the God of Israel: Let My people go that they may celebrate a festival for Me in the wilderness" (Exod. 5:1). Once Pharaoh turns them down, they retort, "The God of the Hebrews has manifested Himself to us. Let us go, we pray, a distance of three days into the wilderness to sacrifice to the Lord our God, lest He strike us with pestilence or sword" (Exod. 5:3).

With guidance, students will be able to discover that the first address is bold and self-assured, whereas the second is humble and apologetic. This discovery will be strengthened if the teacher explains that the term *Hebrews* when used by foreigners was not complimentary to the Israelites (see pp. 40–41).

Stated vs. Implied Meaning

Many facts are stated explicitly in the text. Others, however, can only be understood indirectly. Although not *stated*, they are *implied*. Students should eventually be able to justify an answer by saying that it is either stated in the text or implied by it.

For example: During the second plague (frogs) Moses promises Pharaoh to remove the frogs whenever Pharaoh wishes him to do so. Pharaoh declares, "Tomorrow." Moses leaves Pharaoh's presence and cries out to the Lord to remove the frogs (Exod. 8:8). Moses has committed God to remove the frogs without first consulting Him. The text does not state explicitly that Moses is desperate and insecure. However, crying out is a desperate form of prayer. It is from these words that we can infer Moses' state of mind.

Questioning

The inquiry is conducted by asking a series of questions that direct the students' attention to various aspects of the text. The teacher must prepare questions that guide the students in a logical manner to discover the meaning of the text. The questions that appear in the "Teaching Procedure" sections of this book should be seen as samples and suggestions, and are not to be followed blindly. The teacher must listen carefully to students' responses and form the next question based on those responses.

"Leading questions" should be avoided since they limit the scope of the student's answer. For example: We find three episodes in which Moses intevenes in behalf of the weak (Exod. 2:11–19). The question "How do we know that Moses was a righteous man?" is a leading question, limiting the discussion to one particular character trait. However, the question "What do these three episodes teach us about Moses?" allows the student to explore various aspects of Moses' motivation.

In a meaningful discussion, a question posed by the teacher should trigger a number of responses from the students. Students should have the opportunity to argue for the plausibility of their replies. All attempts at explanation must be taken seriously. Obviously, many of the questions a teacher asks about the text have been asked before. (The same is true of the science teacher who guides students in experiments with magnetism or electricity.) The fact that students may reach conclusions that others have reached before does not invalidate the experience of discovery that the students have shared.

Not every interpretation of the text is admissible or valid. An interpretation is not acceptable if it violates either the content of the text or the reality of the biblical cultural milieu.

Although the teacher must know in advance what ideas conveyed by the text will be the focus of the lesson, the *process* of inquiry should be open and flexible. Students may give answers that the teacher had not anticipated. If the answer is defensible, based on *textual* evidence, it deserves due credit. Incorrect answers should be rejected.

Teacher and students alike will have to defend their answers with textual evidence, by citing the words or verses that substantiate their opinions. It is a good habit to ask: "Where does the text say this?"

3. WHAT DOES THE TEXT MEAN TO ME?

"What meaning does this text have for my life?" This kind of "freewheeling" discussion generally takes place at the end of a guided inquiry. Since it is not based on text, no evidence from the text is required.

In general the biblical narrative is skeletal. It concentrates on *actions*. We are not told *reasons* for people's actions or their *thoughts* or *feelings*. For example, we do not know what Moses' mother felt as she tucked her baby into the basket and left him in the reeds of the Nile. Nor are we told how the Israelites felt as they sat down to eat the roast lamb on their last night in Goshen, before their departure from Egypt. These details are left for us to flesh out, ponder, question, and speculate about. We are assuming that although the cultural milieu has changed since biblical times, the way in which people act and react in general, has not.

Students should be encouraged to volunteer feelings and opinions. At times the teacher may have to direct the discussion since students may lack the life experience to know how people behave in certain situations. Students should discuss human nature and the possibilities for change in conduct. They should try to identify with the feelings and motivations of the characters. This in itself may prove to be a rewarding educational experience.

❐ THE USE OF COMMENTARIES

One of the tasks of the teacher is to teach students to distinguish between what a text says and what others have said about it. What Rashi or other commentators have said about a text is not admissible

Introduction

at the first stage of study. By quoting Rashi we rely on authority rather than understanding. This deprives students of their own struggle with the text.

Once the students have studied and discussed the meaning of the text, teachers may broaden the range of possible meanings by using commentaries of their choice. Students will be delighted to find out that some of their interpretations had been given by commentators hundreds of years earlier. They will also have the opportunity to defend their own point of view or that of one commentator in the face of an opposing interpretation.

Throughout the ages different commentators interpreted the texts in light of whatever they themselves held true, applying the methods of inquiry that were available to them. For instance, Abraham Ibn Ezra (1089–1164) was acquainted with Arabic philology and linguistics and therefore could utilize these tools in compiling his commentary. Knowledge of these subjects was not available to Rashi (1040–1105), who lived within the same century but in a different locale. In making the text meaningful, each had his own approach to textual interpretation.

There has never been a single, timeless and authoritative understanding of the biblical texts. Each generation has added its own interpretations according to its needs. It is an affirmation of our tradition that in our generation we too interpret the Bible in light of current knowledge and contemporary science, and in accordance with our needs.

❏ *PESHAT* AND *DERASH*

Traditionally Jews have interpreted the Bible according to one of two modes of interpretation (or a combination of the two). One mode is called *peshat* (פְּשָׁט); the other, *derash* (דְּרָשׁ).

PESHAT

We use the term *peshat* to refer to the meaning of a particular text *within its original historical and contextual framework.*

In the *peshat* mode, we study the language of the Bible as it was used in biblical times and not as it may have been used in later or modern Hebrew. For example, although we today use the word *Torah* to describe the Five Books of Moses (the חֻמָּשׁ, or Pentateuch), in the Bible the word means "instruction" (Lev. 14:54: זֹאת הַתּוֹרָה אָדָם כִּי יָמוּת בְּאֹהֶל; Num. 19:14: זֹאת הַתּוֹרָה לְכָל־נֶגַע הַצָּרַעַת).

In the above examples we are given the *torah*—the "instruction" of how to behave when *Tzara'at* or death occur. The word *torah* here obviously could not refer the Five Books of Moses.

The *peshat* mode makes use of the *historical approach,* setting the text in its original cultural environment or milieu. Frequently this is done by comparing the biblical world with other cultures that existed at the same time. For example: Moses is instructed by God to perform signs and wonders before the elders of Israel and before Pharaoh. The performing of signs and wonders by sorcerers was a common practice in ancient Egypt, and therefore would be an effective introduction of Moses and God to both the Israelites and to members of Pharaoh's court.

DERASH

The second traditional mode of interpretation is *derash*. By *derash* we mean interpretation of the text that *disregards the linguistic, historical, and contextual limits of the text.*

For example: The text states that Pharaoh enslaved the Israelites בְּפָרֶךְ, "with hard labor" (Exod. 1:13). Later Midrash, however, teaches that Pharaoh enslaved them בְּפֶה רַךְ, "with flattery and seduction" (literally, "with a soft mouth"). According to this explanation, Pharaoh challenged the Israelites to compete with him to determine who could produce the most bricks. After the competition, Pharaoh demanded that Israelites continue to produce that same number of bricks on a daily basis.

This story ignores the linguistic evidence that בְּפָרֶךְ and בְּפֶה רַךְ have no connection to one another. It further ignores the historical background that makes it entirely unlikely that Pharaoh would demean himself to engage in making bricks. Although this story cannot be be regarded as *peshat,* as *derash* it enriches our reading of the text. We are left with the caution that it is possible to be enslaved by the word as well as by the sword.

When such an explanation is taught, students must understand that these stories are not *peshat*. They are not biblical stories, nor do they fit within the historical, contextual, or linguistic limits of the text. These stories should be understood and valued in their own right, in terms of the message they convey.

Our first concern is with the *peshat* meaning of the text. However, when we ask ourselves, "What does this text mean to us today?" we are not any longer dealing with the *historical* meaning of a text. We are in effect engaged in the process of *derash!* For example, if we explain Gen. 1:26 ("Let us make man in our image . . . they shall rule

... the whole earth") as relating to issues of environmental protection, we can assume that this was not the original meaning of the text. Nonetheless, it may be an explanation of significance to us today.

❐ LITERARY DEVICES

It must be emphasized that when we say *peshat* we do not mean the *literal* meaning of the text. The medium of the Torah is language, and language is not always self-explanatory; it often requires interpretation. Words function on many different levels of meaning. Throughout the generations, our Rabbis were aware of the difference between the obvious, literal meaning, and the underlying or metaphorical meanings of a text.

METAPHOR

There are at least two ways of talking about ideas. One is abstract, the other metaphorical. Some texts use philosophical, abstract language to deal with ideas. But the Bible belongs to the style of literature that uses metaphorical means to express ideas. The word *metaphor* is derived from the Greek *meta* ("beyond") *phore* ("carry"). *Metaphor* means "carry beyond." A metaphor transfers expressions from one area of experience to another. Hence, when we say that God took us out of Egypt "with a strong hand and an outstretched arm" (Deut. 4:23) or that God brought us to Him "on eagles' wings" (Exod. 19:4), we do not conceive of God as actually having a hand, an arm, or eagles' wings.

"My love is a red rose" or "My anger is a burning fire" are obvious metaphors. As we use them, we know that we are borrowing the imagery of the rose and the fire from the physical world in order to express our feelings more concretely. Often, however, we are not even aware of the fact that we are using a metaphor. When I ask, "Do you see my point?" and you answer, "Yes," in a literal sense you are wrong. You do not "see my point" at all, since in reality there is no tangible "point" that you can perceive with your eyes. However, inasmuch as I have been using a metaphor, your answer is correct. A metaphor has a true and real meaning, although not a *literal* one.

The more abstract the ideas, the more metaphorical the language used to depict them must be. For example, when we refer to God by calling him *Adonay* (my Lord) or *melekh* (King), we are borrowing terms from the area of human relationships. A metaphor serves to describe the unfamiliar, ineffable, and indescribable—in this instance, God—in terms of a known model (a lord, master or king). It thus becomes easier for us to deal with something as complex and overwhelming as God. For example, when Moses demands to know God's essence (Exod. 33:17–23) in order to know how to appeal to Him, God says that He will show Moses His back but not His face. We do not conceive of a physical God who has either a back or a face. We read the statement as a metaphor, and we understand it to mean that humans can perceive only some but not all of God's attributes.

Metaphors serve as tools for dealing with the abstract, but they are never *identical* to the idea they help to convey. We can never assume that everything that is true of the metaphor can be transferred to the abstract idea. The metaphor has to be taken seriously and understood to be true to a limited degree, but *it must not be taken literally.*

PARABLE

The Bible also uses parables (from the Greek *paraballein*, "to throw beside," "to compare"). A parable is a short fictional story or narrative from which moral or spiritual truth is drawn.

The parable operates on at least two levels of meaning. One level is "within" the text—the story itself, which can be understood in its own terms. Another level is the meaning "beyond" the text, other meanings that are alluded to by the first. For example, the book of Jonah is a parable. It can stand on its own as a story about a man and a big fish. But the story has other levels of meaning at which certain morals or lessons can be learned.

MYTH

The Bible also contains myths. A myth, in the technical sense that we use it, is an extended metaphor. It is a narrative or story that uses subjects and actions from known experience to express the ideas, relationships, and values that are essential to a particular culture or community. (We are not using the term *myth* in its popular sense of "that which is not true," "a fable" or "illusion.")

In the same way that the metaphor says something true about the object being described (love is like a rose in *some* respects), so a myth reflects some truth about God, mankind, and the world. For example: Whether the story of the Ten Plagues did or did not take place in

Introduction xvii

history is irrelevant to us. The story is a myth that teaches us about the ways in which God reacts to human conduct.

BEGINNING MYTHS

Some myths deal with the beginnings of a people—how that people came to be. These myths are called *beginning myths.* Different peoples have different beginning myths. The particular beginning myth of a people has a great deal of influence on their way of life, ethics and observances. Such myths actually express the concerns and values of the people who tell the story. Studying the beginning myth of a people can tell us much about how that people understood themselves, their world, and their God.

The Jewish people have three beginning myths. The first is the story of the creation of humankind (Genesis 1). The second is the choosing of Abraham to become the father of a great nation (Genesis 12). The third beginning myth is the story of the beginning of Israel as a people, culminating in the covenant of the Israelites with God at Sinai (Exodus 19–20).

❐ WHAT IS THE BIBLE?

SACRED LITERATURE

The Bible is a collection of many *books* (in Greek, *biblia*) that were considered holy by the people Israel. They were therefore preserved and recopied by hand countless times, and passed from one generation to the next. Bible scholars differ over the question of when the Bible was finally assembled in the form we know today. Most scholars believe that the first five books, the Torah, achieved its present form after the Babylonian exile (6th century B.C.E.).

We know that many other books existed that were not preserved. Some of them, such as the Book of Jashar (referred to in Josh. 10:13, 2 Sam. 1:18) and the Book of the Wars of the Lord (Num. 21:14) are mentioned within the Bible itself. The books of the Bible were preserved because the people Israel fervently believed that these books were the inspired words of God, a sacred literature. Accordingly, they took great pains in keeping and preserving them.

ORGANIZATION OF THE BIBLE

The Bible (תַּנַ"ךְ) is divided into three major sections. The Hebrew word תַּנַ"ךְ is made up of the first letter of each of the sections: (1) תּוֹרָה, (2) נְבִיאִים, and (3) כְּתוּבִים.

(1) תּוֹרָה—The Torah, the Five Books of Moses, חָמָשׁ, Pentateuch (from the Greek words meaning "five books"). (See below.)

(2) נְבִיאִים—The Prophets.
(a) Early Prophets: Joshua, Judges, 1 Samuel (called "First Samuel"), 2 Samuel (called "Second Samuel"), 1 Kings (called "First Kings"), and 2 Kings (called "Second Kings").
(b) Late Prophets: the so-called Major Prophets (Isaiah, Jeremiah, and Ezekiel) and twelve so-called Minor Prophets.

(3) כְּתוּבִים—The Writings.
Psalms, Proverbs, Job, the Five Scrolls (Song of Songs, Ruth, Lamentations, Ecclesiastes, Esther), Daniel, Ezra, Nehemiah, 1 Chronicles (called "First Chronicles") and 2 Chronicles (called "Second Chronicles).

The Torah is divided into five books:

(1) בְּרֵאשִׁית—Genesis (Greek, meaning "beginnings")
(2) שְׁמוֹת—Exodus (Greek, meaning "going out")
(3) וַיִּקְרָא—Leviticus (Greek, meaning: "concerning the Levites")
(4) בְּמִדְבַּר—Numbers (in part having to do with the census of the Israelites)
(5) דְּבָרִים—Deuteronomy (Greek: "second law")

The Hebrew name of each book is derived from the first verse of the Hebrew text. When the Torah is read in the synagogue, it is read according to a traditional schedule of weekly *parashiyot* ("sections"). However, when we *study* the Bible, it is customary to refer to chapters (a later division of the text into smaller subdivisions by non-Jewish scholars, which has become standard). To identify a particular text, we shall refer to chapter and verse (never to page number, since pages numbers differ from edition to edition and translation to translation).

As in some other Hebrew books, the number of the chapter appears in Hebrew letters at the beginning of the chapter of the Hebrew text. The first letter of the Hebrew alphabet, א, stands for 1; the second, ב, for 2, and so on, up to 9. י stands for 10, כ for 20, and so on, up to 90. ק stands for 100. Letters are combined to represent other values (e.g., קיט stands for 119).

The verses are numbered throughout the text, either with numerals or Hebrew letters. When we want to write chapter 4, verse 20, we write 4:20. A verse is generally composed of one or more sentences; however, there are verses that contain only part of a sentence, as is the case with lists of names.

☐ THE BOOK OF EXODUS

The second book of the Torah is called Exodus ("going out") and שְׁמוֹת in Hebrew. The Hebrew name is derived from the first words of the book אֵלֶּה שְׁמוֹת בְּנֵי יִשְׂרָאֵל הַבָּאִים מִצְרָיְמָה אֵת־יַעֲקֹב, "These are the names of the sons of Israel who came to Egypt with Jacob."

The book's narrative begins with the death of Joseph and ends with the erection of the mishkan (portable sanctuary) in the second year after the exodus from Egypt.

Chronologically, Exodus comes after the book of Genesis, yet it is not a direct continuation of that book. The opening verses of Exodus do not follow the last verses of Genesis; rather, they bridge the two books by summarizing the genealogy of Gen. 46:8–27. The first few verses (Exod. 1:1–7) take us through a period of hundreds of years, enough time to have the seventy members of Jacob's household proliferate and become a people.

In the book of Genesis God created the world and populated it with people of whom He had certain expectations. However, by giving these people "free will," the power to choose between good and evil, He gave them the ability to defy and disobey Him. God chastised the people time and time again. When immediately after the flood humankind again displeased God by building the Tower of Babel (Gen. 11:1–9), He realized that He could not deal with all of humankind. Instead, He chose Abraham and covenanted Abraham to Himself with the intention of making him an example to all others, so that all the families of the earth would bless themselves by him (Gen. 12:3).

God promised the Patriarchs of Israel (Abraham, Isaac and Jacob) progeny and the possession of the land of Canaan. The book of Exodus relates the partial fulfillment of these promises.

God liberated the Israelites from the yoke of Egypt and started them on the way to the land of their ancestors. In doing so, God revealed to the people His extraordinary powers and made them willing to accept His covenant. This acceptance is the highlight of the narrative. The people pledged themselves at Sinai to live according to God's laws and ordinances thereby becoming a special, distinct people, dedicated to God (Exodus 19). The mishkan would house the cherubim and the ark, God's throne, on which He would descend at will to dwell with His people, to care for them, and to guide them.

Like the stories of the Patriarchs, the story of Exodus is placed within historic times. However, it will not be treated here as a historical document but as a religious one. The aim is not to ascertain the historicity of any part of the story. The aim is instead to ask ourselves what the text is telling us about the relationships between God, man, and nature, and how—by what literary means—this telling is accomplished.

☐ SUGGESTIONS FOR THE TEACHER

Leading an inquiry is much harder than lecturing since the teacher is less in control. Students may swamp the teacher with questions or alternate answers. This may be the first time that they will have been encouraged to probe and doubt. Questions that students ask tend to come in categories (e.g., "Bible versus science," "Bible versus historical fact"). Once you have dealt with one problem in a category, the next problem in that category will go much faster.

Not every lesson will take the form of an inquiry. One may occasionally, for the sake of variety or saving time, present only the conclusions of an inquiry, as long as these are based on evidence from the text and not presented as arbitrary opinion.

If you don't know all the answers, be honest. Do not panic and do not pretend. Ask some students to look up the needed information, or offer to do it yourself. The spirit of inquiry is for the teacher as well as for the student.

In some classes teachers will be able to teach the biblical text in Hebrew; other classes will study the Torah in English translation. We strongly recommend that you use the new Jewish Publication Society (JPS) translation of the Torah (1962 or later). All translations in this *Guide* are from that translation.

Before you start teaching a section, it will be necessary for you to read the text of Exodus, as well as all the material in this *Guide* pertaining to it. "In Preparation for Teaching" consists of background information for the teacher that is essential for the teacher's understanding of the text. "Teaching Procedure" is designed to help the teacher lead a guided inquiry in class. The questions that appear should be seen as samples and suggestions, and are not to be followed blindly. It is not expected that students will come up with the answers provided. Teachers will often have to break a question up into smaller ones. The answers will most of the time be reached by combined efforts of students and teacher.

Although the *Guide* is divided into "lessons," you may find that you may need more or less than one class session to deal with the given material.

We recommend using a tape recorder to record your lessons. Listen to your own tapes. Check the quality of your questions: Are they direct? Are they simple or ambiguous? Do they expand or limit students' thinking? Do you answer your students' questions? Or do you veer off the subject? A tape recorder can be an excellent self-teaching device.

UNIT ONE

Enslavement

Exod. 1:1–6:1

LESSON 1

From a Family to a Nation
Exod. 1:1–7

❐ IN PREPARATION FOR TEACHING

The family of Israel multiplied greatly. From a family they grew to be a nation (Exod. 1: 1–7). With the accession of a new king in Egypt, "who did not know Joseph" (Exod. 1:8), the status of the Israelites was changed and they were forced into slavery.

Students may remember that Genesis foresees a time when Abraham's offspring shall be "strangers in a land not theirs and . . . be enslaved and oppressed for four hundred years, but in the end go free with great wealth" (Gen. 15: 13–14). We have discussed elsewhere* the *moral* reason the Bible gives for the delay of hundreds of years in the fulfillment of the possession of the land of Canaan by Abraham's progeny, "for the iniquity of the Amorites is not yet complete" (Gen. 15:16), yet we do not know why these four hundred years have to be spent in the pain and suffering of slavery. Early biblical historiography does not give a moral reason for each and every calamity** (we are not told why there were famines in the days of Abraham, Isaac and Jacob). Defeats in war and other mishaps are not always seen as retributions for misdeeds. One explanation why the Israelites had to undergo those hardships might be to enable God to exercise His saving power so that eventually Israel would feel obliged to recognize Him and accept His covenant.

The question may arise: Why did not Joseph and his brothers return to Canaan once the famine was over? Biblical evidence seems to indicate that exit from Egypt was always regarded as difficult. In Gen. 46:3–4, God assures Jacob. "Fear not to go down to Egypt. . . . I myself will go down with you to Egypt and I myself will also bring you back." Apparently, Jacob feared that he would be unable to

---

* *Genesis: A New Teacher's Guide*, 3rd ed. (New York: Melton Research Center, 1991), p. 162.

** See Moshe Greenberg, *Understanding Exodus* (Melton and Behrman House, 1969), p. 53.

leave Egypt without God's intervention. Joseph, in spite of his high position, had to ask for permission to bury his father in Canaan (Gen. 50:5) and one cannot but wonder why the text chooses to inform us that "their children, their flocks, and their herds were left [as hostages?] in . . . Goshen" (Gen. 50:8). Also, note Joseph's last will and testament (Gen. 50:24–25), "God will surely take notice of you and bring you up from this land to the land which He promised on oath to Abraham, to Isaac, and to Jacob . . . when God has taken notice of you, you shall carry my bones from here" (Gen. 50:24–25). He, too, considers God's intervention essential.

Bible scholars have varied opinions about the date of the Exodus. In these lessons we shall not deal with the possible historical aspects of the story.

Start the lesson with a summary of the end of the book of Genesis. The events of the past presumably forgiven, Joseph and his brothers have become a united family. The brothers had unwittingly served God's plan (Gen. 15:13–14) to bring Jacob's family to Egypt (although this does not in any way make the brothers' behavior toward Joseph in Genesis 37 more acceptable). Joseph had died, as did all his generation. Their families, however, stayed on in Egypt. In the book of Exodus, we shall find out what happened to them. Some students may tell you what they already know from Bible stories or the Passover celebrations. Now they are going to learn the biblical version of the events.

Acquaint your students with Exodus 1. Your first level of inquiry deals with the factual level ("What does the text say?"). One way of achieving this end is to ask your students to read the whole chapter and divide it into sections providing a rationale for their choices. Another way, probably more suitable for twelve-year-olds, is to read the chapter in small sections, selected by the teacher. Students may be invited to provide a title for each section.

❏ TEACHING PROCEDURE

Read the beginning of Exodus 1 and stop when you think you have come to the end of the first section. Where does this section end?

1:7.

What would you call this section?

(Open.)

Draw attention to 1:1.

Lesson 1 — From a Family to a Nation

Whom does the term "The sons of Israel" (בְּנֵי יִשְׂרָאֵל) refer to in this verse?

1:2–5 indicate that it deals with the immediate family of Jacob, his sons.

Now read 1:7. Whom does the term "Israelites" (בְּנֵי יִשְׂרָאֵל) refer to?

The text here is referring to a multitude of people, a nation.

In seven short verses, Jacob's twelve sons have become a nation.

The name of the section, therefore, could be "from a family to a nation" or something similar.

You may remember that we already had a list of those who came to Egypt with Jacob in Genesis 46. How do these two lists compare?

The list in Genesis is longer. Students will note that this list is abridged, it mentions only Jacob's sons, not their progeny.

Why, if the list was already given in Genesis, is it repeated here?

1:1–5 serve as a bridge between past events in Genesis and the future events which are to occur in Exodus.

What does Exod. 1:6 add to our understanding of the events?

It indicates the passage of time. This story does not pick up where Genesis ended, but many years later.

What change has taken place by 1:7?

The Israelites have become numerous, no longer a family but a people.

Had you expected this growth?

(Open.)

Some may say that it is natural for any people to multiply as the years pass. Draw attention to the repetitions in 1:7. "They were *fertile, prolific,* they *multiplied* and *increased* very greatly so that the land was filled with them." We have learned that repetition in the Bible is a very significant technique used for emphasis. The text seems to be incredulous about the increase. It is not seen by the text as a normal population explosion.

Some students may remember that God had promised the Patriarchs that they would become a great nation. Direct students to the verses below in Genesis.

Gen. 17:2   I will make you *exceedingly numerous*.
Gen. 17:6   I will make you *exceedingly fertile*.
Gen. 18:18 Abraham is to become a great and populous nation.
Gen. 22:17 I will make your descendants *numerous*.
Gen. 26:24 I will *increase* your offspring.
Gen. 28:14 You shall spread out to the West and to the East.

The same vocabulary will appear in Exodus.

Read Exod. 1:12.

"The more they increased and spread out," recalls Gen. 28:14, "You shall spread out."(As you continue to study Exod. 1, you will find more repetitions of the Genesis vocabulary.)

What does the text teach us by repeating the vocabulary used by God in His blessings?

That the fertility of the Israelites is not a "normal" development. The Israelites increased greatly *by God's will*. This is the beginning of the fulfillment of the promises made to the Patriarchs.

Summarize the breakdown of Exod.1:1–7 on the board:

From a Family to a Nation
1. 1:1–5   A Bridge from Genesis
2. 1:6   The Passage of Time
3. 1:7   Israel Has Become a Nation

LESSON 2

A New King in Egypt
Exod. 1:8–14

❏ TEACHING PROCEDURE

Last lesson we studied the first section of Exod. 1 and found that the sons of Israel grew from a family to a nation, fulfilling God's promises to the Patriarchs.

What title or name would you give this section?

> (Open.) Suggestions: "A New King," "Enslavement," "Shrewd Dealings."

1:8 tells us that a new king arose who did not know Joseph. Why does this statement strike us as strange?

> We have learned in Genesis that Joseph saved Egypt from starvation. We also learned (in Gen. 47:13–26) that it was Joseph who instituted a feudal system in Egypt, transferring all the land (except that of the priests) to Pharaoh, thereby enriching him greatly.

Pharaoh must have heard of Joseph. What meanings could the statement "did not know Joseph have?"

> It is possible that the statement means that the new Pharaoh did not *want* to know or remember Joseph nor bear him any gratitude.

What reason could Pharaoh have had to become unfriendly to Joseph's descendants?

> The king noticed that the Israelites were a recognizable, distinct minority and was concerned with their number, "they are much too numerous for us," he told his people.

All through history, whenever a new dynasty of kings arose, they did not necessarily consider the allies of the former dynasty their own allies. On the contrary, new dynasties would annihilate all the relatives and allies of the old dynasty, fearing rebellion. (A new president in the United States chooses his own cabinet.)

What does Pharaoh mean by this statement?

Pharaoh makes his people acutely aware of the potential danger of a large minority, too large to contain. Should a war break out—they might join the enemy forces and take over. (The translation of וְעָלָה מִן הָאָרֶץ is not clear. It could mean "take over" or "emigrate.")

What does Pharaoh suggest?

He suggests that they deal shrewdly with the Israelites.

Let us see what Pharaoh means by his suggesting to deal shrewdly with the Israelites. What is his first shrewd act?

He sets taskmasters over them and makes them build Pithom and Raamses.

Does his plan work? And if not, why not?

It fails because Pharaoh unwittingly is opposing the will of the God of Israel (1:12).

You may have to point out that Pharaoh's plan contains an inner tension or conflict. On the one hand he wants to diminish the strength of the Israelites—on the other he wants to utilize them as a source of cheap labor. (Those in charge of the extermination camp Auschwitz intended to make this a "model camp." They complained that the Jewish prison laborers were too weak to work, and that they would die after only a few weeks of hard labor.)

In 1:13 Pharaoh enters the second stage of his "shrewd dealings." How does this differ from the first stage?

It seems that the work in 1:13–14 is harder labor than that of the first stage.

Does Pharaoh's second stage of shrewd dealings succeed? And if not, how do you know that it does not?

Because he initiates a third stage. Had it succeeded, this would not have been necessary. The text does not spell out the result of the second stage.

What is the third stage?

(Have students explain in their own words.)

The midwives are told to kill the baby boys on the birthstool, as the babies are being born. Baby girls are permitted to live. The mothers are to believe their babies were stillborn.

Why do the midwives disobey the king?

They revere God.

What excuse did the midwives give Pharaoh?

They pretended that the Israelite women, who were indeed strong (as Egyptian pictures of Asiatic women indicate), had their babies on their own, before the arrival of the midwives and thus they could not kill the babies surreptitiously.

1:20–21 are not an integral part of this story. We are told that God rewarded the midwives and gave them children (households) in return for their courage.

Did the midwives deserve their reward? And if so, why?

Yes, because the midwives revered God more than they feared the king, although the punishment meted out by a ruler or by a government is more imminent.

The motif of a king or queen being outsmarted by a "mere" woman is a popular one in many cultures.

Give a name to this section.

Possible names would be "the midwives" or "the secret edict."

Why did Pharaoh try to kill the baby boys secretly?

Maybe he was afraid of a revolt among the Hebrews. He might have been afraid of adverse public opinion among his own people.

Why was Pharaoh's decree directed against boys only?

Possibly because only boys were potential soldiers.

It is not clear who these midwives were. Traditionally there are disagreements about whether they were Hebrew or Egyptian. Grammatically, the term מְיַלְּדֹת הָעִבְרִיּוֹת could mean two things: (a) midwives who are Hebrew, or (b) midwives to the Hebrews (הַמְיַלְּדוֹת אֶת הָעִבְרִיּוֹת, as the Greek translation implies).

What do you think they were, Hebrew or Eygptian? Everyone can have an opinion. We don't have to agree or come to a decision.

(Open.) Possible reasons:

Midwives were Israelites	**Midwives were Egyptians**
They revered God. We assume Egyptians did not.	They were rewarded for revering God. Israelites would be expected to revere God.
Egyptian women would not serve the slave women.	Pharaoh would not trust Israelite midwives.
Israelite mothers would not trust Egyptians.	Pharaoh commanded *all* his people to kill the baby boys. We may assume that the midwives were some of his own people.
	God made the midwives fertile. Israelites were already fertile.

LESSON 3

Birth and Survival
Exod. 2:1–10

◻ IN PREPARATION FOR TEACHING

Exodus 2 begins with the birth of Moses and the miracle of his survival. Like Isaac, Jacob and Joseph, he too is a "miracle baby."

Although later on we shall learn that Moses' parents already had a son and daughter when Moses was born, the text places the birth of Moses immediately after the marriage of the parents. This telescoping of events seems to point out that although many newborn babies must have been drowned in the waters of the Nile, Moses and his survival indicate the failure of Pharaoh's fourth stage of oppression.

Some students may be bothered by the mention that Moses was beautiful. Would his mother have cared for him less had he not been good looking? "Looks" are often described in the Bible when they add to the understanding of the story. Looks are all one knows about a newborn. Character is still unknown. The detail about the looks of Moses facilitates the readers' participation in the mother's plight and may explain Pharaoh's daughter's willingness to aid in the saving of his life.

Pharaoh's daughter knows that the child is a Hebrew. Hebrew babies looked different from Egyptian ones. In addition, no mother would abandon a beautiful baby unless she had to.

Miriam's suggestion to find a Hebrew wet nurse stands to reason. Many Hebrew mothers had lost their babies. We are told that Pharaoh's daughter called the boy "Moshe" saying כִּי מִן הַמַּיִם מְשִׁיתִהוּ. Ironically the name means "the one who draws out." Thus the name Moshe is prophetic: Moses will draw the Israelites out of Egypt. The text seems to ignore the fact that Moses is an Egyptian name. According to our story Pharaoh's daughter spoke Hebrew!

❐ TEACHING PROCEDURE

We have seen three stages of oppression. Which verse describes the fourth and final stage?

1:22.

What was that final stage?

The drowning of the Hebrew baby boys. Having failed three times, Pharaoh commanded all Egyptians to drown the Hebrew baby boys in the Nile, but permit the baby girls to live.

At this point the teacher might summarize the class discussion by having the class fill in a chart of the four stages of oppression. For example:

	Verses	Decree	Result
Stage 1			
Stage 2			
Stage 3			
Stage 4			

Is there any progression in the severity of the "decrees."

The decrees become more and more severe.

Note that so far we have not yet read of the result of stage four.

The first section of this chapter is 2:1–10. What title could you give it?

The birth and childhood of Moses.

In Exodus 1 we read the four decrees of Pharaoh. After each of the first three decrees we learned that none of the decrees succeeded.

What was the fourth decree?

Every boy that is born you shall throw into the Nile, but let every girl live.

What is the result of that decree?

Lesson 3 — Birth and Survival

The birth of Moses and his survival.

Now let's look at 2:1-4, the birth of Moses. What happened?

(Students summarize the events in the text.)

Why was it easier to hide a newborn boy than an older baby?

(Open.) Suggestions: A newborn is not as vocal as an older boy. He may be mistaken for a baby girl.

Why are we told of his beauty?

Looks are all one knows about a newborn. Character is still unknown. This detail about Moses' looks makes Moses' mother's plight all the harder and may explain Pharaoh's daughter's willingness to aid in the saving of the baby's life.

What did the mother do?

She made a wicker basket and put the baby in it and put it in the reeds on the banks of the Nile. She placed his sister nearby.

What did she think might happen to the baby?

(Open.)

The Hebrew word for "wicker basket" in which Moses' mother hid him is תֵּיבָה. Where in Genesis did we hear of a תֵּיבָה—but a bigger one—and someone being saved in it?

In the story of the Flood. The word תֵּיבָה is translated there as "ark."

In what way do these two תֵּיבוֹת resemble one another?

Both are meant to save lives, both contain no rudder, in both cases God is the "captain."

In what way do they differ?

Noah's תֵּיבָה was large and made of gopher wood. Moses' תֵּיבָה was very small and made of reeds.

What did happen to the baby?

The baby was found by Pharaoh's daughter who came down to bathe in the Nile surrounded by her maids and slave girls.

What did Pharaoh's daughter know about the baby?

That he was a Hebrew: "This must be a Hebrew child." (2:6)

How did she know that the baby was a Hebrew?

Hebrew babies looked different from Egyptian ones. In addition, no mother would abandon a beautiful baby unless she had to.

What does Miriam suggest to the princess?

That she, Miriam, get a wet nurse to nurse the baby.

What decision is Miriam pushing the princess to make?

To adopt the baby.

Why did Pharaoh's daughter need a wet nurse?

In those days before "baby formulas" a wet nurse was a must, in the absence of a mother.

Did the daughter of Pharaoh know Miriam was an interested party? Did she know she was giving the baby to his own mother to nurse?

We do not know. (Open discussion.)

What tells us that, no matter what the baby's past, Pharaoh's daughter now considers him to be hers?

She says: "Nurse it for me, and I shall pay you wages."

When the baby is weaned (which may be at age three or four as was the custom in the past), he is brought to Pharaoh's daughter who makes him her own and calls him Moses.

You might end the discussion with this speculative question:

It is clear that Pharaoh's daughter considers Moses to be her child and that he grows up in the palace. Pharaoh must have known that Moses was a Hebrew. Why did Pharaoh permit his daughter to harbor the Hebrew child?

(Open.)

The text does not provide an answer. The midrash, however, does.* The Rabbis tell the following story:

> One day the king was dangling Moses on his knees, when the boy lifted the crown from the king's head and placed it on his own. The king was perturbed. Was this a childish act, or an omen for the future? He decided to test the child's intelligence: if dullwitted, he may as well continue to delight his daughter; if, however, he proved to be bright, he would have to die. The king placed a pile of gold on one side of the table and a pile of burning embers on the other. The child was to choose. Moses, being intelligent, of course stretched his hand out toward the pile of gold, but God sent down the angel

---

* For an explanation of the term *midrash*, see pp. xv–xvi.

Lesson 3 — Birth and Survival 15

Gabriel, who pushed Moses' hand into the burning embers. The midrash continues to tell us that Moses placed his burned hand into his mouth, burned his tongue, and stammered ever after.

Make sure your students know that the story is a midrash, not part of the text.

Who are the heroes of the story?

The first heroes are Shifrah and Puah, the two midwives who defy Pharaoh. Next comes the mother of the baby, then the baby's sister, Miriam, and Pharaoh's own daughter.

What do these five have in common?

They are all women.

What is ironic about this?

Pharaoh does not fear women. The female children were allowed to survive. And yet it was the women who were his undoing!

LESSON 4A

The Character of Moses
Exod. 2:11–22

❏ IN PREPARATION FOR TEACHING

The second half of Exodus 2 focuses narrowly on three episodes in Moses' life. From an examination of these three episodes we learn what kind of person Moses is and what motivates him to act. We find that he cannot stand by uninvolved when injustice is taking place. The three episodes build on one another to make this point (see discussion). Have students examine Moses' character based on these three episodes. Clarify it by making a chart on the blackboard. The operative question is: What do we learn about Moses' character from these three events?

The last three verses telescope a long span of time and set the stage for future action: The king died and a new one took his place.

Oppressed people look forward to a change in the power structure. The people cried out to the Lord and their cry was heard. God remembered his covenant with the Patriarchs. (In the Bible "remembering" means "deciding to act." See, for example, Gen. 8:1, "God remembered Noah.") The last paragraph ties God's decision to act in behalf of his people to the man Moses. The reader senses that God will have to find a way to return Moses to Egypt and involve him in the deliverance of His people.

❏ TEACHING PROCEDURE

In the last lesson we read of the birth of Moses and how he came to live in Pharaoh's palace. Now we read of Moses in action as a young man.

Read 2:11–22 to yourself. Divide it into three separate events, and give a title to each.

(Open.) Suggestions:

1. 2:11–12   The Killing of the Egyptian
2. 2:13–15   Two Hebrews Fighting
3. 2:16–22   Moses Rescues the Midianite Women

1. THE KILLING OF THE EGYPTIAN (2:11-12)

What did Moses do?

He went out to his kinsfolk and witnessed their toil.

What does the word kinsfolk seem to indicate?

That Moses identified with the Hebrews, knew he was one of them.

How might he have found out that he was a Hebrew?

(Open.) His mother told him. Pharaoh's daughter told him. The maids and servants present when he was found told him.

Treat this delicately—some of your students may be adopted.

As we continue our reading, we shall find evidence that the Hebrew slaves too know his identity.

What specifically did Moses do?

a. He saw the Egyptian beating a Hebrew.
b. He turned this way and that to see if he was observed.
c. He struck down the Egyptian.

What reason does the text give for the Egyptian beating a Hebrew?

No reason is given.

Can you suggest any possible reasons?

(Open.) It is possible that this was an Egyptian taskmaster who was displeased by the slave's performance.

Was the killing a deliberate act, or had Moses lost his temper?

The text seems to indicate deliberation. Had Moses lost his temper, he might have struck the Egyptian first and *then* looked around to see if he had been observed.

The text in no way judges Moses for having killed the Egyptian, although the Egyptian had beaten but not killed the Hebrew.

Why do you think Moses went so far as to kill the Egyptian? What if he had only beaten him?

It is likely that he could not have just beaten the Egyptian (short of killing him) any more than a Jew could have beaten a guard in a German concentration camp, since the guard would have taken a terrible revenge.

To sum up this first event in Moses' life at the palace: Moses killed the Egyptian in an act of defending the weaker, one of his own, which may be seen in the same light as self-defense. Yet, as we shall see, by this act of homicide, Moses was to remove himself from the scene of action and had it not been for God, Moses' usefulness to his brothers would have come to an end.

2. TWO HEBREWS FIGHTING (2:13–15)

As in the first episode, here, too, we do not know what caused the fighting.

Can you suggest some reason for the fighting?

(Open.)

Later we shall learn that the Egyptian taskmasters appointed Hebrew foremen (Exod. 5:14). Perhaps this was a foreman who was beating a slave in the line of duty. Do not supply this answer now.

How does the second episode differ from the first one?

In the first episode Moses protected one of his own from a foreigner. In this episode both men are Hebrews.

What makes Moses intervene?

Moses does not seem able to stand by when injustice is being done.

What did the Hebrew slave say to Moses? (Read the Hebrew text of this verse aloud, emphasizing the repetitions of the ש and ר sounds.

"Who made you chief and ruler over us? Do you mean to kill me as you killed the Egyptian?" מִי שָׂמְךָ לְאִישׁ שַׂר וְשֹׁפֵט עָלֵינוּ? הַלְהָרְגֵנִי אַתָּה אֹמֵר כַּאֲשֶׁר הָרַגְתָּ אֶת־הַמִּצְרִי? (2:14).

No Hebrew slave would speak to an Egyptian prince in such a manner! What must the slave have known about Moses?

That he was a Hebrew.

How did the Hebrew slave feel toward Moses?

Angry and resentful.

Why did he resent Moses?

Lesson 4A — The Character of Moses

(Open.) Maybe because Moses was a Hebrew but lived the life of a prince.

What else does the Hebrew seem to know about Moses?

That he killed an Egyptian.

Considering that Moses made sure nobody was around when he saved the slave from the Egyptian, how did this Hebrew know what Moses did?

(Open.) Possibly the villain in the second episode is the same man Moses had saved in the first episode.

It is possible that the Hebrew in the first episode had exposed Moses by telling what Moses had done.

Once he knew that word was out, Moses became frightened. Was his fear justified?

Yes, Pharaoh wants to kill him. (2:15)

What do we learn from this about Moses' position in the palace?

His position was not secure.

What did Moses do once he saw that his life was in danger?

Moses escaped across the border to Midian.

Where in Midian did he go?

He went to the well, like other travelers before him (the servants of Abraham and Jacob).

3. MOSES RESCUES THE MIDIANITE WOMEN (2:16–22)

What are the daughters of the priest of Midian trying to do?

Draw water from the well to water their flocks.

What problem do they have?

Shepherds come and drive them off and use the water for their own sheep.

How do we know this is a recurring situation?

The father is surprised that the daughters have returned home so early. (2:18)

Who is the only person who stepped in to help them?

Moses.

What nationality do the women believe Moses to be?

Egyptian. (2:19)

Why might they have thought he was Egyptian?

His dress, his speech.

Now that we've seen Moses in three separate episodes, what can we learn about him? What similar motive for action moves him in all three stories?

In each case he rights the wrong. Moses is unable to observe injustice without trying to stop it. He gets himself involved.

From these three stories we learn how strong Moses' sense of justice was. In the first story, his intervention might be explained as his desire to protect his own kin from foreigners.

In the second story, the motive of protecting his own against a foreigner is missing. Since both men are Hebrews, one might think that Moses' interest is only with the Hebrews.

In the third case, however, Moses is a disinterested party. Midianite men mistreat Midianite women, yet Moses gets involved on behalf of the downtrodden.

Moses' concern is that justice be done, no matter who the parties are.

We had noted that all heroes in this story were women. Who is the first male hero?

Moses.

How was Moses different from other Israelite men?

(Open.) He was not a slave. He grew up in the palace. He experienced freedom, and observed leadership and power. Perhaps his spirit was not broken as those of his brothers were.

LESSON 4B

The Death of Pharaoh
Exod. 2:23–25

☐ TEACHING PROCEDURE

Exod. 2:23–25 makes us aware of the passing of time. How?

"A long time after that . . ."
"The King died."
The groaning, moaning, and crying out seem to have been going on for some time.

What change is to occur now?

God is to take an active role.

God has not been mentioned until this time (except in connection with the midwives' reward). How many times is he mentioned here?

Five times:
"Their cry for help . . . rose to God." (2:23)
"God heard." (2:24)
"God remembered His covenant." (2:24)
"God looked upon the Israelites." (2:25)
"God took notice." (2:25)

What does this unusual emphasis on God seem to indicate?

That God is going to act on behalf of the people. The fact that three stories about Moses are followed by a passage describing God's decision to take action seems to indicate that Moses will be involved in whatever actions God will take.

The following discussion is optional.

We noted that the Bible does not criticize Moses for killing the Egyptian in defense of the Hebrew. How would the story have differed had Moses not killed the Egyptian?

(Open.)

Could he have helped his brothers by his position in the palace?

(Open.)

Would he sooner or later have run afoul of the king anyway?

(Open.) Probably, since he was unable to tolerate injustice.

After a while people get used to injustice, treating it as if it is unavoidable and just a fact of life. For instance, thousands and thousands of men and women in this country are homeless. They sleep in the streets or in bus and train terminals, and they carry their property around in paper bags. Few people are concerned enough to try to do anything about it.

Would Moses, had he stayed on in the palace, become callous to the plight of his people? Would he possibly have gotten used to the situation?

(Open.)

LESSON 5

The Burning Bush
Exod. 3:1–6

☐ IN PREPARATION FOR TEACHING

In Midian Moses has become a shepherd. Foraging with his sheep for grass near Mount Horeb, his attention is caught as "an angel of God" appears to him in a blazing fire out of a bush. He gazes "and there was a bush all aflame yet the bush was not consumed" (3:2).

Students may inquire about the nature of the fire: was it real? Did the sheep see it? How come the bush was not consumed?

At the burning bush the life of Moses was to take a new turn: He will be compelled by God, very much against his own wishes, to become God's messenger to the people of Israel, their leader and prophet.

The encounter with God is an overpowering experience. Never will his life be the same again! This is a highly subjective emotionally charged encounter, and it is therefore expressed in extraordinary terms. Were we, the teachers, to explain the phenomenon of the burning bush in "realistic" or "scientific" terms, we would be countering the intention of the text, destroying its meaning.

Remind your class that the Bible uses metaphors. Fire is one of the many metaphors the Bible uses for God's heralds. A burning torch passed between the pieces in Genesis 15, and fire and smoke will be present at the revelation at Sinai. Fire is not God, but it symbolizes God's presence. Fire is, in some ways, like God—it is beneficial. It warms us and cooks our food; in ancient times it served to protect humans from wild beasts. Yet it has to be handled with care. Fire can burn with consuming fury. Fire purifies and illuminates. It can be seen, yet it has no form. It is real, yet has no substance. One may approach it but never come too close!

Instead of posing the question: What did actually happen at the bush? Ask why the fire metaphor is used here, and in what way the life of Moses is to be changed by the burning bush episode.

We shall see that Moses is reluctant to accept God's mission, but God's will shall prevail.

☐ TEACHING PROCEDURE

We have already noted two stages in the life of Moses:

1. He lived in a palace, as a prince.

2. He became a fugitive.

Assuming that one's life experiences prepare one for the role one is to play, how might these two phases of his life have prepared Moses for leadership?

(Open.) Some suggested answers:

1. Life in the palace:
   a. taught him to value freedom.
   b. taught him about power and leadership.
   c. made him more rebellious than his brothers, the slaves, were.

2. Life as a fugitive:
   a. taught him humility.
   b. taught him that one's life can change in an instant.
   c. taught him to fend for himself.

In Exodus 3 we will find Moses a shepherd. What is the life of the shepherd like?

Remind your students of the hardships of a shepherd's life that Jacob mentioned in Gen. 31:38–40. Shepherds wander from one place to another, in search of water and grazing land. They may stay away from home for weeks or months at a time, without shelter from the heat of summer and the cold of winter. They have to protect the flocks from marauders and wild beasts, nurse the sick animals, go after the strays and return them. Theirs is a hard and lonely existence.

What character traits does it take to be a good shepherd?

Compassion, determination, courage and integrity are but some of them.

Abraham, Isaac and Jacob were shepherds, as was David, the ideal king. The Bible uses the metaphor of the shepherd for the leader,

Lesson 5 — The Burning Bush

even for God! "The Lord is my shepherd," says the Psalmist (Psalm 23). The וּנְתַנֶּה תֹּקֶף prayer, which we read on the High Holy Days, also uses the shepherd motif to describe God.

Read 3:1–6. In his wanderings after grazing land, Moses arrives at Horeb, "the dry mountain" (also called Sinai). Which words tell us, the readers, that something exceptional is going to happen here?

We, the readers, are told that this is "The mountain of God." We are prepared for the exceptional.

Does Moses expect something exceptional? And if not, how do you know that?

No. He approaches the bush wondering why it is burning but is not consumed.

Was Moses frightened by the sight?

No, it seems that he was curious.

Do you think the fire was a small one or a big roaring one?

Probably a small one. Had it been a big, roaring fire, Moses would have been frightened.

Can you think of a reason why God may not want to frighten Moses?

God manifests Himself in many different ways. At Sinai He will appear amidst thunder and lightning on a trembling mountain. Here, however, God considers Moses' frailty. He is led gently, permitted to express doubts and trepidations.

Notice that the text does not distinguish between God, the angel and the fire. All three seem interchangeable.

Fire is often used as a metaphor for God. Why?

It's beneficial but also dangerous. It can be seen, but does not have a constant form. It cannot be touched or held.

When does Moses experience fear for the first time?

When God identifies Himself: "I am the God of your father, the God of Abraham, the God of Isaac and the God of Jacob" (3:6).

All ancient people believed that it was fatal to encounter God.

How does God introduce Himself?

As the God of Moses' own father, the one Moses knows and recognizes.

Why does He introduce Himself as an intimate, known God?

It is less threatening to Moses.

Next God informs Moses that He is also the God of Abraham, Isaac and Jacob. What might Moses know about the God of the Patriarchs?

That throughout the book of Genesis God had made promises to the Patriarchs: promises of covenant, of people hood and land!

What might be God's purpose in refering to Himself as the God of the Patriarchs?

Moses will remember the promises and understand that the time of fulfillment is at hand.

LESSON 6

Encounter with God
Exod. 3:7–4:17

❐ IN PREPARATION FOR TEACHING

The encounter between God and Moses may be seen as a "dialog of negotiations." A detailed explanation of this dialog for the teacher follows:

1. God declared His purpose; namely, to rescue Israel through Moses (3:7–10).

2. Moses' first difficulty: He considers himself inadequate for the task. "Who am I that I shall go?" he asks (3:11). Moses is a humble man.

3. God promises, "I will be with you" (3:12). It is of no importance who you are. The task is not yours alone, it is also mine. God gives Moses a "sign": on their way to Canaan the people shall worship at the mountain. The sign, however, will come about after the exodus so that in essence the sign does not give Moses the support he is seeking.

4. Moses' second difficulty: he is ignorant of God's name (3:13).

If Moses started by questioning who he himself was, he now turns to God and asks, "Who are you?" Unless the people know God's name, they cannot be expected to deliver their fates into His hands. When passing on information we inspire confidence by quoting a reliable source.

5. God was known to the Patriarchs by various names: Elohim, El Roi, or El Elyon, as well as by the Tetragrammaton (the four-letter name of God). It must be assumed that in the manner of ancient religions, originally different aspects of the divinity were alluded to by the different names. By what name are the people of Israel to evoke God's name during prayer and worship?

Students may remember that the angel who wrestled with Jacob (Gen. 32:25–33) refused to reveal his name. God *does* reveal his name to Moses; it is, however, a name that does not define and limit God (as other names do): אֶהְיֶה אֲשֶׁר אֶהְיֶה (*Eheyeh Asher Eheyeh*, "I shall be what I shall be"). God declares that He is not to be limited by a definite name. The people shall know about God as His nature unfolds in human history. They shall know about God by what He does."

The people of Israel already know some of God's attributes. They know Him as the God who made promises to the Patriarchs. However, they have not yet experienced God's saving powers. These they shall learn about throughout the book of Exodus.

What is the name אָהְיֶה? God is talking about Himself, in the first person, "I will be" (3:15). When *we* talk about God, we use the third person, "He shall be"* (3:15).

Moses is to tell the elders that *Eheyeh* sent him.

6. Moses' third difficulty: The people will not believe him (4:1). How could he prove that God had sent him?

7. Accordingly, God enables Moses to present three signs as evidence that he is indeed God's messenger: leprosy, a serpent, and blood (4:6–9).

In biblical times people did not differentiate between "natural" and "supernatural" events. The Pharaohs employed magicians at their court. They performed magic and produced signs of the kind Moses was now to produce. The ability to produce signs which others could *not* produce, was considered as evidence of God's power. If Moses could "out perform" Pharaoh's magicians the divine authority of the God of Moses would be established. The fact that the signs themselves are loathsome and fear-evoking would serve to depict God Himself as awesome and fear-evoking. Initially both Israel and Egypt would have to learn to fear God!

As in other cases we have studied, here too the historiocity of the story is not what we are interested in. We do not ask if Moses did indeed produce the signs or not. Instead, we read the story and ask ourselves: Why is the story here? What does it come to teach us? In this case the story comes to teach us that God will indeed support Moses, and that His powers are greater and more awe-inspiring than the powers of all the gods of Egypt.

8. Moses' fourth difficulty: He is not an orator (4:10). Moses realizes that negotiations will have to take place, yet he is painfully aware of the fact that he is not eloquent, he is neither a polished speaker nor an orator. Your students are no doubt aware of the

---

* The verb "to be" in biblical Hebrew is expressed by two roots, the more common היה and the less common הוה. The name אהיה uses the more familiar root, היה, while God's personal name, the Tetragrammaton, uses the more distinctive root, הוה. We have similar variations with the Hebrew name of Eve (חוָּה). We would expect her name, explained as meaning "life giver" (אֵם כָּל־חָי), to be חַיָּה, derived from the root חיה. Instead, her name is derived from the root חוה.

power of "advertising" and "presentation." None of us is immune to the lures of television jingles and announcements. What do your students drink or eat for breakfast?. What jeans or sneakers do they ask their parents to buy? Much of what we think we want or need depends not on the intrinsic value of the object but on smooth salesmanship.

Moses considers it of vital importance that the case be presented to Pharaoh by an eloquent speaker.

9. God answers Moses (4:11): "I will be with you as you speak." He will instruct Moses on the spot in what he is to say. God could have chosen an orator to do His bidding, but He did not. It is God and not Moses who is going to make things happen.

10. God has tied up all of Moses' "loop holes." Exasperated, Moses asks God to send someone else. He seems to lack the faith to realize that God would stand by him no matter what (4:13).

11. As Moses continues to refuse to act on God's behalf, God's anger is aroused (4:14). Yet even now, aware of Moses' human frailty, he meets him halfway. His brother Aaron will speak for him. Yet it will not be Aaron's fluidity of speech, but God's word mediated through Moses that will free the Israelites from their Egyptian bondage (4:15–16).

In 3:20, God tells Moses that when the Israelites finally leave they will "borrow" silver and gold from the Egyptians. Your students may find this "borrowing" of money with no intention of returning it offensive. Remind them that the Hebrews were slaves for hundreds of years. They worked hard and received no remuneration. Now was their chance to get some compensation for their hard labor. The Bible considers this "borrowing" as a partial restitution for the Israelites and a well-deserved punishment for the Egyptians.

❏ TEACHING PROCEDURE

Read 3:7–4:17 with your students. Then let them reread it for themselves. Discuss the details of this dialog. When this discussion is completed, have the students complete a worksheet like the one on p. 33.

Now we are going to read a long dialog between God and Moses. Let's first read through the entire dialog with one student reading God's words, and another student reading Moses'. As we read, try to pay attention to each objection Moses raises to God's plan, and also note how God attempts to reassure Moses.

After the reading is completed, discuss it section by section.

1. (3:7–10) What information does God give Moses here?

God tells Moses that He cares for His people. He makes Moses aware of His plan to rescue them—and tells Moses what his part in that plan is.

2. (3:11) What is Moses' first reaction?

"Who am I that I should go?"

3. (3:12) How does God reassure Moses?

Moses, you may not think you are important enough for this task, but it does not matter who you are, since I, God, will be with you.

What sign does God give Moses?

That on their way to Canaan the Israelites will worship God at this very place where God is now speaking to Moses.

Why doesn't this sign give Moses enough confidence?

Because the sign—worshipping at Horeb, Sinai—will take place only later, after the Exodus.

4. (3:13) Moses is not reassured. What is the next problem he raises?

The Israelites will want to know God's name.

Unless the people know God's name they cannot be expected to deliver their fates into His hands. (When we pass on an order or instructions from a third party, we inspire confidence through being able to quote a reliable source: "The President has announced" or "The Rabbi told me!")

5. (3:14–22) God tells Moses his name. By what names did the Patriarchs know God until now (3:15)?

Elohim; El Shaddai; El Ro'i; El Elyon; the four-letter name of God.

Different names of God probably refer to different aspects of God. But the special name that God now tells Moses does not limit God to just one certain aspect. "Ehyeh Asher Ehyeh" means "I shall be what I shall be." "You shall learn about me as my nature will unfold in human history. You shall learn about me by what I do." Until now the Israelites knew God only as the one who made promises to Abraham, Isaac and Jacob. Now they will experience God's saving powers. They will learn that God fulfills His promises (3:16–22). God

Lesson 6 — Encounter with God

then tells Moses exactly what He will do to save the Israelites and what Moses' part will be in the coming events.

6. (4:1) Does the telling of his special name reassure Moses?

No.

What does Moses fear?

That the Israelites will not believe that God had spoken to him. He needs proof.

7. (4:2-9) What "proofs" does God give Moses?

Three signs: a serpent (4:2–5), leprosy (4:6–8), and blood (4:9).

According to God, what will be the effect on the Israelites of seeing these signs?

They will believe that God really did appear to Moses, and that he is truly God's messenger.

In biblical times people considered the ability to produce signs which others could not produce as proof of God's support. These signs will prove to the people that God will support Moses, and that God's powers are greater and more awe inspiring than the powers of all the gods of Egypt.

8. (4:10) Moses is still worried that he will not be effective in dealing with Pharaoh. He knows negotiations will have to take place. What worries him?

He is worried since he is not an orator.

We can understand Moses' hesitation. He knows he is not a good speaker. We know that often it's not what a person says, but how he says it that convinces his audience. Can you think of any examples of this?

Television ads, other salesmanship gimmicks. Presidents are made by television.

9. (4:11-12) How does God reassure Moses about his speaking ability?

God states that it is He and not Moses who is going to make things happen.

10. (4:13) What is Moses' final objection?

He gives no further concrete reason, but begs God to send someone else. He seems to lack the confidence that he will be able to carry out his mission.

11. (4:14–17) How does God react to Moses' final objection?

He is angry but agrees to have Aaron speak on behalf of Moses.

Sum up this discussion by asking:

What have we learned about God from the way he has dealt with Moses in this dialog?

God's plan is set, but He responds to Moses' human frailties. He is reassuring and patient.

As a final exercise, students can summarize the entire dialog by completing a worksheet like the one on p. 33.

The Negotiation between God and Moses

In Exod. 3:7–4:17 God and Moses speak to one another.
Each time God speaks, Moses raises a problem.
Complete the following summary of the negotiation:

1. (3:7–10) God explains His purpose. He tells Moses to go to Pharaoh.

2. (3:11) Moses says that _____
   _____.

3. (3:12) God reassures Moses, telling him that _____
   _____.

4. (3:13) Moses now says that the Israelites _____
   _____.

5. (3:14–15) God reveals His _____.

6. (4:1) Moses says that the Israelites might not _____.

7. (4:2–9) God gives Moses three _____.
   They are _____
   _____
   _____.

8. (4:10) Moses complains, saying that he _____
   _____.

9. (4:11–12) God says that He will _____
   _____.

10. (4:13) Moses begs God to _____.

11. (4:14–17) God becomes angry with _____.
    Then God says that _____ will speak for Moses.

LESSON 7A

Moses in Midian
Exod. 4:18–23

❏ IN PREPARATION FOR TEACHING

Moses is told by God that he will not easily succeed at the task he has been given. God will stiffen Pharaoh's heart and make him stubborn. There is also a foreshadowing of the last plague—the death of the first born. Your students may consider God's "hardening" or "stiffening" Pharaoh's heart a moral problem. It is not fair to punish Pharaoh if he does not have the ability to repent and change his ways. If possible, postpone this discussion until you read the plagues story and discover that only at the sixth plague (inflammation) does God intervene and render Pharaoh unable to repent.

Students have been led to believe that "one can always repent," "it is never too late." Neither the Bible nor our modern day justice system backs this assumption up. In the Bible we find occasions when God manipulates people. He makes sure that people *cannot* repent but have to suffer the full measure of their deserved punishment. Thus God says to Isaiah (Isa. 6:10):

Dull that people's [the Israelite's] mind	הַשְׁמֵן לֵב הָעָם הַזֶּה
stop its ears	וְאָזְנָיו הַכְבֵּד
and seal its eyes	וְעֵינָיו הָשַׁע
lest, seeing with its eyes	פֶּן יִרְאֶה בְעֵינָיו
and hearing with its ears	וּבְאָזְנָיו יִשְׁמָע
it also grasp with its mind	וּלְבָבוֹ יָבִין
and repent and save itself.	וָשָׁב וְרָפָא לוֹ.

There comes a time in the life of a person or a people when repentance is no longer possible: full punishment has to be meted out. For instance, a mass murderer cannot tell the judge, "I'm sorry, and I won't do it again," and expect to be exonerated. It is important to realize that Pharaoh and the Egyptians well deserve their punishment for the hardships and tortures they inflicted upon the Israelites and for the murder of innocent Hebrew babies. By God's punishment of Pharaoh, Israel will learn of His saving powers and will eventually be obliged to enter into a covenant with Him.

❏ TEACHING PROCEDURE

Read 4:18–21. What reason does Moses give his father-in-law for wanting to return to Egypt?

"Let me go back to my kinsmen in Egypt and see how they are faring."

Why does he not tell the truth?

(Open.) Suggestions: Perhaps he is too modest and humble, or he doesn't want to appear ridiculous.

What new information does Moses receive now?

"The men who sought to kill you are dead." (4:19)
(We, the readers, were already informed of the death of Pharaoh who sought Moses' life in Exod. 2:23.)

How does this information change his plans? (Check 4:20.)

It is possible that the decision to take his family along was based on knowing that he was relatively safe in Egypt.

Read 4:21–23. Initially (4:2–9) Moses was to perform the signs in the presence of the elders. What new use for the signs does God reveal?

He is to perform the signs before Pharaoh so that Pharaoh might allow the Israelites to go.

According to God's prediction, what will it take to convince Pharaoh to let the Israelites go?

It will take the killing of the Egyptian firstborn sons.

Your students who already know the Passover story may be able to tell you that the slaying of the firstborn is the last of the ten plagues. Moses, and we too, are told that neither leprosy, serpents, or blood will be sufficient to teach Pharaoh to fear God—by the death of his own firstborn will he have to learn of God's powers.

God reveals to Moses that his task will be difficult and that Pharaoh will not let the Israelites go. Why does God give Moses this discouraging information even before Moses has started?

This knowledge should serve to save him from disappointment. He is forewarned that Pharaoh will not be easily persuaded.

LESSON 7B

The Night Encounter
Exod. 4:24–26

❐ IN PREPARATION FOR TEACHING

This is a nightmarish, disturbing story. Why should God attack Moses and his family as they are returning to Egypt as God had commanded Moses to do? What had he done wrong? Bible scholars do not all agree on who the victim of God's attack/assault is. It is commonly assumed that it is Moses, but it could also have been his son. Zippora seized a flint knife (stone) and circumcised her son. She then touched the prepuce to the genitals of either Moses or that of his son ("feet" is a polite word for genitals in the Bible), bringing immediate relief.

It is possible that this is an ancient story, going back to a time before circumcision had become the sign of the covenant between God and His people. It is possible that once upon a time circumcision was considered apotropaic (meant to ward off evil). It might have been understood as a means for averting disaster. Some scholars see in this story an indicator of the fact that God has also dark and dreadful sides. There are things about God which we fail to understand. It is possible that this story prepares us for all the seemingly unfair and immoral things God will do in the future, like killing all the innocent Egyptian firstborn babies, and all the cattle in Egypt.

You may want to read the story as one would read a strange fairy tale. Or you might decide to skip it altogether. Leaving it out will not interrupt the story line.

❐ TEACHING PROCEDURE

If you decide to teach this section, read it to your students and deal with the plot of the story. Let them express their wonder about the meaning of it.

Lesson 7B — The Night Encounter

Who attacked Moses?

God. (4:24)

What exactly did Zippora do?

She circumcised her son and touched Moses' legs (or perhaps the son's) with the foreskin.

What was the result of her act?

It kept God from killing Moses.

How does Zippora know how to save Moses?

We do not know.

This story may reflect an ancient rite that people used to enact in times of danger.

Why did God attack Moses?

We do not know.

Here are some possibilities:

1. It is possible that this is God's way of teaching Moses that His ways indeed do not always seem fair and logical.

2. We have learned that Moses will have to be instrumental in acts of violence. He will be instrumental in God's slaying of the Egyptian firstborn. It is possible that Moses has to became aware of the meaning of death before he metes it out to others. You may want to give an example: Some time ago, a group of judges voluntarily spent several days in jail. They thought that since it is their task to sentence felons to varying length of prison terms they should experience prison life firsthand. (Can any of us *really* conceive of what a five-year prison sentence means? Twenty-four hours a day in a cell?)

3. Blood is apotropaic (it wards off evil). When we learn about the tenth plague we shall learn that the Israelites will put blood on their doorposts to prevent death. Here the blood of the circumcision may serve the same purpose.

What does this story teach us about God?

(Open.) Suggestions: God does not make sense; He seems unfair; He is "unpredictable."

You might even want to refer back to some of the conclusions you came to about God when you dealt with the God as fire metaphor. Some of the aspects of God you talked about then may fit in here.

LESSON 7C

Back in Egypt
Exod. 4:27–31

❐ TEACHING PROCEDURE

The meeting between Moses and Aaron (4:27) is expected since in Exod. 4:14 Moses was told, "There is your brother Aaron. . . . Even now he is setting out to meet you."

Does this meeting help to encourage Moses?

It should.

How?

If one of God's promises comes true, the rest should follow.

Moses performs the signs in the sight of the elders. What is the effect?

The elders believe that Moses is the messenger of an awe-inspiring God. They bow low to him in homage.

Which of the objections that Moses had raised to God in Exodus 3 and 4 has now been resolved?

What if the Israelites don't believe me? (Exod. 4:1)

What does Moses feel at this point (after the positive reaction of the elders)? Compare the way he feels now with the way he felt in the midst of God's dialogue with him (Exodus 3–4.)

(Open discussion.)

Use this as a culminating question for this session. Remind your students that Moses has been through a great deal since his objection to God's task. He has made the decision to return to Egypt. He has encountered a near fatal attack on the way. He has faced the Israelite elders and they have accepted his message.

LESSON 8

The First Encounter with Pharaoh
Exod. 5:1–6:1

◻ IN PREPARATION FOR TEACHING

In Exodus 5 we encounter a reversal of the preceding verses (Exod. 4:27–31).

Bolstered by the previous success, Moses and Aaron now demand of Pharaoh that he heed the words of the God of Israel and let the people go and worship God in the Wilderness. It is important to remember that Pharaoh had the status of a god in Egypt and that the Hebrew word עֲבוֹדָה means both work and worship. Thus Moses and Aaron are actually demanding from Pharaoh that he let the slaves replace him with their God.

Furiously Pharaoh declares that he does not recognize their God! Pharaoh increases the slaves' work burden. They in despair turn against Moses, who turns against God, complaining, "Why did you send me?"

Moses had become a leader and prophet. An important part of his task is to protect the people and plead for them to God. He is the spokesman of the people. Now that he realizes that he had actually harmed them by his interventions, he is wondering if God's plan is indeed working. The students already learned in Genesis (Gen. 14:13 and 39:14) that the term "Hebrew" was used by non-Israelites in reference to Israelites and was not a complimentary one. Explain that such terms of identity mean different things to different people at different times. Nowadays there are non-Jews in the United States who call Jews by the term "Hebrews," believing that the word "Jew" is derogatory. We Jews, of course, do not feel this way. By the same token there was a time when black people wanted to be called "colored people" but then they preferred to be called "Blacks." Today the accepted term is African American.

Moses, sensing Pharaoh's anger, now uses the term "Hebrews" which the Egyptians used when referring to the Israelites.

A question may be raised: Why was Moses to present his request to Pharaoh pretending that all the people wanted was to worship

God for three days in the desert and then return to Egypt. If in reality, the plan was to leave Egypt forever, why was Moses to use deception? Discuss. Some possible answers: In any negotiation one has to discuss issues which can be resolved. When one demands the "impossible," negotiations cannot even begin. As we shall see, Pharaoh will not consider freeing the people of Israel even for three days in order to worship in the desert. Had Moses asked that the king free the people altogether, the king would most certainly have turned Moses down. Also, Israel's position was weak. They could hardly approach Pharaoh with *demands*. Moses had to use diplomacy or deception.

People in biblical times viewed deception somewhat differently from the way we do. Throughout the Bible we find the weaker deceiving the stronger, and being applauded for "getting away with it." For example, Michal, daughter of Saul, deceived her father when she put *terafim* in David's bed and allowed him to escape (1 Sam. 19:11–17). Also, Ehud, son of Gera, killed the Ammonite king using deception and he is considered a popular folk hero (Judg. 3:15–26).

❑ TEACHING PROCEDURE

Reread 4:29–31. How did Moses feel after his success with the elders?

Confident.

(5:1) Encouraged by their acceptance by the elders, Moses and Aaron confront Pharaoh. What do they say?

"Thus says the Lord God of Israel: Let My people go that they may celebrate a festival for Me in the wilderness."

What is their tone?

Confident, demanding.

(5:2) What is Pharaoh's reaction?

Pharaoh, livid with anger, declares that he does not recognize the Lord, nor will he heed Him and let the slaves worship Him in the wilderness.

(5:3) Moses, taken aback, immediately changes his tone. Compare 5:3 to 5:1. What differences in tone do you see?

(See sample worksheet, p. 41.)

Moses and Aaron Change Their Tone

When Moses and Aaron first spoke to Pharaoh (Exod. 5:1) their tone was full of confidence: they demanded that Pharaoh let the Israelites go. After Pharaoh's reaction (Exod 5:2), their tone changed (Exod. 5:3).

Exod. 5:1

1. Thus says the Lord, the God of Israel:
2. Let my people go
3. that they may celebrate a festival for Me in the wilderness.

Exod. 5:3

1. The God of the Hebrews has manifested Himself to us.
2. Let us go, we pray,
3. distance of three days into the wilderness to sacrifice to the Lord our God,
4. lest He strike us with pestilence or sword.

List any differences you find that indicate a change in tone or attitude. You should be able to find *at least three*.

(Remember that the term "Hebrew," when used by non-Israelites in reference to Israelites, was not a complimentary term.)

1. _____
2. _____
3. _____
4. _____
5. _____

1. Moses now refers to "the God of the Hebrews," instead of the Lord, God of Israel. (The term "Hebrew," when used by non-Israelites in reference to Israelites, was not a complimentary term.

2. "Let us go, we pray" is a request, a plea. (In 5:1 it was a demand.)

3. In 5:3 Moses claims that should they *not* go the Lord might strike them with pestilence or sword (no mention of *having* to go in 5:1).

4. Moses now limits the distance they would venture into the wilderness to a distance of three days. This can be understood as three days going and three days returning, and maybe three days of celebration. (In 5:1 no mention is made of a limit of time or distance.)

5. In 5:1 Moses and Aaron quote God directly to Pharaoh. In 5:3 they merely say He has appeared to them and because of this they feel they must go.

In general what is the difference in tone?

In 5:1 they were confident and demanding.
In 5:3 they are subservient, make excuses, almost begging.

At this point you may want to get into the issue of Moses' asking for a trip of three days' distance when he really intends to take the Israelites out of Egypt for good.

Is Moses sincere in his request? Does he actually intend to return? If not why does he pretend? Is such a ruse morally permissible?

These questions have no answers in the text You may find the discussion of deception on p. 40 helpful.

(5:4–5) What is Pharaoh's reaction to Moses and Aaron's plea?

Pharaoh is not moved by Moses and Aaron's plea. "The people of the land [the Israelites] are already too numerous," he says, "and you would have them cease from their labor!"

What further decree did Pharaoh make in his anger?

You shall no longer provide the people with straw . . . but the same quota of bricks as before will be made (5:4)

What excuse did Pharaoh make for this decree?

Pharaoh told Moses that the people were grumbling because they had too much time on their hands.

To whom did Pharaoh issue this command?

To the taskmasters and the foremen.

(5:6–19) At this point discuss the organization of the Egyptian work force. List the following on the board: Pharaoh, slaves, foremen, taskmasters.

Arrange these in order from highest rank to lowest rank:

Pharaoh, taskmasters, foremen, slaves.

Which of the four groups were Israelites?

Foremen and slaves.

What happened when the Israelites didn't complete the quota of bricks?

The Israelite foremen were beaten.

Why?

Pharaoh had appointed Egyptian taskmasters and these in turn chose some of the Israelite slaves and elevated them to foremen. The task of the foremen was to see to it that the slaves produced their allotted work quota. When the slaves failed to produce, the foremen were punished by the taskmasters.

Explain the precarious position of the Israelite foremen.

The anger and hatred of the slaves were directed against the Israelite foremen, their direct and immediate tormentors. The foremen were very much aware of their tenuous position: should they fail, they wound soon be reduced to slavery themselves. Naturally they were eager to please their masters. (Your students may know that in the German concentration camps the Nazis too, employed Jewish "kapos" (or "foremen") who were directly responsible for the prisoners and the running of the camps.)

To whom did the Israelite foremen come with their complaints?

The foremen came to Pharaoh to explain why they had failed but Pharaoh would not listen to them.

(5:17–18) What was Pharaoh's response?

You are shirkers. No straw.

(5:19–23) Whom did the foremen meet as they were leaving Pharaoh's presence?

They met Moses and Aaron.

(5:21) The foremen vented their anger on Moses and Aaron. What did the foremen actually say to Moses?

"May the Lord look upon you and punish you for making us loathsome to Pharaoh and his courtiers—putting a sword in their hand to slay us."

In what sense are they right?

Life *had* become harder for the Israelites.

What do they fail to realize?

That one often has to suffer before a situation is changed or mended.

Freedom does not come easily. There is often a price to pay. The United States had to engage in war to obtain it and so did the State of Israel in 1948.

Was Moses angry with the foremen?

Moses, understanding their position, was not angry with them.

What was Moses' mood after this encounter?

Moses despaired. He had failed all along the line. Pharaoh in his arrogance had failed to recognize God. The Israelites who had initially accepted Moses and Aaron, rejected them with the first difficulty. They were not ready or willing to suffer for their freedom.

Moses and Aaron were confident at the end of Exodus 4. In this chapter they suffered a complete reversal. It seems that everybody concerned has to learn a great deal about God. Pharaoh has to learn to recognize Him. The Israelites and Moses too have to learn that God's powers have no limits.

UNIT TWO

The Ten Plagues
Exod. 6:2–11:10

LESSON 1A

God Encourages Moses
Exod. 6:2–13

❐ IN PREPARATION FOR TEACHING

The events of Exodus 5 psychologically overshadowed those of the "burning bush" episode. Whatever confidence Moses might have gained was eroded by Pharaoh's refusal to recognize His authority. The people of Israel had rejected Moses and Aaron as messengers who had come in His name. Moses himself had accused God of impotence and blamed Him for failing.

6:2–13 deals with the tie between God's name and His essence, and the Israelites' experiencing God's essence: an active redeeming God, who fulfills his covenant. The students will need some guidance in establishing this fact.

Some may remark that the explicit name of the Lord (the tetragrammaton) had been used in the book of Genesis and is not new to Exodus. This is true. God, however, had no occasion to display all His facets in Genesis. The people did not yet *experience* the many meanings of His name. Also, the events in Genesis had receded into the past. The people did not think that God was still aware of them and of their plight.

❐ TEACHING PROCEDURE

By the end of Exodus 5, whatever confidence Moses had gained through God's revelation at the burning bush was lost. The Israelites had turned on Moses and Aaron, and Moses had accused God of failing His people. Now God addressed Moses again.

Read 6:2–8. What phrase is repeated three times?

I am the Lord. (6:2, 6, 8)

The Hebrew word translated as "the Lord" is the four-letter name that God had revealed to Moses at the burning bush.

By what name, according to the text, had the Patriarchs known Him?
By the name El-Shaddai.

What, according to the text, had God done for the Patriarchs?
He had made a covenant with them to give them the land of Canaan sometime in the future.

When, according to 6:5, will the promise be fulfilled?
The time is close at hand. "I have remembered my covenant"—remembering means taking action.

According to 6:5, up to this point God had not made himself known to Abraham, Isaac and Jacob by His four-letter name יְ־הֹ־וָ־ה. 6:7 elaborates on God's name by telling us what God will do in the near future.

Read 6:6–8. What will God do now?
1. "I will free you." (6:6)
2. "I will deliver you." (6:6)
3. "I will redeem you with outstretched arms and through extraordinary chastisement." (6:6)
4. "I will take you to be my people." (6:7)
5. "I shall be your God." (6:7)
6. "I will bring you to the Land I swore to give to Abraham, Isaac and Jacob." (6:8)

What will the people know by these actions?
That He is Adonai (יְ־הֹ־וָ־ה).

Just as people know one another by observing what they do, so shall the people know the Lord as the one who saves and redeems (by experience). To emphasize this point you may want to use the following example (or think of a similar one):

We learn about God, or for that matter about people, by watching what they do and how they act. The longer we know people, the better we know them. Let's imagine: a little village in the United States, several hundred miles west of Chicago. A new family has moved into the area, somebody notes that they bear a Jewish name. There are no other Jews in the area. Most inhabitants are apprehensive: what are Jews like? Are they going to be different from the other, "normal," people of the village? What kind of neighbors will they make? You can tell your students how the village discovers what Jews are like or—you can have your students make up the story.

The people knew, of course, that the Jews will not join the church. Somebody says that Jews have long noses and dark hair and eyes. Dan and Sarah, the family's young children, don't have long noses. Dan's hair is dark but Sarah's is light brown—so much for that!

Dan puts a "beanie" on his head before lunch but Sarah does not. Soon the kids know that Jewish males cover their heads when they eat but females usually do not. They also notice that Dan and Sarah stay out of school quite often in the early fall because of Jewish holidays. Eventually they will learn that Dan and Sarah do not celebrate Christmas or Easter. The mother seems to be very interested in the ingredients on the packages of food she purchases. She never buys meat or foods that contain meat by-products in the store. Are Jews vegetarians? One day a truck pulls to the curb and unloads a big cardboard box marked "Kosher Meat" and "Chicago." Stephen checks on the word *kosher* in the encyclopedia and finds that Jews keep a complex kitchen. They avoid certain meats and fish and separate between meat and dairy dishes.

You may want to continue the story in this vein. Nancy and Richard find out about the life of the family and the objects they keep—the *mezuzah*, the *kiddush* cup and *havdalah* candle—the festive meal and the *zemirot*. They envy Dan and Sarah for the warmth of their family life and are sorry for them for some of the limitations Judaism enforces. Dietary laws, Sabbath, the study of Hebrew. The village is aware of the fact that the family takes part in civic affairs. They willingly contribute their time and money to worthy affairs. They care about learning and books. You can go on with the story (but do not spend more than half an hour on it).

What you want to emphasize is that one can learn about others (or even about God) by observations and experience. Make sure your students understand that from observing one family one cannot learn everything there is to learn about Jews. Our family here is a family of practicing Jews, but not all Jews practice the same way. Some Jews are kinder, smarter, neater than others. The village learned some things, but not everything about Jews by watching the family.

The story in Exodus will teach us some things about God—namely, about His love for His people Israel and about His saving powers. Many aspects of God, however, will remain unknown and often puzzling.

Does the knowledge of God's essence restore Moses' confidence? (6:9)

We do not know for sure, but he has enough confidence to bring the message to the Israelites.

Why were the Israelites not convinced by Moses?

Their spirits were crushed by the slavery.

(6:10–11) What were God's next instructions to Moses?

To go to Pharaoh and tell him to let Israel go!

(6:12) What is Moses' reaction?

He is still dejected. He appealed to the Lord saying "The Israelites would not listen to me. How then should Pharaoh heed me, a man of impeded speech?!"

What section does this bring to mind, and what does it tell us of Moses' mood?

Moses' objections at the burning bush. Clearly the second rejection by the Israelites has undermined Moses' confidence. (4:10)

Moses had several changes of mood. When did he feel most confident?

In 4:31, after his first meeting with the Israelites.

When did he feel least confident?

After the foremen accused him of making the life of the Israelites harder, and right here (6:12).

Think about all the people involved—Moses, Aaron, the Israelites, the Egyptians. Has any of them come to "know the Lord," that is, to feel His redeeming powers?

None. Moses and Aaron feel rejected. The burden of the Israelites has increased. Pharaoh has not been impressed.

LESSON 1B

The Genealogy
Exod. 6:14–30

❏ IN PREPARATION FOR TEACHING

The story comes to a halt with the introduction of the genealogy of Moses and Aaron. This passage is bracketed by 6:13: "So the Lord spoke to Moses and Aaron in regard to the Israelites and Pharaoh King of Egypt, instructing them to deliver the Israelites from the land of Egypt," and 6:26–27: "It is the same Aaron and Moses to whom the Lord said: Bring forth the Israelites from Egyptians. These are the same Moses and Aaron."

These verses come to tell us of the importance of these two men. The text pinpoints Levi, the ancestor of Moses and Aaron as the third son of Jacob (born after Reuben and Simeon). Some of the people named in the genealogy of Levi will play a role in the future life of the people of Israel.

We learn here that the parents of Moses and Aaron were Amram and Jochebed, and we learn the names of Aaron's wife and progeny. We already know about the wife and sons of Moses. This section should be read and briefly explained.

❏ TEACHING PROCEDURE

A quick reading and a few questions will suffice.

What does this section add to our knowledge of Moses and Aaron?

They are very important men, whose ancestry can be traced back to Abraham. It gives them official "accreditation."

What is unusual about the placement of this genealogy?

It comes long after we have already met Moses and his family. Because of the dramatic story of Moses in the Nile, following Pharaoh's decrees, no genealogy was given there.

LESSON 2

The Signs
Exod. 7:1–13

❏ IN PREPARATION FOR TEACHING

The Lord continues to reassure Moses. Aaron will serve Moses as an intermediary to Pharaoh. Just as Moses (the prophet) mediates between God and Pharaoh, so will Aaron mediate between Moses and Pharaoh. God repeats that He will harden Pharaoh's heart and He explains why: "That I may multiply my signs and marvels . . . I will lay my hands upon Egypt and deliver my people . . . with extraordinary chastisement . . . *and the Egyptians shall know that I am the Lord.*"

We have already learned that the Israelites will "know God" through their experience of Him.

The Egyptian experience will differ from that of the Israelites. They shall learn of His power and His ability to mete out punishment. Pharaoh, who denied God, will have to learn that there is a power greater than his own.

Moses and Aaron perform the signs in the sight of Pharaoh and his courtiers in order to establish that they are indeed the messengers of God. The magicians, too, are able to produce "signs," yet God's signs are greater than those of the magicians.

Some ancient cultures depended more than others on "magic" and "signs." Pharaoh had professional "magicians" at court who used rites and incantations: "spells" (Exod. 7:11) as the Bible calls them.

The Bible does not doubt the effectiveness of "spells" (the witch of Ein Dor (I Sam. 28) does produce the ghost of Samuel), but forbids their use. Witches were not tolerated in Israel (Exod. 22:17).

We find "magic" in many children's stories: Alladin rubs the magic lamp to have the genie appear. Anyone who possesses the lamp can rub it with the same result. In the story of Ali Baba *anybody* who knows the incantation "Open Sesame" can open the stone wall.

The Bible, however, attributes all miracles to God, Moses and Aaron will never become magicians. They will be able to produce signs and plagues only by God's direct order and by His consent.

Lesson 2 — The Signs

The Bible, in this story, chooses tools familiar to the Egyptians and likely to impress them most.

☐ TEACHING PROCEDURE

Remember that Moses and Aaron have already appeared before Pharaoh. What was the result?

They had been rebuffed. (Exod. 5:1–5)

How did Moses and Aaron react to Pharaoh's rejection?

They had lost confidence. (Exod. 6:12, 30)

How did the Israelites react?

They were angry at Moses and Aaron (Exod. 5:21) and impatient because they were overworked.

How did Pharaoh react?

He was angry at the Israelites and at Moses and Aaron. He had called the Israelites shirkers. (Exod. 5:17)

Read 7:1–2. According to God's instructions to Moses, between which two figures will the confrontation take place?

The confrontation is between God and Pharaoh. Moses is to represent God. He will use Aaron as his spokesman. Therefore it is Aaron who will confront the king.

Read 7:3–4. What is God's prediction of what will happen?

Pharaoh will not listen, God will harden his heart and deliver the Israelites by means of special chastisements (punishments) of the Egyptians.

Why does God warn Moses in advance?

We've seen Him do this before (4:21, 6:1). Perhaps God warns Moses so that he will not be surprised and discouraged.

Read 7:5. What is the purpose of this performance?

To let the Egyptians know that "I am the Lord"—to teach them. It is a learning experience.

We have already learned that the Israelites will "know that I the Lord am your God" through experiencing His saving powers (6:7).

Read 7:8–13. What sign is Moses and Aaron to use to prove that they are messengers of God?

The rod turning into a serpent.

When had Moses and Aaron used this sign before? Why?

When they first approached the elders, in order to convince them that Moses and Aaron were God's agents. (Exod. 4:30–31)

What causes the rod to change into a serpent?

God's direct order and consent.

What changes the magician's rod into serpents?

Magic spells.

What should the fact that Aaron's serpent swallowed those of the magicians have proved to Pharaoh?

That Aaron represented a power far greater than the power of Pharaoh's and his magicians.

Why do you think God chose to prove his power by changing the rod to a serpent?

God chose what was familiar to the Egyptians and therefore most likely to impress them.

Read 7:13. What was Pharaoh's reaction?

Pharaoh stiffened his heart even though God had shown that Moses and Aaron were truly His representatives. He had greater power than Pharaoh. Pharaoh did not obey God's command, issued through Moses and Aaron, to let the Israelites go.

Pharaoh could have recognized and obeyed God at this time, but he didn't. This was, in a sense, a test for Pharaoh. Since Pharaoh did not learn of God's power from this experience, he will have to experience further demonstrations of God's power: the plagues. Summarize this point by asking for a title for this section that shows the purpose of the section (e.g., "Testing Pharaoh," "Pharaoh Misses the Opportunity to Learn of God's Power").

LESSON 3

Blood, Frogs, and Lice
Exod. 7:14–8:15

❏ TEACHING THE PLAGUES: AN OVERVIEW

Your students have been exposed to the story of the Ten Plagues before. They have been told the story of the Exodus from Egypt in connection with the Passover holiday. They have recited the names of the plagues while dipping their fingers in wine during the celebration of the seder. When they were younger they may not have questioned the miracles of the plagues. Now, however, at age eleven or twelve they may find the story problematic: What did actually happen in Egypt? Did the plagues really occur? And if so, what caused them to be?

Traditionally, teachers have answered these questions in two different ways: the fundamentalist approach and the scientific approach. Each has signficant drawbacks.

THE FUNDAMENTALIST APPROACH

Using the fundamentalist approach, the teacher usually will say that whenever God wants miracles to happen, they will happen. The problem with this answer is that the students are given a message: one may not question the biblical text when it refers to God and His deeds. According to this view, if the students find this difficult to accept, they must keep their doubts to themselves.

THE SCIENTIFIC APPROACH

A teacher using the scientific approach might say that the plagues did indeed occur. However, they were not miracles but natural occurrences. The teacher will explain the plagues in terms of our modern concept of "cause and effect." For instance, a tidal wave or an earthquake caused strange phenomena in nature. Some will explain the turning of the Nile's water into blood as an effect of algae that at times make the Nile's water appear red as blood. Plagues such as frogs, lice, locusts, and hail will be explained in terms of natural phenomena that strike the area periodically. Most teachers will be stumped by the last plague, the death of the "firstborn" and will admit that this last one may have indeed been a miracle.

The problem with this kind of interpretation is that it *contradicts the thrust of the biblical narrative*. The Bible views these events as extraordinary feats, ones that cannot be explained as natural phenomena. The text itself makes the scientific explanation of the plagues untenable. For example, regarding the plague of darkness we read:

> The Lord said to Moses, "Hold out your arm toward the sky that there may be darkness upon the land of Egypt, a darkness that can be touched." Moses held out his arm toward the sky and thick darkness descended upon all the land of Egypt for three days. No one could get up from where he was, but all the Israelites enjoyed light in their dwellings." (Exod. 10:22–24)

The Bible takes great pains in telling us that this was *not* an ordinary event. A teacher who explains the darkness as merely a solar eclipse has negated the very message of the text.

The Bible does not differentiate the "supernatural" from the "natural." According to the Bible, every event in nature is directly caused by God. God makes the sun rise and set each day. These events may be quite ordinary, but they are still acts of God. God can also do *extraordinary* things to the sun. God can stop the sun in its path (Josh. 10:12–13) or, as here, make it disappear. The darkness in our story occurs at a time set by God, and it is brought about by a symbolic gesture performed by Moses. (This is biblical "cause and effect.") It is an extraordinary darkness, one that can be touched, and it lasts for three full days. Moreover, it is a local phenomenon: in Goshen, where the Israelites dwelled, daylight prevailed.

But if we rule out both the fundamentalist and the scientific interpretations of the plagues, how then are we to teach the story of the plagues?

THE PLAGUES AS SACRED HISTORY

We do not know what actually happened in Egypt before the Israelites left. Historians are of no help, since no Egyptian sources about the events exist and no other documents dealing with the Exodus have ever been found. The Bible is highly subjective. It does not tell us what happened in a historical sense, but rather how events were perceived and understood by our people. The story is emotionally laden with the feelings and perceptions of those who experienced the great miracle of gaining their freedom after years of cruel oppression, and with the emotions of their children and children's children who were told the story and who repeated it from one generation to the next. Those who departed from Egypt knew that God in His great love for them had performed extraordinary feats in freeing them from slavery. This act of redemption will in turn oblige the people of Israel to covenant themselves to Him at Mount Sinai in an everlasting bond.

The story, then, is not objective history but what may be called "sacred history." It is a subjective, poetic expression of awe and gratitude to God. The story as it appears in the Torah is the result of generations of Israelites telling and retelling and embellishing the perceptions of those who participated in the exodus from Egypt.

This approach eliminates the drawbacks of the approaches discussed previously. First, unlike the fundamentalist approach, the reader is not bound by the literal meaning of the text, which is frequently untenable to the modern mind. Second, unlike the scientific approach, it enhances rather than contradicts the intent of the Torah, namely, to attribute the redemption from Egyptian slavery to the extraordinary powers of God.

WHY TEN PLAGUES?

Why, if God is so powerful, did it take God *ten* plagues to free His people? Do not ten plagues indicate nine failures? Would not one longlasting plague that devastated the land have been more inidcative of God's power?

At the onset of the plagues, we meet a Pharaoh who does not recognize God. We meet a people who retreat at the first obstacle that they encounter, and a Moses who is doubtful of his own powers and those of God. The plagues will serve as a learning experience. Everybody will have to learn—Pharaoh, Egypt, Israel, and Moses.

We shall see that the the succession of plagues is not mere repetition but a progression. At first, it is Aaron who will bring forth the plagues. He opposes the magicians who perform on Pharaoh's behalf. In the early plagues the magicians seem to be able to reproduce the feats Aaron performs, but soon their powers wane until eventually they themselves are inflicted with the plague and fade from the scene.

At this point, Moses will take over from Aaron, having gained confidence in God and in himself by witnessing the first plagues. He will directly confront Pharaoh, who in turn slowly but surely will come to fear and recognize the God of Israel, whose existence he had denied.

The Egyptians watch their land being devastated and learn to fear God.

The people of Israel watch and learn the power of God and His special concern for them. This will serve as a learning experience not only for the generation of the Exodus but for all generations to come.

◻ IN PREPARATION FOR TEACHING

Students may inquire if the plagues really happened? Remind them that the Bible is not to be read as if it were a book of history but rather as a religious document. The biblical text is not a photograph of reality but the product of the enthusiastic retelling of events by those who experienced them and those who passed them on.

To make this clearer to students, remind your class of an event you all experienced together. Suppose you went on a class trip to a museum. Ask students to jot down what about that trip impressed them most. You will get diverse answers. Some students were most impressed by one or another of the exhibits. Some students might have been most impressed by the bus ride, an accident they witnessed, or the soda they had in the drug store. Our impressions and memories are selective. How we view a city like Philadelphia or New York may be colored by our specific experiences in that city. Did I have fun? Did I make new friends? Was the sun shining? Or did I lose my wallet on the bus and not know anybody to lend me money for a telephone call?

The story of the exodus from Egypt is similarly colored by the experiences of those who were there. The exodus from Egypt meant more to the Israelites than to the Egyptians. The Egyptians had many groups of slaves; the Israelites were one among many. The loss of their services meant less to Egypt than redemption and freedom meant to the Israelites. That explains why this story is so central to our lives, while apparently remaining undocumented in the annals of Egypt.

The plague story is a long one, covering several chapters. Do not spend more than three lessons on the first nine plagues.

The succession of plagues is not mere repetition. An overall pattern emerges, in which all of the characters in the story develop. It is not necessary for students to discover this pattern all by themselves since this might prove to be tedious. Lead your students through the narrative, pointing out the evidence in the text. This is

Lesson 3 — Blood, Frogs, and Lice

quite acceptable as long as your statements are supported by the text.

As the class discussion of the plagues proceeds, have your students fill in a chart like the one on pp. 73–75. The students' charts should resemble the sample completed chart on pp. 76–78. You may want to divide your class into small groups. Tell them that the plagues are a "teaching device" and that as they read they are to look for development of the characters. Explain what is meant by each of the seven column headings in the chart. Use the first plague as an example so the students understand what is expected of them.

You may want to enrich this plague story, depending on your own talents and inclinations. Teachers have made murals of the plagues with their students. Some have published a "newspaper" containing articles written by students pretending to be Egyptians or Israelites describing what they felt or thought or anticipated during the plagues.

❐ TEACHING PROCEDURE

1. BLOOD (7:14–24)

Who announces this plague to Pharaoh? Where does this announcement take place?

> The plague is announced by Moses as Pharaoh is standing on the banks of the Nile, surrounded by his courtiers.

What is the stated purpose of this plague?

> The purpose of the plague is to teach Pharaoh a lesson (7:17): "By this you shall know that I am the Lord."

Who brings on the plague?

> Aaron performs the sign that commences the plague—striking the water in the Nile with the rod.

What is the extraordinary miracle element in this plague?

> 1. The plague is announced before it happens.
> 2. The Bible makes sure that we, the readers, know that this is an extraordinary occurrence: even the water that had been hauled to the homes of the Egyptians prior to the onset of the plague and that was stored in vessels of stone and wood turned to blood.

What is Pharaoh's reaction?

> Pharaoh stiffens his heart!

What made Pharaoh react this way?

> The fact that the magicians, too, could turn water into blood diminished the impact of the plague, so that Pharaoh could disregard it.

Some "practical" students may want to know where the Egyptians found water to turn to blood if all the water had already been turned to blood by Moses and Aaron. Point out 7:24: "The Egyptians had to dig round about the Nile for drinking water. . . ."

Whom is the confrontation between?

> Aaron and the magicians.

We are not told how and when the waters of the Nile reverted back to normal. How do we know that they did?

> Because we are told that seven days later the Nile was able to bring forth frogs. (8:1)

After this discussion of the first plague the teacher might fill in the chart together with the students.

2. FROGS (7:25–8:11)

Who announces this plague? Where?

> The plague is announced by Moses in the palace of Pharaoh.

Whom is the confrontation between this time?

> The magicians and Aaron.

Is there any difference between what Aaron can do and what the magicians can do?

> Like Aaron, the magicians, too, are able to produce frogs, but 8:4 indicates that they are not able to remove them.

What is Pharaoh's reaction?

> Pharaoh, realizing the connection between the frogs and the God of Israel, pleads with Moses to remove them. Later, once they are removed, he becomes stubborn again.

What is the miracle element this time?

> The "miracle element" is indicated by the fact that (1) the plague had been announced by Moses, and (2) by the fact that Moses promises to remove the plague at a time indicated by Pharaoh (as soon as possible! Tomorrow!) and is able to do so.

How does Moses feel once he promised to remove the frogs? (8:8)

(Open.)

Note that Moses promises Pharaoh to remove the frogs before "clearing it" first with God. He is now worried that God might not heed him. Moses cries out to the Lord ("crying out" is an anxious prayer). After this discussion of the second plague students to fill in the plague chart.

3. LICE (8:12-15)

In what way is the onset of this plague different from the others?

The third plague comes about without prior warning.

Whom is the confrontation between?

Aaron versus the magicians.

What is different about what the magicians can do this time?

The magicians tried to produce lice, but they failed. They conceded the superiority of God's power and declared it was "the finger of God."

What do you think the expression "a finger of God" might mean?

Eventually God will redeem His people with a strong hand and an outstretched arm. The first three plagues were only "a finger," a foretaste of the havoc God will play with Egypt.

Did Pharaoh react the same way as the magicians?

No. His heart stiffened.

Fill in the plague chart. You might end the lesson by drawing conclusions from the chart so far:

The confrontation has so far been between Aaron and the magicians. The magicians have been moved—they have come to recognize God's part in the plagues. But Pharaoh—who had the same opportunity to do so—has not.

LESSON 4

Insects, Pestilence, and Inflammation
Exod. 8:16–9:12

☐ TEACHING PROCEDURE

4. SWARMS OF INSECTS (8:16–28)

Where does Moses present himself to Pharaoh?

> At the water.

To which plague is this similar—in this respect?

> To the first plague.

Who announces the plague?

> Moses.

What new element does Moses announce in advance this time?

> God will make a distinction between the people of Israel and the Egyptians. No insects will invade the region of Goshen. Thus, the miracle will be even greater.

What is the stated purpose of the plague?

> "That you may know that I the Lord am in the midst of the land."

What is the Pharaoh's first reaction after the insects arrive?

> Initially Pharaoh is willing to let the Israelites sacrifice to their God but only within the borders of the land of Egypt.

What is Moses' reaction to Pharaoh?

> Moses tells Pharaoh that they could not sacrifice their goats and sheep in Egypt since sheep were untouchable to the Egyptian cattle breeder.*

What does this reply, by Moses, teach us about his state of mind?

> (Open discussion.) Suggestion: He has become bolder as the plagues progressed.

* See *Genesis: A New Teacher's Guide,* 3rd ed., p. 299.

Lesson 4 — Insects, Pestilence, and Inflammation

How does Pharaoh react to Moses' refusal to sacrifice in Egypt?

Pharaoh relents.

Why?

He is obviously desperate.

How were the insects removed?

Moses, upon Pharaoh's request, pleaded with the Lord to remove the insects.

How does "pleading with the Lord" differ from "crying out to the Lord" (8:8)?

"Pleading" is less desperate than "crying out."

What was Pharaoh's reaction once the plague was removed?

Once the plague was removed, Pharaoh became stubborn once more.

5. PESTILENCE (9:1–7)

Little information is given in connection with this plague that needs to be recorded in the chart.

Where did Moses speak to Pharaoh this time?

Moses encountered Pharaoh in the palace.

What was the miracle element of the plague?

1. The plague was announced in advance and carried out at a fixed time.
2. The pestilence was to strike the livestock of the Egyptians. Nothing, however, of what belonged to the Israelites was to die.

What was Pharaoh's reaction?

Pharaoh remained stubborn.

6. INFLAMMATION (BOILS) (9:8–12)

Who performs the miracle?

For the first time Moses takes over from Aaron the performance of the symbolic act that will bring on the plague. Moses throws handfuls of soot from the kiln toward the sky which causes inflammation, boils on man and beast throughout the land of Egypt.

Why didn't the magicians confront Moses?

The magicians found themselves unable to confront Moses since they themselves were afflicted with boils (irony).

What was Pharaoh's reaction?

Here for the first time we are told that God intervened and stiffened Pharaoh's heart.

When the chart is completed you might ask a summary question:

What major changes have come about by the sixth plague?

1. Moses has confronted Pharaoh. (Moses will continue confront Pharaoh until the tenth plague, when God will take over.
2. By the sixth plague both Aaron and the magicians have faded out of the picture. (The magicians have admitted to the plagues being "the finger of God".)
3. The separation of the Israelites from the Egyptians in suffering the effects of the plague has become part of the miracle element (fourth and fifth plagues).
4. For the first time now, God is responsible for the stiffening of Pharaoh's heart.

LESSON 5

Hail, Locusts, and Darkness
Exod. 9:13–10:29

❑ TEACHING PROCEDURE

7. HAIL (9:13–35)
Where does Moses announce the plague?

Moses stations himself in the palace before Pharaoh to announce the coming hail.

What is the stated purpose of the plague?

"In order that you may know that there is none like me in all the world," ". . . to show you my power and . . . that my fame may resound throughout the world."

Hail can be a natural event. What is the miracle element in this plague? That is, what about this plague makes it clear that it was perceived as a miracle?

1. It is announced in advance.
2. This hail, we are told, will be "heavy . . . such as has not been in Egypt from the day it was founded."
3. "Only in the region of Goshen, where the Israelites lived, there was no hail."

In what way does God give the Egyptians a chance to show that they have learned to fear God?

The Egyptians are warned to take their slaves and livestock indoors.

What tells us that some Egyptians came to recognize God's power and some did not?

Those who feared the Lord heeded Moses' words and saved their property, others did not.

What was Pharaoh's reaction?

Pharaoh admitted to being "guilty this time" and asked that Moses intercede for him with God. However, once the hail stopped, Pharaoh's heart stiffened.

How did Moses stop the hail?

Moses left Pharaoh's presence and spread out his arms in a symbolic gesture of prayer. In terms of confidence he had come a long way from the day when he cried out to the Lord in anguish (second plague).

Not all vegetation was destroyed (9:31–32). Within the grand scheme of the plagues planned by God, the wheat was not blighted but was saved to serve as food for the locusts.

8. LOCUSTS (10:1-20)

Again Moses and Aaron appeared before Pharaoh to announce the plague. What was the stated purpose of the plague?

The stated purpose of the plague: "in order that I may display my signs among them and that you may recount in the hearing of your sons and your sons' sons how I made a mockery of the Egyptians in order that you may know that I am the Lord."

What is the miracle element of this plague?

1. It is announced in advance and is predicted: This is not an ordinary locust invasion, but "something that neither your fathers nor your fathers' fathers have seen from the day they appeared on earth to this day."
2. When it actually happens: "Never before had there been so many [locusts] nor will there ever be so many again."

What is the reaction of the courtiers?

The courtiers are aware that "Egypt is lost." (10:7)

They realize this even before the plague actually comes. What is Pharaoh's reaction before the onset of the plague?

Moses and Pharaoh negotiate. "Who is to go?" Pharaoh wants to know. When, however, Moses boldly answers, "We will all go, young and old. We will go with our sons and daughters, our flock and herds" (10:9), Pharaoh refuses to let the families join their menfolk on their journey and Moses marks the onset of the plague.

What is Pharaoh's reaction after the onset of the plague, and how does this reaction compare to his reaction to the seventh plague, hail?

In the hail episode he admits to being "guilty this time" (9:27). Now he admits to being "guilty before the Lord." "Forgive my offense just this once," he pleads. But God stiffened Pharaoh's heart and he will not let the Israelites go.

What is Moses' reaction?

During the negotiations he stood his ground—"We will all go: young and old." (10:9)
After Pharaoh admits guilt, Moses pleads with the Lord on Pharaoh's behalf. (10:18)

9. DARKNESS (10:21–29)

The ninth plague comes unannounced. There is a pattern to the way the plagues are announced which we will see in the chart at end of this lesson. The discussion of the plague continues:

What is the miracle element?

1. This is no ordinary eclipse. Upon Moses' raising his arm a "touchable" darkness envelopes the land of Egypt.
2. The Israelites enjoy light in their dwellings.

What is Pharaoh's reaction?

Pharaoh agrees to let the Israelites go provided they leave their livestock behind as surety. After Moses refuses to leave the livestock, the Lord stiffens Pharaoh's heart. He will not consent to let the people go.

What is Moses' reaction?

Moses declares, "You yourself must provide us with sacrifices . . . to offer up to the Lord our God . . . our own livestock too shall go with us—not a hoof shall remain behind." Moses, who shrank from Pharaoh in Exod. 5:3, now stands up to him.

Although the ninth plague in Exodus 10 ends with the declaration by Moses to Pharaoh, "I shall not see your face again," we shall note that Moses "left Pharaoh's presence in hot anger" only in Exod. 11:8. Yet, in Exod. 11:1–2 we find God addressing Moses. It is unlikely that God would have done so in the presence of Pharaoh.

These two verses (11:1–2) probably have to be understood as a past perfect: God *had given* Moses these instructions sometime in the past. We do not find any new information here.

LESSON 6A

Announcing the Tenth Plague
Exod. 11:1–10

❐ TEACHING PROCEDURE

Moses tells Pharaoh that God Himself will go forth among the Egyptians and smite from the firstborn of the Pharaoh to the firstborn of the cattle. Yet the Israelites' firstborn and the firstborn of their cattle shall be untouched "in order that you may know that the Lord makes a distinction between Egypt and Israel."

What will be the lesson of the tenth plague?

The tenth plague shall teach Pharaoh about God's powers and His special relationship to the people of Israel.

LESSON 6B

The Plagues: A Literary Device

☐ TEACHING PROCEDURE

Ask students to look back over the first nine plagues, noticing how each plague is announced. As the information is gathered, organize it on the board as in the following chart:

Announced at the Nile	Announced in the palace	Not announced
1. Blood	2. Frogs	3. Lice
4. Insects	5. Pestilence	6. Inflammation
7. Hail	8. Locusts	9. Darkness

Notice the orderly sequence. This arrangement is a lovely literary device. This is part of the poetic structure of the plague story.

LESSON 6C

The Plagues: Review

❐ TEACHING PROCEDURE

Now that nine plagues have been completed, ask students to review their completed plagues chart (see pp. 76–78). Have them study the information in the second column ("Performer of Miracle"), looking for changes and progressions that took place over the course of the first nine plagues. Then have them repeat this investigation for each of the remaining columns. The class should reach the following conclusions:

PERFORMER OF MIRACLE

Aaron brings on the first three plagues, confronting the Egyptian magicians. The sixth through ninth plagues are brought on by Moses. (The tenth plague will be brought on by God Himself.) Moses gains in confidence and is willing to confront Pharaoh directly, without Aaron's help.

STATED PURPOSE OF THE PLAGUE

The plagues are intended to teach the Egyptians and the Israelites about God:

1. There is a God of Israel, even though Pharaoh has refused to recognize him.

2. God has great powers.

3. There is none like God throughout the world.

4. The Israelites are to teach their children how God defeated the Egyptians. (One of the explicit purposes of the tenth plague will be to show that God has a special relationship with the Israelites.)

MIRACLE ELEMENT

1. The plagues are announced in advance, showing that they are not accidents of nature. Nor is the removal of the plagues an accident of nature.

2. Beginning with the fourth plague it is explicitly mentioned that the Israelites do not suffer from the plagues.

3. Beginning with the seventh plague we are told that the severity of these plagues is unique. Such plagues have never before afflicted Egypt, nor will they ever be seen again.

REACTION OF PHARAOH

Pharaoh gradually learns to recognize God's powers:

1. At first Pharaoh refuses to recognize the authority of the God of Israel.

2. He is stubborn. only slowly he begins to acknowledge the power of God.

3. He makes gradual compromises with Moses in order to escape further punishment. After the third plague he is willing to let the Israelites sacrifice within Egypt. After the seventh, he is willing to let only the men go to the desert to sacrifice. After the eighth, he is willing to let all the people go, leaving their cattle and sheep behind. (At the tenth plague Pharaoh will urge the Israelites to depart, taking with them all their belongings.)

REACTION OF EGYPTIANS

The magicians and other Egyptians gradually learn to recognize God's powers:

1. At first the magicians match Aaron's feat.

2. The magicians can reproduce the second plague, but they cannot remove it.

3. They cannot reproduce the third plague, recogzinging God's "finger" in the plague.

4. In the sixth plague the magicians themselves are afflicted and drop out of the contest.

5. In the seventh plague those Egyptians who heed God's warning are spared the lost of their slave and livestock.

6. In the eighth plague they realize that Egypt is lost. (In the tenth plague they will urge Pharaoh to expel the Israelites.)

REACTION OF MOSES

Moses gradually gains confidence in God and in himself:

1. In the second plague Moses insecurely "cries out" to God.

2. Already more secure, Moses is willing to talk back to Pharaoh. He is less desperate in appealing to God (he "pleads" with God).

3. In the seventh plague he chides Pharaoh. Now he addresses God by spreading out his hands, a standard gesture of prayer.

4. In the remaining plagues he becomes very outspoken and demanding before Pharaoh.

It should be noted that there is no column for the reaction of the Israelites. Before the plagues began they retreated at the first obstacle they encountered. There is no mention of their reaction to the plagues until Moses approaches them to announce the tenth plague.

Plague	Performer of Miracle	Stated Purpose of Plague	Miracle Element	Pharaoh's Reaction	Reaction of Egyptians	Moses' Reaction
1. Blood (7:14–24)						
2. Frogs (7:25–8:11)						
3. Lice (8:12–15)						
4. Swarm of Insects (8:16–28)						

Plague	Performer of Miracle	Stated Purpose of Plague	Miracle Element	Pharaoh's Reaction	Reaction of Egyptians	Moses' Reaction
5. Pestilence (9:1–7)						
6. Inflammation (9:8–12)						
7. Hail (9:13–35)						

Plague	Performer of Miracle	Stated Purpose of Plague	Miracle Element	Pharaoh's Reaction	Reaction of Egyptians	Moses' Reaction
8. Locusts (10:1–20)						
9. Darkness (10:21–29)						
10. Death of Firstborn (11:1–10)						

Plague	Performer of Miracle	Stated Purpose of Plague	Miracle Element	Pharaoh's Reaction	Reaction of Egyptians	Moses' Reaction
1. Blood (7:14–24)	Aaron	"By this you shall know that I am the Lord."	Plague is announced in advance. Even water already in vessels turns to blood.	His heart stiffened.	The magicians matched Aaron's feat.	Not mentioned.
2. Frogs (7:25–8:11)	Aaron	Not mentioned	The quantity of the frogs is announced in advance. Plague is removed at time set by Pharaoh.	He asks Moses to plead for him with God. Later he becomes stubborn.	Magicians can produce frogs but cannot remove them.	He "cries out" to God.
3. Lice (8:12–15)	Aaron	Not mentioned	*All* the dust of the land turned into lice.	His heart stiffened.	They cannot produce lice. They say, "This is the finger of God."	Not mentioned
4. Swarm of Insects (8:16–28)	Not mentioned	"That you may know that I the Lord am in the midst of the land."	Plague is announced in advance. Israelites will be spared suffering.	He is willing to let Israelites sacrifice in Egypt. He says, "Do not go very far."	Not mentioned	He talks back to the king, insisting on going into the desert. He pleads with God to remove plague.

Plague	Performer of Miracle	Stated Purpose of Plague	Miracle Element	Pharaoh's Reaction	Reaction of Egyptians	Moses' Reaction
5. Pestilence (9:1–7)	Not mentioned	Not mentioned	Plague is announced in advance. Most of Egyptian livestock dies. The livestock of the Israelites is spared.	He remained stubborn.	Not mentioned	Not mentioned
6. Inflammation (9:8–12)	Moses	Not mentioned	Handfuls of charcoal dust cover *all* the land of Egypt and become boils throughout the land.	God stiffens Pharaoh's heart.	The magicians themselves are afflicted.	Not mentioned
7. Hail (9:13–35)	Moses	"That you may know that there is none like me in all the world." "To show my power." "That my fame may resound through the world."	Plague is announced in advance. "Hail such as had not fallen on the land . . . since it had become a nation." There was no hail in Goshen.	He says, "I stand guilty this time. The Lord is right and I and my people are wrong."	Some Egyptians heed God's warning and protect their slaves and their livestock.	He says, "I shall spread out my hands," and "I know . . . that you do not yet fear God.

Plague	Performer of Miracle	Stated Purpose of Plague	Miracle Element	Pharaoh's Reaction	Reaction of Egyptians	Moses' Reaction
8. Locusts (10:1–20)	Moses	"That you may recount to your sons and sons' sons how I made mockery of the Egyptians. That you may know . . . I am the Lord."	"Never before had there been so many [locusts] nor will there ever be so many again."	He is willing to send the males. He insists that the Israelites are bent on mischief.	They say to Pharaoh, "Are you not yet aware that Egypt is lost?"	He says, "We will go, young and old."
9. Darkness (10:21–29)	Moses	Not mentioned	It was darkness "that could be touched." The Israelites had light in their dwellings.	He says, "I stand guilty before the Lord your God. Go! Only your livestock will remain."	Not mentioned	He says, "Not a hoof shall remain behind."
10. Death of Firstborn (11:1–10)	God	"That you may know the Lord makes a distinction between Egypt and Israel."	"Every firstborn [Egyptian] shall die." "Not a dog shall snarl at any of the Israelites."	His heart was stiffened.	The Egyptians try to hurry the Israelites to leave. (Exod. 12:33)	Not mentioned

UNIT THREE

The Exodus
Exod. 12:1–15:21

LESSON 1

The Festival of Pesaḥ
Exod. 12:1–13

▢ IN PREPARATION FOR TEACHING

Up to now the (announced) plagues happened shortly after they were announced. Not so the tenth plague. Since the Israelites are to depart from Egypt during this plague, preparations will have to be made.

BLOOD ON THE DOORPOSTS

God commanded the Israelites to put blood on their doorposts in order to designate an Israelite house. We have already learned that in the Torah the spilling of blood serves an apotropaic measure (see p. 73): the spilling of blood can avert danger.

The Rabbis noted that the Israelites in Egypt had no mitzvot to fulfill, thus no chance to acquire merit. By telling the Israelites to put blood on their doorposts they had a mitzvah to fulfill so they could acquire the merit they needed in order to be redeemed.

One may ask if Egyptians observing the Israelites could have emulated them and saved their households too. The text does not say. However, the plagues being a "learning experience," this may be so. The fear of God, we are told, had saved some Egyptians from the hail plague. It therefore stands to reason that the fear of God and obedience to His commands might have saved some Egyptians, or non-Israelites from the plague of מַכַּת בְּכוֹרוֹת.

THE ORIGIN OF MATZOT AND MAROR

Matzot and maror are part of the Pesaḥ ceremony on the eve of the fourteenth of Nisan. The command to take a lamb to a household came early in the month. The lamb was to be taken on the tenth of the month and slaughtered on the fourteenth, thus the reason for the eating of matzah (namely the lack of time to let the dough rise) does not hold true here. Why then eat matzot on the fourteenth? In Exod. 23:18 (also in Lev. 2:11 and 6:10) we learn a general rule, "You shall not offer the blood of my sacrifice with anything leavened." The Pesaḥ is a sacrifice and therefore eaten with unleavened bread. According to some Bible scholars, anything that has to do with the cult has to remain as natural as possible, the way God made it. Matzot are more "natural" than bread since matzot do not rise. By the same token Zippora and also Joshua used flintstone knives for the ritual of circumcison, although metal was used at the time. We still write the Torah scroll by means of a quill on parchment although today we have far more efficient devices for copying written documents.

Maror (or lettuce) was the normal accompaniment of meat. Thus the eating of matzah and merorim on the night of the Pesaḥ sacrifice had nothing to do with the departure from Egypt.

SACRIFICES

You may at this point have to teach something about sacrifices in general. By and large students view sacrifices as a burnt offering to God. This form of sacrifice was called עוֹלָה. However, there were also other kinds of sacrifices.

There was a time in the life of the Israelites that meat could only be eaten as part of a ritual act. Whenever people wanted to eat meat they had to go to one of the many temples (Gilgal, Shilo, Bethel and others) and have a priest slaughter the animal as a sacrifice (the prophet Samuel went on a temple circuit to do just this). The blood of the animal (its source of life) would symbolically be returned to God, the source of all life, by pouring it on the altar. The hard fat (חֵלֶב) surrounding the inner organs would be burned to God. The priests would then receive their alloted portions, the rest of the meat to be consumed by the owner of the animal and his family (see 1 Samuel 1). שְׁחִיטַת חֻלִּין (the secular slaughtering of animals) was later on permitted, the reason being that the cult of God became centralized in the Temple in Jerusalem and the small temples were abandoned. It became unreasonable to expect everybody who wanted to eat meat to travel all the way to Jerusalem. The Israelites were, however, instructed that when slaughtering animals for food in their village, they should pour the blood on the ground and cover it with earth. Thus, far from being "disgusting" and "blood thirsty" as many students view the sacrificers, people did not eat meat as casually as we do today. They were aware of the fact that the life of the animal, although permitted to be taken for food, was nevertheless God-given and valuable.

In Exodus 11 we last read of Moses' announcement to Pharaoh about the tenth plague. This time, however, Moses' announcement

Lesson 1 — The Festival of Pesaḥ

of the plague is not followed immediately by the plague itself. Since the Israelites will depart from Egypt during this plague, they have to make some preparations first. Therefore we will find that more than the first half of Exodus 12 deals with the preparation made by the Israelites before the tenth plague.

❐ TEACHING PROCEDURE

What is the name of the month referred to (it is the month in which Pesaḥ falls)?

Nisan.

According to 12:2, Nisan was, at the time, the first month of the year. Think about what you learned in your history class about Egypt, and the Nile. Can you think of a reason why in Egypt the new year was celebrated in the spring?

In Egypt, the Nile, fed by melting snow in central Africa, overflows in the spring bringing new fertility to the land. Thus spring is the month of renewal of nature and agriculture.

In later times, in Canaan, the new year celebration was moved to the month of Tishrei, in the fall. Can you think of a reason why?

In Israel fall brings with it the first rains which in turn bring new fertility to the parched earth which received no rain all through the long sun-drenched summer months.

Can you think of another agricultural new year?

The fifteenth day of Shevat is the new year of the trees, since around that time of year the almond tree and some other fruit trees start bearing blossoms, anticipating warmer weather.

Can you think of another, new, reason that made the Israelites view Nisan as the first month of the year?

There was now an historical reason. In Nisan the people were freed from slavery. They experienced a "new beginning."

Do you know of any other national "new years" that spring from historical events?

The American people count their national age from the Fourth of July of their liberation, and the Israelis count their "political age" from the date on which they signed their declaration of independence from Britain.

What exactly are the Israelites bidden to do?

The Israelites are to take a lamb on the tenth of Nisan from the goats or sheep, a male yearling without a blemish, and slaughter it on the fourteenth of Nisan. The lamb may not be cut up into portions or cooked in water. It has to be roasted whole over the fire. It has to be consumed the same night, none of it may remain until morning.

Why are the instructions so specific? Why does the animal have to be male? Why three years old? Why does the meat have to be roasted?

These specific instructions indicate that this was not a regular meal, it was a family sacrifice. At regular meals many different cuts of meat, prepared in a variety of ways, were eaten.

Can you think of a reason why the text emphasizes that no raw meat be eaten?

Because pagans ate the meat of their sacrifices raw or only half cooked, Israelite sacrifices are to be *roasted*.

What are the people to do with the blood?

They are to put it on the doorposts and lintels of their houses.

Explain apotropaic powers of blood. See above, p. 37.

What are the people to eat with the roasted meat?

Unleavened bread (matzah) and bitter herbs.

When are they to take the lamb?

On the tenth day of Nisan.

When are they to slaughter it?

On the fourteenth of Nisan.

Why matzah?

See above, pp. 81–82. If your students say, "Because there was no time to bake bread," refer them to 12:3. Obviously there is enough time to bake bread.

Why maror?

It was the normal accompaniment of meat.

Since some of your students may have the notion that all sacrificial animals were totally burned up you may tell them about the family sacrifices (see above, pp. 82–83).

LESSON 2

The Festival of Matzot
Exod. 12:14–20

☐ IN PREPARATION FOR TEACHING

As you read 12:14, you may notice that "this day" is out of place. The Israelites have not yet left Egypt. A close reading of the text will show that the text deals with *two festivals:*

1. The Festival of Pesaḥ, already discussed, involving the eating of the roast lamb on the eve of the fourteenth of Nisan (with matzah, because this is a sacrificial meal).
2. The Festival of Matzot, the holiday of unleavened bread from the morning of the fifteenth of Nisan to the eve of the twenty-first. We find the etiology for eating the Pesaḥ sacrifice here in 12:5–10; the etiology for eating matzah for seven days however will only come in 12:39:

The holiday of Passover as we celebrate it today is a merger of rituals of the Festival of Matzot with some of the rituals of the Festival of Pesaḥ (the blood on the doorpost, for example, is omitted).

THE MERGER OF THE TWO FESTIVALS

Lev. 23:6 states:

> In the first month, on the fourteenth day of the month, at twilight, there shall be a passover offering to the Lord and on the fifteenth day of the month—the Lord's feast of unleavened bread for seven days.

In Num. 28:16–17 we find a passage that is almost identical. In Ezek. 45:21 (a much later text), however, we find that these two festivals have completely merged:

> In the first month, on the fourteenth day of the month, you shall celebrate the feast of the Passover, and for seven days unleavened bread shall be eaten.

The two festivals have become one, no seams show anymore. The matzah eaten on the fourteenth (with the Pesaḥ sacrifice) has now merged with the matzah of Ḥag Hamatzot, and the etiology of 12:39, the lack of time to bake bread, will imperceptibly cover also the matzah eaten on the fourteenth (although this had not been the fact on the first eventful eve of the fourteenth of Nisan).

Some Bible scholars have noted that the Pesaḥ sacrifice on the eve of the fourteenth might correspond to an already existing Egyptian shepherd holiday. Similarly, the Festival of Matzot, beginning on the morning of the fifteenth, may correspond to an already existing farmer's holiday. Both holidays took place when the moon was full.

Since on that same full moon night the Israelites departed from Egypt and gained their independence, they adopted these two Egyptian holidays and made them their own, giving them a new religious and national connotation. This is the festival known to us today as Pesaḥ, or Passover. (In this connection it is important to point out that in the past, days (including holidays) were considered to begin in the *morning,* not, as they do today, in the evening. Yom Kippur, and Pesaḥ for the reasons stated above, were two exceptions.)

You may find this difficult to teach. Do not attempt an inquiry. Lecture it frontally. No teaching procedure has been prepared for this section.

LESSON 3A

Moses Instructs the People
Exod. 12:21–28

❐ IN PREPARATION FOR TEACHING

Moses relates God's instruction to the people of Israel. He adds practical instructions of his own. He also adds that the sacrifice will be celebrated throughout the generations as a memorial to the Exodus.

❐ TEACHING PROCEDURE

In what way do the instructions Moses gives to the people differ from the ones he received from God?

> He adds details. For instance, how to put blood on the door. He admonishes the people not to leave their homes and explains how this rite will serve as a memorial for all generations.

What is the main lesson the Israelites are to derive from the Exodus for future generations?

> This is a learning experience for all generations. When your children ask you why we celebrate these rites (the eating of the meat, the matzah, the maror) you will have a chance to teach them that God smote the Egyptians but passed over the houses of the Israelites.

Have the plagues taught the Israelites anything?

> They now trust God and Moses (12:27–28). "The people bowed down in homage. . . . They did . . . just as the Lord had commanded Moses."

LESSON 3B

Pesaḥ Mitzrayim and Pesaḥ Dorot
Exod. 12:1–28

❐ TEACHING PROCEDURE

Which verses in Exodus 12 tell the Moses and the Israelites how to prepare for the departure?

12:3–13, 21–23.

What are the people to do in preparation for the departure?

1. Take a lamb on the tenth. (12:3)
2. Sacrifice the lamb on the fourteenth and roast it. (12:6)
3. Put blood on the doorposts and lintel. (12:7)
4. Eat the meat with unleavened bread and maror. (12:8)
5. Eat it hurriedly, wearing sandals and carrying a staff. (12:11)
6. Burn the leftovers. (12:10)

This is called Pesaḥ Mitzrayim.

Now find the verses that tell us how the people are to celebrate the holiday in the future.

12:14–20, 24–28.

How are the people to celebrate the holiday in the future?

1. Sacrifice the lamb on the day of the fourteenth and roast it. (12:27)
2. Eat the sacrificial meat that evening together with unleavened bread and maror. (implied by 12:27 and 12:8)
3. Eat unleavened bread for seven days, from the night after the morning of the fourteenth (today referred as the eve of the fifteenth) until the twenty-first of Nisan. (12:15, 18)
4. Hold a sacred convocation on the first and seventh days of the Festival. (12:16)
5. No leaven shall be found in the houses throughout the Festival. (12:19)

Lesson 3B — Pesaḥ Mitzrayim and Pesaḥ Dorot

This is called Pesaḥ Dorot (Pesaḥ for the Ages). It is the result of combining some of the laws of Pesaḥ Mitzrayim with the laws of the Festival of Matzot.

Pesaḥ as we celebrate it today is different from Pesaḥ Dorot. Since the destruction of the Holy Temple in Jerusalem, we do not offer sacrifices any longer. Therefore the Pesaḥ sacrifice is not a part of our seder meal. The meat we eat is simply part of a festive meal and need not be roasted. Some Jews make a point of not eating roasted meat at the seder to emphasize that that meat is not the Pesaḥ sacrifice.

Some have added additional customs based on Pesaḥ Mitzrayim. Yemenite Jews attend the seder wearing sandals on their feet and carrying a staff, "ready" to depart from Egypt.

LESSON 4

Capitulation and Exodus
Exod. 12:29–42

❐ IN PREPARATION FOR TEACHING

This section looks backward to Exodus 11, the events taking place having been predicted before.

As Moses had foretold Pharaoh, the Egyptians and the king himself wished the Israelites to leave, taking along all their possessions: flocks and herds. The passage bears no surprises. God's plan is fulfilling itself exactly as anticipated (12:37–42).

The life of the Israelites had reached the turning point. The Exodus was at hand. As often in the Bible when important changes are to take place, the narration stops for "taking stock."

Four hundred and thirty years had gone by since the Israelites came down to Egypt (note that this span of time is contradicted elsewhere in the Bible and is not to be regarded as historical data). Six hundred thousand men, aside from children, women and the elderly, and a "mixed multitude" went up with them.

Who was this "mixed multitude"? Why did they hitch their fate to that of the Israelites? The text does not say, but we may wonder: were these other slaves, or were these Egyptians? If they were indeed slaves, were they using this unique opportunity to seek their own freedom? Had they been convinced that the God of Israel was more powerful than any other gods, or had they decided to join the Israelites since they recognized them as the elect of God?

Here (12:39) we find for the first time the etiology (the reason) for eating matzot. On the fifteenth day of Nisan, the day after the Pesaḥ (the sacrifice of the fourteenth of Nisan) "they baked unleavened cakes . . . since they had been driven out . . . and could not delay nor had they prepared any provision for themselves."

Note that the "learning experience" of Pesaḥ continues. The experience of the Exodus will be transmitted by the Israelites to future generations.

Moses had not confronted the Israelites since they had rejected him in Exodus 5. We are told that Moses had gained great stature among the Egyptians. The Israelites now bow low to Moses, just the way they did when he first showed them the "signs" in Exodus 4.

In preparation for the Exodus the people had "borrowed" objects of gold and silver and articles of clothing—as Moses had commanded them (11:2).

☐ TEACHING PROCEDURE

Read 12:29–36. Does the text surprise you?

No, it was predicted in 11:1–8. God's plan is fulfilling itself as predicted.

Read 12:36–42. According to the text how many Israelites left Egypt?

Six hundred thousand men, aside from children, women and the elderly, and a "mixed multitude" went with them.

Who do you think these "mixed multitudes were and why did they join the Israelites?"

The text does not say, but we may wonder: were they other slaves, or were they Egyptians? If they were indeed slaves, were they using this unique opportunity to seek their own freedom? Had they been convinced that the God of Israel was more powerful than any other gods, or had they decided to join the Israelites since they recognized them as the elect of God?

LESSON 5

On Slavery
Exod. 12:43–51

❑ IN PREPARATION FOR TEACHING

Students may be appalled to find out that the text foresees an Israelite slave-owning society, and this so soon after gaining their own freedom. Present this material on slavery to your class without attempting to justify the institution.

❑ TEACHING PROCEDURE

Read 2:43–51. What is the passage about?

It is about the celebration of Pesaḥ Dorot, specifically the sacrifice on the fourteenth of Nisan in the future.

How do you know that this passage deals with the future?

1. Because the text refers to the citizens of the country (at this point there is no country and therefore no citizens).
2. It refers to strangers who shall dwell with Israel.
3. It deals with slaves and resident hirelings (at this point the Israelites are wanderers, not residents).

What are the different groups or classes of people mentioned here?

Foreigners, slaves, resident hirelings, the assembly of Israel, strangers, citizens.

What two categories do these groups fall into?

Those who can offer and eat the Pesaḥ sacrifice, and those who cannot.

Who may offer the sacrifice and eat of it?

The whole assembly of Israel (also referred to as citizens of the country).

Who may not?

Foreigners, slaves, resident hirelings, strangers.

Why not?

They are not circumcised.

How can those in this second group become eligible?

By undergoing ritual circumcision they become citizens, i.e., members of the assembly of Israel.

It should be emphasized that the seder meal that we conduct today does not include a sacrifice, and therefore anyone is permitted to attend and participate.

Discuss slavery. Explain it without attempting to justify the institution of slavery.

It is surprising to find the Israelites at the point of their own redemption contemplating a slave-owning society.

In biblical times slavery was accepted by all people, including the Israelites. There were, however, two kinds of slavery:

1. Slaves owned by the king (e.g., the Israelites in Egypt, slave in the Roman Empire). In Egypt all the Israelites were slaves to the king, who owned them as he owned his cattle, and who could do with them whatever he pleased.

2. Household slaves (e.g., slaves owned by Israelites in Canaan, slaves in Greece). These slaves were attached to a family and were often treated as part of the family. Exod. 12:44 indicates that these slaves were treated humanely. They could, for instance, join the family for the Pesaḥ sacrifice, provided they were circumcised.

HOW DID PEOPLE BECOME SLAVES IN THE FIRST PLACE?

Debtors — People without Money or Resources

Sometimes, when heavily in debt a person may sell himself or his child into slavery. A farmer who suffered repeatedly from bad crops may have to borrow money to sustain his family or for seed and for animal fodder. When he found himself unable to repay this debt he might sell himself into slavery. The Bible limits the servitude of an Israelite slave to six years. This limitation in effect changed his position from that of a slave to that of an "indentured servant."

An indentured servant is one who works in order to repay money he owes. (A slave labors without being paid.)

Many people who had no means came to the United States as indentured servants. They found a "master" who paid their passage. In return they worked for the "master" until they repaid their debt.

It might be pointed out that one of our ancestors became an indentured servant in order to pay for his wife. Jacob, lacking the funds for the "bride-price" for Rachel whom he wished to marry, went into servitude to Laban and served him fourteen years for Rachel and Leah.

Thieves

Sometimes a thief, when caught, was unable to restore the property he had stolen and unable to repay the fine imposed on him as punishment. He would be sold into slavery for six years until his work had compensated his victim for his loss.

HOW WERE SLAVES TREATED BY ISRAELITES IN CANAAN?

The slave's master could not treat him as if he were his property, his ox or cow. If the slave was harmed in any way by his master, and made to lose an eye or a tooth, the master had to set him free immediately. Thus the notion that a slave was not mere "chattel" but created in "God's image" and had certain rights and privileges in society is already implanted in the book of Exodus.

We shall deal with slavery in detail in Exodus 21. You do not have to deal with the subject now unless your students demand it. The idea will be further explored in Deuteronomy.

After presenting the material on slavery, you may want to discuss with your class how the Israelites, themselves once slaves, could become slave owners.

Slavery was a way of life in all societies. (Slavery was not abolished in the United States until the middle of the nineteenth century!)

Israelites treated their slaves differently from the way they had been treated in Egypt. For example, they could partake of family sacrifices (if they were circumcised), they could be freed after repaying debts, and if they were harmed they had to be set free.

Eventually Jewish law did away with slavery altogether.

LESSON 6

Laws for the Future
Exod. 13:1–16

❐ IN PREPARATION FOR TEACHING

Exodus 13, like parts of the previous chapter, deals with laws to be followed in the future. These topics are best introduced through a frontal presentation. Read the background material that follows and determine what you will present.

PIDYON HABEN (13:1–2)

The ceremony of the redemption of the firstborn (פִּדְיוֹן הַבֵּן) is not often taught in school. Many students are not aware of its existence. You may therefore want to take the opportunity to teach about it now.

Primogeniture (the special rights of the firstborn son) is a widespread institution, whose legal, social, and religious features are reflected in the norms of ancient Israel. (Although biblical law favors the firstborn, in the stories of Genesis, the younger son is favored—e.g., Jacob, Joseph, Ephraim.)

In the ancient world the firstborn male had a special status with respect to inheritance rights and certain cultic regulations. The firstborn son of a woman (a man could have several wives) belonged to God. In societies where human sacrifices were brought to the gods, the firstborn son was deemed to be the most desirable sacrifice (2 Kings 3:27).

The firstborn Israelite son has a special obligation to God as a consequence of having been saved at the time of the tenth plague. It is likely that early in the history of the people Israel, all firstborn sons actually served as temple servants. At some point, however, the firstborn Israelites were replaced by the Levites, who as a group were responsible for the service in the sanctuary (Num. 3:12). Each firstborn son to this day must be redeemed from his obligation to serve in the sanctuary through the ceremony called *pidyon haben*.

Rabbinic sources discuss at length the redemption ceremony (Mishna Bekhorot and Temurah). Only a son who is the first child of his mother is redeemed. Neither *kohanim* nor *leviyim* need to redeem their firstborn sons. Nor do men married to a daughter of a *kohen* or a *levi*. Any *kohen* may be chosen to perform the redemption.

The ceremony is held on the thirty-first day of the child's life. If that day is a Shabbat or a holiday, the ceremony is moved to the next weekday. The son is presented to the *kohen* (sometimes on a special tray) who asks in Aramaic if the son is to be redeemed or left with the Kohen. (The ceremony is symbolic and has no legal consequences. The parents cannot declare that they prefer to turn their son over to the *kohen*).

The parent expresses the desire to keep the son and hands over to the *kohen* five *shekalim* (usually five silver dollars in the United States). Paper money, checks, or credit cards are not acceptable. The Bank of Israel mints special coins to be used for this occasion.

The *kohen* recites a *berakha* for the fulfillment of the commandment of redemption and also the *sheheheyanu*. The *kohen* pronounces "You are redeemed" three times and returns the baby to the parents.

Ask your students what, if anything, they know of the redemption of the firstborn. Use the above information in class to the extent you deem necessary.

If possible, take your class to a *pidyon haben* ceremony or invite a *kohen* who officiates at such events to speak to the class. (A text of the *pidyon haben* ceremony may be found on pp. 99–101.)

Another custom associated with firstborn sons is the fast of the firstborn sons, held on the fourteenth day of Nisan (the morning before the first seder). This commemorates the fact that Israelite firstborn were saved during the tenth plague. A custom has evolved whereby the study of a Talmudic tractate is concluded on that morning. The firstborn are invited to participate at a meal celebrating the completion of the tractate (*siyyum*), which takes precedence over the minor fast.

EATING MATZOT IN THE FUTURE (13:3–8)

These verses deal with the eating of matzot in the future as a memorial to God's "mighty hand." While on the day of the Exodus the eating of matzot was a one-day affair, the matzot in the future shall be eaten for seven days (although the mitzvah of eating matzot is only for the seder, not the following days).

TEFILLIN (13:9–10)

You may have dealt with the custom of the wearing of *tefillin* in other parts of the curriculum. The box worn on the hand, and the other worn on the forehead, contain four biblical passages (written on parchment in square letters like the Torah). The passages are: (1) Exod. 13:1–10; (2) Exod. 13:11–16; (3) Deut. 6:4–9; (4) Deut. 11:13–21. The paragraphs in Exodus and Deuteronomy are almost identical.

These paragraphs can, of course, be understood symbolically. To have something "between your eyes" can mean to have it on your mind, to remember it. Something that is "on hand" means "it shall be a constant reminder." The Rabbis, however, have understood these passages literally, as the *tefillin* indicate.

Josephus, a Jewish historian in the second century C.E. already mentions the wearing of *tefillin* (*Antiquities of the Jews*, 4:213). It is noteworthy that *tefillin* were found in Qumran (where the Dead Sea Scrolls were found).

Tefillin are only worn by day. It is suggested that in the past some particularly pious rabbis wore them all day long. *Tefillin* are not worn on the Sabbath.

You might ask someone knowledgeable about *tefillin* to come to the class and show how *tefillin* are worn. Perhaps he could open up an old pair of *tefillin* and show what is inside.

THE FIRSTLING OF THE CATTLE (13:11–16)

In the ancient world, just as firstborn sons had a special cultic standing, so the firstlings of domesticated animals had a special cultic status. They had to be sacrificed to God (e.g., in Gen. 4:4, Abel brought the firstlings of his flocks as a well-received offering to God).

In Israelite lore, since the firstborn of the cattle and flocks of the Israelites (like the human firstborn) were saved by God in Egypt, the firstlings belonged to God.

Sheep and cattle were to be sacrificed in the Temple. Parts were burned to God, parts were eaten by the *kohanim* serving in the Temple, and the rest were eaten by the family of the owner of the animal. Animals not permitted for sacrifice or eating (e.g., a donkey or a camel) had to be redeemed by substituting money or a permitted animal.

It should be noted that this practice has been discontinued. Animal sacrifice was discontinued with the destruction of the Second Temple in Jerusalem (70 C.E.).

IN CONCLUSION

The reason for keeping all customs elaborated on in this chapter is found in 13:14–16. "When, in time to come, your son asks you, saying, 'What does this mean?' you shall say to him, 'It was with a mighty hand that the Lord brought us out from Egypt, the house of bondage. When Pharaoh stubbornly refused to let us go, the Lord slew every firstborn in the land of Egypt, the firstborn of both man and beast. Therefore I sacrifice to the Lord every first male issue of the womb, but redeem every firstborn among my sons."

❐ THE CEREMONY OF PIDYON HABEN

The following is a sample of a ceremony of the redeeming of the firstborn son.*

The rabbi may wish to begin as follows:

In very ancient times, the firstborn son in every Israelite family was vested with special responsibilities. From the day of his birth he was consecrated to the vocation of assisting the priests in the conduct of worship.

Later, when a portable sanctuary was built in the wilderness, this vocation of the firstborn was transferred to the Levites, a priestly tribe. The Torah then decreed that every father release his firstborn son from the duties incumbent upon all firstborn sons by redeeming him from a Kohen (a descendant of Aaron). The ancient obligations of the firstborn son thus continue to be recalled. This practice, ordained as a recollection of the Exodus from Egypt, further serves to make vivid for us the liberation from bondage of the people Israel, an event which has been an inspiration to all freedom-loving people.

It is now our privilege to participate in the mitzvah of redeeming a firstborn son.

The father may say:

Our God and God of our fathers, Source of all blessing, we are grateful for this blessing of a son born to us, and for the privilege of participating in this mitzvah. Throughout our lives may we be worthy of Your favor.

---

* Reprinted from *A Rabbi's Manual*, edited by Jules Harlow, published by The Rabbinical Assembly. Copyright © 1965 by The Rabbinical Assembly. Reprinted by permission.

Lesson 6 — Laws for the Future

Father (addressing the Kohen, and presenting child to him):

זֶה בְּנִי בְּכוֹרִי הוּא פֶּטֶר רֶחֶם לְאִמּוֹ, וְהַקָּדוֹשׁ בָּרוּךְ הוּא צִוָּה לִפְדּוֹתוֹ, שֶׁנֶּאֱמַר: וּפְדוּיָו מִבֶּן חֹדֶשׁ תִּפְדֶּה בְּעֶרְכְּךָ כֶּסֶף חֲמֵשֶׁת שְׁקָלִים בְּשֶׁקֶל הַקֹּדֶשׁ, עֶשְׂרִים גֵּרָה הוּא. וְנֶאֱמַר: קַדֶּשׁ־לִי כָל־בְּכוֹר, פֶּטֶר כָּל־רֶחֶם בִּבְנֵי יִשְׂרָאֵל בָּאָדָם וּבַבְּהֵמָה, לִי הוּא.

This is my son, firstborn of his mother. The Holy One, praised be He, has commanded to redeem him, as it is written in the Torah: When he is one month old, you shall redeem him for five *shekalim*. And it is written: Consecrate unto Me every firstborn of Israel; he is Mine.

Kohen (taking child from father):

מַאי בָּעִית טְפֵי, לִתֵּן לִי בִּנְךָ בְּכוֹרְךָ שֶׁהוּא פֶּטֶר רֶחֶם לְאִמּוֹ, אוֹ בָּעִית לִפְדּוֹתוֹ בְּעַד חָמֵשׁ סְלָעִים, כִּדְמְחַיַּבְתְּ מִדְּאוֹרַיְתָא?

What is your preference—to give me your firstborn son, or to redeem him for five *shekalim*, as you are obligated to do according to the Torah?

Father (handing the five coins to the Kohen):

חָפֵץ אֲנִי לִפְדּוֹת אֶת־בְּנִי, וְהֵילָךְ דְּמֵי פִדְיוֹנוֹ כִּדְמְחַיַּבְתִּי מִדְּאוֹרַיְתָא.

I want to redeem my son. Here is the equivalent of five *shekalim*, fulfilling my obligation according to the Torah.

בָּרוּךְ אַתָּה יְיָ אֱלֹהֵינוּ מֶלֶךְ הָעוֹלָם, אֲשֶׁר קִדְּשָׁנוּ בְּמִצְוֹתָיו וְצִוָּנוּ עַל פִּדְיוֹן הַבֵּן.

Praised are You, O Lord our God, King of the Universe, who sanctified us with your commandments and commanded us concerning the redemption of the firstborn son.

Father and mother:

בָּרוּךְ אַתָּה יְיָ אֱלֹהֵינוּ מֶלֶךְ הָעוֹלָם, שֶׁהֶחֱיָנוּ וְקִיְּמָנוּ וְהִגִּיעָנוּ לַזְּמַן הַזֶּה.

Praised are You, O Lord our God, King of the universe, who has kept us in life, sustained us, and enabled us to reach this day.

Kohen (holding the coins):

זֶה תַּחַת זֶה, זֶה חָלוּף זֶה, זֶה מָחוּל עַל זֶה. וְיִכָּנֵס זֶה הַבֵּן לַחַיִּים,
לְתוֹרָה וּלְיִרְאַת שָׁמָיִם. יְהִי רָצוֹן, שֶׁכְּשֵׁם שֶׁנִּכְנַס לַפִּדְיוֹן כֵּן יִכָּנֵס
לְתוֹרָה וּלְחֻפָּה וּלְמַעֲשִׂים טוֹבִים. אָמֵן.

I accept the five *shekalim* and hereby declare your son redeemed. May he be granted a full life, lived in devotion to Torah and reverence for God. As this child has attained redemption, so may it be God's will that he attain the blessings of Torah, marriage, and a life of good deeds. Amen.

יְשִׂמְךָ אֱלֹהִים כְּאֶפְרַיִם וְכִמְנַשֶּׁה.
יְבָרֶכְךָ יְיָ וְיִשְׁמְרֶךָ,
יָאֵר יְיָ פָּנָיו אֵלֶיךָ וִיחֻנֶּךָּ,
יִשָּׂא יְיָ פָּנָיו אֵלֶיךָ וְיָשֵׂם לְךָ שָׁלוֹם.

May the Lord make you like Ephraim and Menasseh.
May the Lord bless you and guard you.
May the Lord show you favor, and be gracious to you.
May the Lord show you kindness and grant you peace.

יְיָ שׁוֹמְרֶךָ, יְיָ צִלְּךָ עַל יַד יְמִינֶךָ.
כִּי אֹרֶךְ יָמִים וּשְׁנוֹת חַיִּים וְשָׁלוֹם יוֹסִיפוּ לָךְ.
יְיָ יִשְׁמָרְךָ מִכָּל־רָע, יִשְׁמֹר אֶת־נַפְשֶׁךָ. אָמֵן.

May the Lord be your Guardian, your Protector at your right hand.
May He grant you length of days and peace.
May He guard you from every evil, may He protect your soul. Amen.

LESSON 7

Into the Wilderness
Exod. 13:17–22

❐ IN PREPARATION FOR TEACHING

All through the plagues God had been in control of the situation. As we shall see, this control is to continue. Israel's journey will not be that of a band of freed slaves, haphazardly searching for a homeland. God will guide them through their hazardous trip through the wilderness until they reach Canaan.

The trip from Egypt to Canaan through the coastal plain, later to be known as Philistia, would have been the shortest. It was for that reason that God avoided it. It would have forced Israel to immediately engage in war with the inhabitants of Canaan. Would they, at that stage of their nationhood, be able to face a war, or would they turn tail and return to Egypt and to slavery? Later events show that they needed more time to gain confidence in God's protection and His ability to do for them, no matter how hopeless the situation seemed to be from a human point of view.

❐ TEACHING PROCEDURE

On the following page is a simplified map of Egypt, Canaan, and the Sinai Peninsula to help students understand the geography of the area.

The following points should be noted:

1. Since "reeds" grow in many lakes in Egypt, it is impossible to locate the "Sea of Reeds." Some think it was Lake Sirbonis.

2. The shortest way from Egypt to Canaan was through what was later to be known as the Land of the Philistines. The Israelites, however, turned south, into the Sinai Peninsula.

3. There are many theories about the route they took, and there are at least seven theories about the location of Mount Sinai.

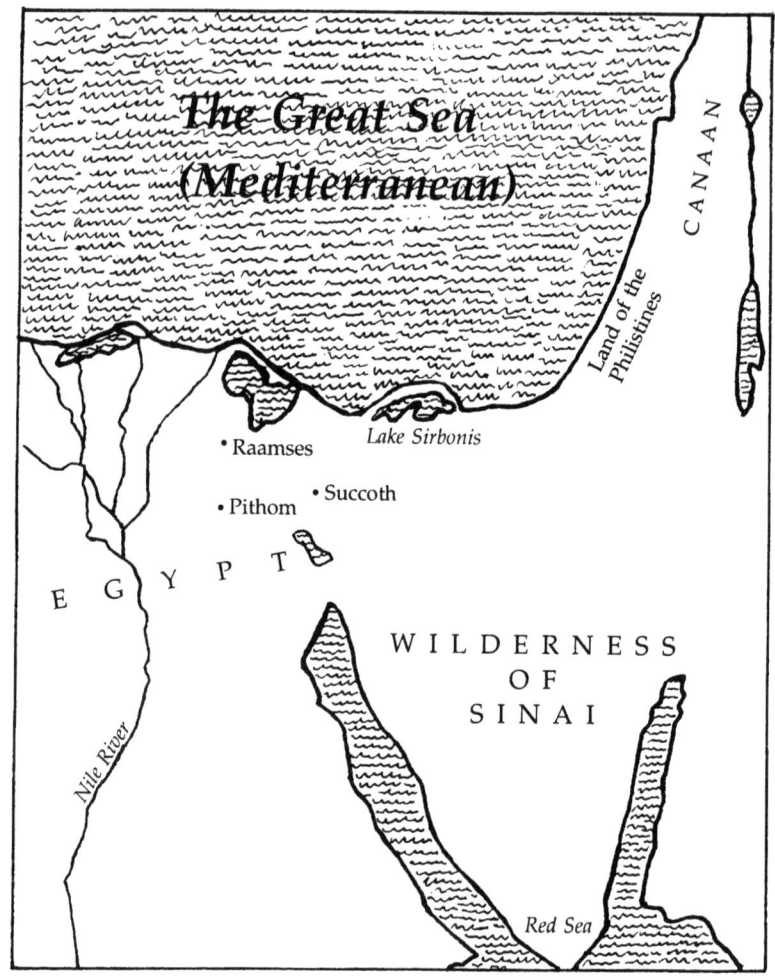

Who is in charge of events?

God. (13:17)

Find the coastal route on the map.
What reason does God have for avoiding the coastal route?

This coastal route, through what is today the Gaza Strip, was not hazardous in itself. The Philistines who were later to dwell there (Gaza was one of five Philistine cities) did not yet arrive on the scene at the time of the Exodus. This route was deemed too short. It would take the Israelites to Canaan before they were ready and able to fight for their freedom.

What would the Israelites have to learn before facing a war in Canaan?

To depend on God for help and not be overwhelmed. They had not yet learned to rise above the logistics of a given situation. They had not yet learned that with God's support seemingly massive obstacles can be overcome.

To clarify this point you may want to use the example of Israel in 1948. The outcome of a war is not always logically and strategically predictable, but can depend to a great extent on the faith and determination of the fighters. Had Israel in 1948 heeded the advice of the military experts she may never have fought against the five Arab nations that closed in on her, and never gained her independence.

The 500,000 Jewish inhabitants of the area had no army, no navy or air force, no arms to speak of, no funds or uniforms or food supplies. However, they were fighting a desperate battle for their homes, their land, their lives. They knew this land was the only possible haven for the thousands of Jews displaced by Hitler and the second World War, and deep in their hearts they knew that God was with them (although they may not have articulated this.)

Read 13:18b–19.

חֲמֻשִׁים in modern Hebrew means "armed," but we do not know what it means in biblical Hebrew. If indeed "armed" is here the correct translation, we do not know where they obtained the arms.

What did Moses carry out of Egypt?

He took with him the bones of Joseph.

This was in response to Joseph's request. Joseph had exacted an oath from the Israelites on his deathbed (Gen. 50:25).

What was Moses indicating about his intentions when he took Joseph's bones with him?

> The finality of the departure. Israel had left, never to return.

Read 13:20–22.

At the end of Exodus 13 we are told that God led the Israelites by a pillar of cloud by day and a pillar of fire by night. We shall not attempt to explain these pillars by "scientific" means.

What is the Bible trying to tell us by the means of the pillar metaphor?

> That the Israelites are aware of the fact that God is leading them. They express their trust in God's leadership in poetic form by means of the pillar metaphor.

You might want to summarize along these lines: In the last section of Exodus 13 we are given the overpowering message that God, who has just orchestrated the ten plagues, is in charge of the Israelites and is guiding them.

LESSON 8

The Final Blow
Exodus 14

❐ IN PREPARATION FOR TEACHING

The translation of the Hebrew יַם סוּף yields "The Sea of Reeds," not "the Red Sea." There are many bodies of water in Egypt which grow reeds and we cannot identify which of these the story in this chapter refers to.

The story in Exodus 14 is not the event itself but the retelling of the event, and like the plague story it is highly subjective, colored by emotions. As with the plagues, here too the Egyptians may have encountered a mishap. There may be certain coastal strips of land which at flood time are covered by water and at ebb are dry. Regardless, as the story stands, with walls of water on the left and on the right the story is poetic, and not meant to be taken literally. It is there to indicate God's power and His love for His people Israel. Let your students, therefore, enter the spirit of the story, suspending their disbelief, and enjoy its poetic beauty.

We have broken the chapter into several small sections to enable a close reading.

❐ TEACHING PROCEDURE

GOD'S PLAN (14:1-4)

According to 14:4, why will God stiffen Pharaoh's heart?

God informs Moses he will stiffen Pharaoh's heart in order to "assert His authority": win recognition of His power by dealing a final blow to Pharaoh and all his hosts, so that the "Egyptians will know that I am the Lord."

The learning experience had not yet been concluded. It was God's plan that Pharaoh and Israel would meet once more for a final showdown.

PHARAOH'S PLAN (14:5-8)

When did Pharaoh change his mind about letting the Israelites go?

When he was told that the Israelites had fled.

How does the narrator describe the departing Israelites?

"The Israelites were departing boldly." (14:8)

Describe the difference between a "fleeing" person (as the Israelites were described to Pharaoh) and one who "departs boldly" (as the narrator describes the Israelites).

The fleeing person runs, looks around in a furtive manner, takes cover behind bushes and rocks. One who departs boldly walks erect, in full view, at his own pace.

What is Pharaoh's army ("host") made up of?

1. chariot
2. horses
3. horsemen
4. warriors

THE CONFRONTATION (14:10-14)

The "boldly departing" Israelites caught sight of the Egyptians advancing upon them and were greatly frightened. Whom do they accuse?

Moses.

Why do they accuse Moses?

(Open.) He is their leader. He has brought them to this point. Insecurity is worse than the hard life of being slaves.

What do they tell Moses?

That they would rather be back in Egypt.

What do they fail to realize?

That God is with them and will save them (as Moses tells them).

What do we learn about the Israelites from their reaction?

That they still have a lot to learn. They are by no means ready to confront the inhabitants of Canaan.

What do we learn about Moses from his answer to them?

Moses is confident. He tells them that God will fight their battle. "Stand by!" he tells them, "for the Egyptians whom you see

Lesson 8 — The Final Blow

today, you will never see again!" As leader, he shows confidence in God.

INSTRUCTION TO MOSES (14:15-18)

From 14:15 we learn that Moses himself finds the situation difficult. What words tell us that?

"Why do you cry out to Me?"

Why is the situation particularly trying for Moses?

He is confronted not only by Pharaoh and his hosts, but also by Israel.

What are God's instructions to Moses?

To lift his rod and hold his arm over the sea and split it so the Israelites may march into the sea on dry ground.

What will be the purpose of this miraculous feat?

To "let the Egyptians know that I am the Lord" (just as with the plagues). (14:18)

THE NIGHT BEFORE (14:19-20)

What happened to the pillar (God's guiding presence) as the Egyptians approached that night?

The pillar shifted its position and placed itself between the camp of the Israelites and that of the Egyptians (although the text says this was a pillar of cloud, being nighttime this probably meant a pillar of fire).

What effect did the position of the pillar have on the Egyptians?

The text tells us that a magic spell was cast upon the night. The Egyptians were frightened and did not approach the Israelites.

CROSSING THE SEA (14:21-25)

What happened once the Egyptians entered the sea?

God threw them into panic. The wheels of their heavy chariots sank into the mud and would not turn. They locked tight. "Let us flee," the Egyptians cried. "The Lord is fighting for them." But by then it was too late.

THE DROWNING (14:26-31)

Moses held out his arm over the sea. The sea returned to its normal state. The Egyptians abandoned their chariots and tried to flee on foot, but God hurled them into the sea. They were toppled by the water and drowned. You can imagine what it was like. If you have ever been thrown by a wave at the beach, whirled by the water, your head is stuck in the sand at the bottom of the sea, you are struggling to get to the surface. The Egyptians, moreover, were armed and wearing coats of armor (show pictures of Egyptian chariots and their riders). "The waters turned back and covered the chariots and the horsemen of Pharaoh's entire army that had followed after them into the sea—not one remained."

Reread Moses' prediction (14:13). Was he right?

> Yes, Israel was never to see the mighty Egyptian army again, what they saw instead was the dead on the shore of the sea.

You may want to read the chapter to your class dramatically as a final activity or give a separate lesson on retelling the crossing of the sea in the first person. You can do this orally with your class (as described below) or in writing.

CROSSING THE SEA — A FIRST-PERSON REPORT

Have your students retell the crossing of the sea, pretending they were there. Take one short section, have a student describe it, then have others add to the description before you move to the next. You may be able to record the students' descriptions and then write a composite record of the students' "recollections."

The story could develop along the following lines: You have just spent the night trapped between the sea and the hosts of the Egyptian army. By the light of the pillar of fire that stood between you and them you watched the glimmer of the polished chariots, the armor, the helmets, the spears. You heard the neighing of their horses.

All that night a strong wind was blowing. You watched the waters in the sea diminishing and drying up. In the early morning you waded through the muddy sea floor, your sandaled feet slowed down by the squishy soft earth. Your heart was pounding, the Egyptians were close behind you. Your father was carrying your little sister and your mother was urging you to hurry. The lambs, prodded by the men, were bleating. The first Hebrews were clambering ashore.

Now the entire Egyptian army had entered the dried-up sea, the chariots, the horses, the horsemen, the warriors, but things did not seem to go well with them. You could hear them swear and curse, the wheels of the heavy chariots sunk into the soft mud. The charioteers were whipping their horses. You looked back and saw some horsemen pulling their horses, but these, their mouths foaming, were breaking at the knees and kneeling in the mud. The Egyptians, their heavy armor weighing them down, were up to their knees in the mud.

Then, with a tremendous roar and thunder the waters came crashing down on them: on the men, the chariots, the horses. You had just climbed out on the other shore exhausted, and now, watching, you could not quite believe your eyes. Pharaoh's might was covered by the waters, sinking like lead to the bottom of the sea. As Moses had told the people (14:13), Israel was never to see the mighty Egyptian army again.

Exodus 14 ends with the statement, "the people feared the Lord. They trusted in the Lord and in his servant Moses." What does "trusting in the Lord" mean here?

(Open.) Suggestions: They believed in the Lord's existence and were convinced of His superior powers. They knew that God loves Israel. He had kept His promises and will keep them in the future too.

What would trusting Moses imply?

(Open.) Suggestion: They would be convinced that Moses was God's agent and therefore they would obey him.

How has the Israelites' opinion of Moses changed since they first encountered Moses?

(Open.)

LESSON 9

The Song at the Sea
Exod. 15:1–21

❐ IN PREPARATION FOR TEACHING

It is believed by some that the original song consisted of 15:1 only: "I will sing to the Lord, for he has triumphed gloriously; horse and driver he has hurled into the sea" (repeated in slightly changed form in 15:21).

Many scholars believe that much of this hymn was a freestanding poem composed after the conquest of Canaan and the establishment of the Sanctuary. It was included here because it can be read as a prophesy.

❐ TEACHING PROCEDURE

In the last lesson we tried to identify with what the Israelites felt at the Sea of Reeds. Today we are going to read, in Exodus 15, a hymn that the Israelites may have sung at that time.

Does anyone know what a hymn is?

> A hymn is a song of praise to God, glorifying Him. It is also called a psalm.

Read the entire hymn (Exodus 15) now. Then go back and look at it in sections. As we read, try to notice which lines are said directly to God, addressing God, and which ones tell why he is praised.

Now let's go back to 15:1–3. Who speaks in 15:1?

> A single person.

Who is singing?

> It could be anybody who had crossed the sea.

Whom does he or she sing to?

> God.

Lesson 9 — The Song at the Sea

Why?

Because of God's triumph in defeating the Egyptians and saving the Israelites.

How is God viewed in these verses?

He is the Lord, the warrior. He is strength, might and salvation.

It is important to remember that God has manifold aspects. He is one God who supports His people and ministers to all their needs whatever they might be. In this case, faced by the Egyptian army it is God the warrior who is praised.

What is described in 15:4–5?

The drowning of mighty Pharaoh.

In 15:6 the singer turns to God and address Him directly. What words tell us that?

Your right hand. *You* send forth, etc.

Read 15:7–10. Whom is the singer quoting in 15:9?

The enemy—the Egyptians.

How do the Egyptians sound?

Confident. Glorying in what they imagine to be their triumph.

According to this description, in splitting the Sea of Reeds God set a trap. Who was the trap set for?

The Egyptian army.

Who was the bait?

Israel and their property.

What are 15:11 and 13 about?

They are the spontaneous thanks of the Israelites who were saved as a result of the Egyptians' being drowned when the trap closed.

What is odd about 15:12?

The *earth* swallowed the Egyptians. In reality it was the *waters* that swallowed the Egyptians. It is possible that 15:12 serves as a bridge between the first part of the hymn and the second one, since 15:13–18 deal with Israel's passing over land (earth).

Bible scholars believe that this hymn was not written in the desert and proclaimed after the crossing, but was written in later times.

15:1–11 deal with the events that have just taken place at the Sea of Reeds. What do 15:14–18 deal with?

With the effect of the drowning of the Egyptians on others. The people of Canaan shall hear that Israel is approaching and shall tremble.

(15:15) Why will the dwellers of Canaan be aghast?

Because they will have heard of the mighty deeds that God had performed for His people in Egypt and at the Sea of Reeds. God has made His reputation!

Eventually God will bring His people to His holy abode.

What part of the hymn did Miriam sing as a song?

"Sing to the Lord for He has triumphed gloriously; horse and driver He has hurled into the sea." (15:21)

You might conclude with the following discussion:

This hymn of praise is an outpouring of thanks by the Israelites for God's having saved them from what looked like certain death at the hands of the Egyptians. Reading this hymn we feel their relief and joy at having been saved. However, there is a midrash—an explanation written by the Rabbis many generations after the event—which expresses another point of view. It says that at the time of the drowning of the Egyptians the ministering angels wished to sing a song of praise to the Lord but He scolded them saying, מַעֲשֵׂה יָדַי טוֹבְעִים בְּיָם סוּף וְאַתֶּם אוֹמְרִים שִׁירָה לְפָנַי? "My own creation is drowning in the sea. Would you utter song before me?"

What difference is there between the God described in the text and the God of the midrash?

(Open discussion.) God in the text is concerned with His own people. He is a God of war. In the midrash He is a universal God, unable to rejoice when any of His creatures are destroyed.

What is this midrash trying to teach?

This midrash was written many generations after the events. The author of this midrash does not deny that the destruction of the Egyptians was just and necessary, nor does he condemn the Israelites for rejoicing. He does, however, try to teach that a "godly" reaction (which humans presumably should emulate) is to value all human life and feel sorrow at its destruction.

Can anyone call to mind something we do with our full cup of wine at the seder that is related to the concept that this midrash is trying to teach?

At the seder we equate wine with joy. At the mention of the ten plagues suffered by the Egyptians we diminish our joy by spilling out some of the wine in our overflowing goblet, lest "our cup of joy runneth over."

UNIT FOUR

Revelation at Sinai
Exod. 15:22–20:23

LESSON 1A

The Bitter Water
Exod. 15:22–27

◻ GOD THE PROVIDER: OVERVIEW

The next four lessons, covering Exod. 15:22–17:16, describe different events that occurred at several stopping places during Israel's early wandering in the wilderness. These events are not connected to one another yet they all fulfill the same purpose: they tell us about the special relationship between God and Israel. In each of the stories there is the same sequence of events:

1. The Israelites run into difficulties.
2. They turn against Moses. They do not seem to remember from one difficulty to the next that it was God had saved them previously.
3. In response to the people's complaints, Moses turns to God.
4. God helps His people.

These stories teach a lesson: God has the power to help. He is concerned with Israel, and the life of the people depends on God. Since God has done so much for his people they must obey Him and follow His instructions.

Read each one of these stories with your students. They are difficult and do not contain enough new and interesting material to dwell on them for more than a brief time. Once you read them all, you may want to ask why these stories have been grouped together. What do they have in common? Have students discover that they are a learning experience for the people of Israel.

◻ IN PREPARATION FOR TEACHING

Regarding the episode of the bitter water, Bible scholars in the past and in modern times have found great difficulties. What was the test, and what are the "fixed rules" (15:25)? One explanation suggests that God put the Israelites through a learning experience.

The ordeal at Marah was a *teaching device* through which God taught the people the "fixed rules," namely: (1) how to sweeten water, and (2) that in all situations God will protect His people, if only they follow His instructions (practical and moral).

◻ TEACHING PROCEDURE

Read the section. Some questions to be asked are:
1. What was the misfortune that befell the people?
2. Whom did they complain to?
3. What did Moses do?
4. What did God tell Moses to do?
5. Why wasn't God angry with the Israelites?

Which words here tell us that God is using this water problem to educate the Israelites?

"He put them to the test." (15:25)
"If you will heed the Lord." (15:26)
He is using this experience to teach them faith: In all situations God will protect His people if they only follow His instructions.

Do not ask students to struggle with the meaning of 15:25b–26.

LESSON 1B

Manna and Quail
Exod. 16:1–36

❐ IN PREPARATION FOR TEACHING

This story is told twice in the Torah. Here and in Numbers 11. In this story the people are not criticized for their grumbling. They have consumed whatever they had brought with them from Egypt and they are parched and hungry. They complain to Moses. God supplies the people with both manna and quail, thus the story parallels the Marah story insofar as it establishes God's ability to fulfill all the people's needs.

Not so in the story in the book of Numbers. There it seems that the people already have manna to eat but felt a "gluttonous craving" (Num. 11:4) for meat. In that story God is angry with the people and as they start eating from the huge mounds of quail they had collected in their "depraved craving" they died of a severe plague (food poisoning?).

Bible scholars have noted that the Exodus stories that are placed *before* the Sinai covenant, do not involve God's anger or His punishment. They seem to be part of the "learning experience" in which Israel learns about God's love for Israel and about God's saving powers. In the stories placed in the post-Sinaitic times, however, punishment does play a part.

Manna, we are told, appeared every morning but melted in the sun later in the day. Note that the word "bread" refers to "food" in general.

Quail are birds that do not fly well. They cover distances only when a strong wind blows. When the wind subsides the birds sink to the ground and can be easily gathered. The evening wind was to bring the quail.

Note that this is the first time the Torah mentions the Sabbath as an institution to be kept by the people (Gen. 2:1–4a deals only with God's ceasing from work). It appears as if the people are already aware that the Sabbath has to be kept, although the commandments have not yet been received.

Traditionally, commentators understood that אֵין מֻקְדָּם וְאֵין מְאֻחָר בַּתּוֹרָה, "there is no early or late in the Torah." That is, the episodes in the Torah do not necessarily follow a chronological sequence. Thus, they may contain anachronisms. These inconsistencies should not concern us too much, since the Torah itself ignores them. Our purpose is not to figure out exactly what happened historically, but to draw out the message that the text itself conveys by telling its story the way it does (such as placing all the episodes of deprivation and rescue together).

☐ TEACHING PROCEDURE

(16:1–3) Describe the predicament of the Israelites.

A month after the departure from Egypt, the people have run out of bread.

לָחֶם means "food," as in the phrase הוּא נוֹתֵן לֶחֶם לְכָל־בָּשָׂר in Birkat Hamazon.

Whom do they turn against?

Moses and Aaron.

What do they disregard?

They disregard the fact that God is "in charge," and that He is the Provider (the same lesson as at Marah).

(16:4–12) How does God react to the complaint of the Israelites?

The Lord promises "bread" to the people.

There is a test involved (16:4) "to see whether they will follow My instructions or not." We do not yet know what this test entails, except that they are to collect a double portion of manna on the sixth day. God will supply the people with meat in the evening and bread in the morning so that "you shall know that I the Lord am your God" (16:12).

(16:13–21) What were Moses' instructions to the people?

Gather as much of it as each of you requires to eat, an omer to a person. (16:16)
Let no one leave any of it over unto morning. (16:19)

How did some people fail the test?

They didn't pay attention to Moses' instructions. They hoarded the food, and it became infested. (16:20)

What was being tested here?

Their trust in God's ability to provide for them on a continuous basis.

Ordinarily, people who have gone hungry for a while and suddenly come upon food might well want to keep some of it for the next day. These, however, were not normal circumstances. The people were supposed to demonstrate their trust in God's ability to provide for them by following His instructions.

(16:22–36) For five weekdays the people were to collect one omer per person. How did the rule differ for Friday? for the Sabbath?

On the sixth day the people were to collect a double portion. (16:22–24)
On the Sabbath day they were to refrain from collecting manna. (16:25–26)

(16:27) How did some people fail this test?

Some people went out to gather manna on the Sabbath but found none.

(16:28–30) What is God's reaction to those who failed the test?

"How long will you men refuse to obey My commandments?"

(16:31–36) How were the people to remember God's providence for all generations?

They were to store a jar of manna in the ark of the covenant (once it was built).

LESSON 1C

Water from the Rock
Exod. 17:1–7

❐ IN PREPARATION FOR TEACHING

This story of Moses hitting the rock appears also in Numbers 20. See above, p. 119, for comments about stories that appear in two versions.

❐ TEACHING PROCEDURE

Why do the people grumble now?

There is no water to drink.

What is familiar in the way they word their complaint to Moses?

"Why did you bring us out of Egypt . . . to kill us . . . with thirst?" (17:3)

Of what previous complaints does this remind you?

Exod. 16:3 (and Exod. 14:11).

Moses seems exasperated. What does he say?

He says to God (17:4): "What shall I do with this people? Before long they will be stoning me."

What does God tell Moses to do?

To hit the rock with his staff and water will come out of it.

The episode is called a test (17:7). Who is testing whom?

This time it is Israel that sets up the test to see if God is present in their midst or not.

LESSON 1D

Amalek
Exod. 17:8–16

◻ TEACHING PROCEDURE

The first three episodes show Israelites encountering difficulties because of lack of food and water. The difficulty here is of a different kind.

What new difficulty do the Israelites encounter?

The Israelites are attacked by the Amalekites.

How does God rescue the people?

Moses is to hold his arms up. As long as he does so, the Israelites will prevail.

What do you think the holding up of Moses' arms symbolizes?

(Open.) The meaning of this symbol is not clear, but it is a powerful image however we understand it.

God tells Moses, "I will utterly blot out the memory of Amalek from under heaven.... The Lord will be at war with Amalek throughout the ages." Usually such bitterness against an enemy prevails when one *loses* the battle. Israel wins this battle. Nevertheless, there is great bitterness.

This ancient hatred of Amalek is carried on throughout Jewish history. Saul, first king of Israel, fights numerous battles against Amalek. Later, the author of the book of Esther describes Mordecai as coming from Saul's tribe (Benjamin) and family (Kish), while Haman is called an Agagite (Agag being the king of Amalek in Saul's time (1 Sam. 15:8).

A possible explanation for this longlasting hatred toward the people of Amalek is the additional information found in Deut. 25:17–19 (a passage that is read in the synagogue on Shabbat Zakhor, the Shabbat before Purim):

Remember (זָכוֹר) what Amalek did to you on your journey, after you left Egypt—how, undeterred by fear of God, he surprised you on the march, when you were famished and weary, and cut down all the stragglers in your rear. Therefore . . . you shall blot out the memory of Amalek from under heaven. Do not forget.

According to this passage from Deuteronomy, what is the reason for the special bitterness toward Amalek?

Amalek's attack was a surprise attack on the weakest of the Israelites just after they left Egypt. It was unprovoked and cowardly.

GOD THE PROVIDER: CONCLUSION

What lesson should the Israelites learn from the episodes of the bitter water, manna and quail, water from the rock, and Amalek?

God has the power to help. He is concerned with Israel, and the life of the people depends on God. Since God has done so much for his people they must obey Him and follow His instructions.

Can you think of a reason for God's not being angry with the Israelites in these episodes?

These are "learning experiences," from which Israel learns about God's love for Israel and about God's saving powers. Once the Israelites have entered into the covenant with God at Sinai (Exodus 19–20), God becomes angry and punishes the people when they lack faith.

LESSON 2

Jethro
Exodus 18

☐ IN PREPARATION FOR TEACHING

Biblical tradition attributes the administrative organization of the people into thousands, hundreds, fifties and tens to Jethro, Moses' father-in-law. This organization was to simplify the administration of justice, prior to giving the law. The Israelites were to use this order in their travels and camping through the years in the wilderness. Thus Jethro is viewed as a "technical advisor" or "consultant" to Moses.

☐ TEACHING PROCEDURE

JETHRO ARRIVES WITH MOSES' FAMILY (18:1-7)

What new information about Moses' family do we gather here?

Moses had at some point sent his wife Zippora and his two sons back to Midian. Now the family is reunited.

Why might Moses have done that?

(Open.) Suggestion: Moses feared danger in Egypt.

JETHRO RECOGNIZES GOD'S SAVING POWERS (18:8-12)

What is Jethro's reaction to hearing the amazing things that God has done for the Israelites during Exodus?

Jethro, a Midianite, comes to realize that "the Lord is greater than all other gods."

This recognition of the God of Israel as greater than all gods represents the fulfillment of one of God's purposes as stated during the plagues. What purpose was that?

"In order that my name resound throughout the world." (9:16)

Does Jethro's statement recognizing God's power make him an Israelite?

No, since he does not recognize God as the one and only God.

What specifically convinced Jethro of God's greatness?

For one thing, he had already heard (18:1) all that God had done for Israel His people. In addition, Moses now "recounted to his father-in-law all that had befallen them on the way, and how the Lord had delivered them"; (18:8) how they lacked food and water and how they were attacked by the Amalekites.

It may be interesting for your class to speculate on the difference between the Israelites' reaction to God's wonders (Exodus 15–17) and Jethro's. The Israelites, for whom the wonders are performed, seem less convinced of God's power than does Jethro.

JETHRO ORGANIZES THE PEOPLE (18:13–27)

What does Jethro notice as he observes Moses?

Since Moses is the sole authority to which the people can turn with their questions, he is overworked and the people have to wait a long time to see him.

Why, according to Moses is he overworked?

Moses explains that he works so hard because the people come to him to "inquire of the Lord":

1. Moses is a judge. Whenever there is a dispute, Moses, knowing the laws of God, decides who tells the truth and judges between the people.

2. Moses is a prophet. He consults with God and then conveys to the people God's laws and teachings in cases where there is no precedent.

Jethro recognizes that Moses is fulfilling these two separate functions and is working too hard. What does he suggest Moses should concentrate his own efforts on?

Moses should concentrate on his role as a prophet.

What about his role as a judge?

These duties can be taken over by judges whom Moses appoints.

What kind of people are these judges to be?

אַנְשֵׁי חַיִל—"men of means," substantial people who command respect by their socioeconomic position.

What qualities does the text mention that these people should have?

They should be capable (efficient), God-fearing, trustworthy, and capable of spurning ill-gotten gain (bribes).

How was the community organized?

Moses divided his people into units of thousands, which in turn were divided into hundreds, and those into fifties, and those into tens. Each unit and subunit had a leader.

How did this new organization solve the original problem that Jethro had seen?

It took part of the burden off Moses and established a chain of leadership that would organize the people throughout the desert years.

In the next chapters we will learn of God's revealing his laws to the Israelites. Why is it important that administrative problems—the chain of command—be set up ahead of time?

The implementation of the laws depends on a workable administrative and judicial system.

LESSON 3

Revelation at Sinai
Exodus 19

❐ IN PREPARATION FOR TEACHING

The following background material is based on "Understanding the Sinai Revelation" by Edward L. Greenstein. The entire essay can be found in the appendix, pp. 273–317 below. Teachers are urged to read it in its entirety.

The teaching of revelation to today's young generation is a difficult task. It may not be necessary to teach revelation as a subject, but we know from experience that students are baffled by the story and ask many questions: Did it really happen? Can God talk to a multitude of people? How much of the Torah did He proclaim at Sinai? How can we believe that mitzvot are revealed by God when scholars tell us that some mitzvot are similar to laws of other ancient nations?

It is therefore necessary to provide the teacher with the background material to satisfy some of the students' questions. The examples used in this material can probably be used for students too.

The Revelation at Sinai is the most significant event in the story of the Jewish people. At Sinai the people of Israel entered into a covenant (בְּרִית) with God. This covenant made the Hebrews into a nation dedicated to fulfilling the mission of God. It is this common mission which binds the people together. Without it, the formation of the Hebrew people is no more than an accident of history that could be undone just as accidentally as it was done. The Torah, however, teaches that the covenant with Israel was the intention of God from Genesis on.

The Bible, in its description of the events at Sinai, imposes itself upon its reader with bold directness. It tells us "This is what happened!" Yet there are elements in this story which make it difficult for us, modern people, to read the story literally, as an historic event. God appears as fire in the midst of smoke. He speaks in a human voice amid thunder and lightning to a large multitude

Lesson 3 — Revelation at Sinai 129

simultaneously. We may be able to conceive of God talking to one person, but can one see and hear God outside of oneself?

Our understanding of what happened at Sinai is restricted by our personal belief about what *could* have happened. Our concept of what God could or could not do differs from what our ancestors believed that God could or could not do. It is also true that we do not all agree with one another on this point.

Nowadays events that happen are often recorded on videotape. Once the event is over, we can replay it over and over again. We can also slow it down and study each frame separately. By studying the videotape we may be able to learn more about the event than if we had been present at the time it happened. Not so when we read about an event in the Bible. The event happened, it is over! It was not recorded! All that people who were present at the time can do is tell about it. This telling is not an exact replica of the event but an explanation of it. Ancient Israelites explained the Sinaitic events in the light of their own enthusiasm. They believed that these events *could have happened.* (If you believe in the existence of U.F.O.'s you may explain what you saw in the sky during an evening ride in your car differently than your friend, who refuses to believe in U.F.O.'s, would.)

Every culture explains certain phenomena in certain ways. These descriptions are a matter of *convention.* We use some of them although we know they are not accurate. We say "the sun sets" although we know in reality the earth rotates and not the sun. Young children will always paint the sky blue, although it is often white or gray or even pink.

Similarly the Israelites used conventional ways to describe God's appearance on Mount Sinai. The description of the events at Sinai had been passed from generation to generation before it was written down, and must have changed in transmission. We have many times before discussed the fact that our memories are selective. We remember some things and forget others. In addition, different cultures will elaborate different aspects. For instance, biblical heroes meet the women they are to marry, at the well. Rebecca was found there by Abraham's servant and Jacob and Moses met their wives at the well. Therefore, when we read the story of the Revelation we must be aware of the differences between a) the event as it actually happened, and b) how the Torah describes what happened.

In Exod. 19:1–2 we are informed of the time and place of the event, thus presenting it as an historical fact. Exodus 19 contains two parts, 19:1–16 and 19:16–25. In the first part Moses speaks to God on the mountain. In the second part God appears to the entire people and speaks to them. The Torah describes God's appearance in physical terms. Although there is no claim that Israel saw God directly, His appearance was accompanied by certain phenomena that could be seen or heard. The Israelites witnessed thunder and lightning. He surrounded Himself in cloud. He appeared in the form of smoking fire radiating light. To the sound of thunder the sound of the shofar blast was added. The people trembled and so did the mountain! Moses addressed God, and He answered with "voice" (בְּקוֹל).

The above description is not unique. In other places in the Bible God appears in the form of fire and smoke, for instance, at the "covenant between the pieces" (Genesis 15) and at the "burning bush" (Exodus 3). He also guides Israel in a pillar of fire by night. Thus describing God in the form of fire and smoke or fog is a *convention* which we need not take literally. (Why fire is a suitable metaphor for God we have discussed before. See above, p. 25.)

The Israelites believed in one God, and to this one God they attributed all the powers and many of the qualities that other people attributed to their pagan gods. The people of Israel living in Canaan were dependent on rain. Rain was life itself. When they spoke of God in respect to His powers as the provider of wind and rain they borrowed the imagery of the pagan *storm god.*We find many examples of this in the Bible (see 2 Samuel 22). At Sinai God appears as "fire" and also as "storm," the radiance (כָּבוֹד) is also borrowed from ancient Near Eastern imagery.

The ancient storm god was also a warrior, thus the shofar blast described in Exodus 19 represents the trumpet blasts that signal the battle charge. The blasts of the shofar are a *conventional* way to describe a war god and need not be taken literally. Had we written the story today we may have used imagery current in our own culture. Are we to understand that God spoke in a human "voice" to all those assembled?

The Israelites believed that God could appear in human form, as he appeared to Abraham (Genesis 18). They also believed that He could, if He so wanted, communicate in human voice. (When God called Samuel by name, Samuel thought Eli was calling him. See 1 Sam. 3:4–5.) God's speaking to people is another conventional image, as God's seeing or hearing is, and we do not take his seeing or hearing literally, since we do not attribute human organs to God.

What do we mean by "God"? God has so many aspects that we can never perceive Him wholly. We have difficulty, as a matter of fact, of perceiving wholly even people we think we know well. We are often surprised when friends do something we would not have expected of them. We know our friends by their conduct, by what they do. By the same token, we know God by observing His behavior toward us and toward the world. We conceive of God as having a personality. He "sees," "hears," "remembers," and He has the will and the power to carry out His plans. Revelation is a willful act by God who wants to convey a message to a group of people.

For this communication to take place we have to have a sender, a message, and a receiver. In our case the sender is God; His message is His mitzvah or command. The receivers are the people of Israel. Should one of these three elements be missing no communication could take place.

In order to be able to receive revelation one has to believe in the existence of a sender (God) and one has to believe that He can reveal Himself by sending His message.

A person who can receive revelation holds a world view which allows for divine intention behind the event observed. From biblical times until present times Jewish tradition has understood all events as taking place on two levels simultaneously: the natural level and the supernatural or divine level. For example, Joseph was brought down to Egypt because he did not get along with his brothers. They were so angry with him that they sold him as a slave. This is the natural level. On the supernatural, or divine level, Joseph said to his brothers that it had been God's plan to have him brought down to Egypt so he could save Jacob's clan.

Some people recognize only the first, natural, human level of events. Others see history as being guided toward a purpose and a destiny by divine forces.

In order to be able to experience revelation at Sinai it was necessary that the Israelites explain history as God's plan (in terms of the divine). In the first part of Exodus 19 God has Moses sensitize the people to understand their recent history as the mighty acts of God. "You have seen what I have done to Egypt, how I bore you on eagles' wings and brought you to me" (Exod. 19:4).

Revelation need not be verbal. It can also occur through deeds. We know God by what he *does*, provided we attribute events to Him and not to "accidents."

THE RECEIVER

Let us consider an example. Imagine that two photographers take the same picture of an event. One photographer develops his film, thus getting his picture. The other does not develop the film, and therefore has no picture. The first photographer can be likened to a religious person who has learned to interpret events as acts of God. This "development" enables him to experience an event as a revelation, while the other comes away with nothing at all.

THE SENDER

Let us also compare revelation to the viewing of a film. There has to be a sender. In this case, a projectionist is necessary to show the film, and there have to be viewers who are capable of seeing, hearing and understanding the film. The viewers may understand the film in many different ways, depending on their personalities, education and background. By the same token, different people might view revelation in different ways. The message will differ according to the viewer.

Some people believe in a literal revelation. God spoke, the people heard and Moses wrote it down, word for word. Careful study of the Bible, however, indicates that different parts of the Bible are written in different styles and different stages of the Hebrew language. There is, therefore, reason to believe that the Israelites recorded their impression of revelation in their own language.

If revelation of the Torah is not word for word what God actually spoke, then how *did* God communicate? How can the laws of the Torah be understood as the message of God? Revelation is an intense religious experience in which a person feels moved by God to do something special. It is not exactly like any other experience, but it is in certain ways like something more familiar to us, such as music and illumination.

Listening to Music

Someone must produce the music and someone else must listen to it. The listener, however, does not only hear the music, he is also moved by it. Different people respond to the same music in different ways. Yet, some music is so clear, so bold that we would all respond similarly. We will recognize a certain passage as a storm, another as a dance. God's deliverance of Israel from Egypt came across as bold music with a clear message: Israel will be God's people. The people were moved by this and responded by binding themselves to God in the covenant, by adopting God's mitzvot as their responsibility. Thus the Revelation, like music, was an interaction between the source of the Revelation and the audience of the Revelation.

The Torah simplifies the story of revelation by attributing nearly everything in it to the source, God. *We* have greater appreciation of the role of the audience, Israel. Without Israel's sensitivity to "see" and to "hear" God, there could not have been revelation. Nevertheless, although the Torah may have understood the process of revelation differently than we do, we can still share our faith in the Revelation although we may explain it differently.

The ancients believed the sun literally rose and set. We know that the earth rotates—yet we agree with the ancients that the sun *appears* to rise and set.

Revelation not only moves people to respond, it makes them see things in a new or different way.

Illumination

God's presence may be likened to a source of light. Seeing things in the presence of God is like seeing them illumined, permitting us to see that which we could not see before. An X ray light permits us to see our bones which we cannot ordinarily see. However, the X ray light is not enough. We need a viewer who can look at our bones under the X ray and interpret the picture. A doctor who is trained to view X ray images will be able to do so, but a lawyer or plumber will not. However, if the image showed a clear break in the bone, even a lay person may be able to interpret it.

COMPARISON WITH SINAI

Once the Israelites were sensitized to interpret the Exodus as God's acting in history, they were able to "see" their relationship with God as special. They could now apply their intelligence and cultural concerns in the "light" of God's presence, to adopt His mitzvot. The mitzvot can be understood as *Israel's response to God's presence*. This response is a combination of (1) human understanding of how people should live, and (2) the additional special "light" that is thrown on human experience by God's acts in history.

Neither of the two above examples is exactly like revelation. No example is ever like the model that is described; that is why several examples are needed. The special relationship between God and Israel was formalized at Sinai in the *brit*.

Israel understood that they had been liberated for a purpose: Israel will accept the Lord as God, God will remain Israel's guardian, and Israel will have a special status as "a kingdom of priests." In all nations the priests had to maintain a high degree of ritual purity. In Israel, the entire citizenry must observe a level of holiness and nearness to God that is proper for a priest. For example, the ban of not eating meat torn by a beast (Exod. 22:30) which originally was applied to priests only, was extended to apply to every Israelite.

Which of the mitzvot were actually revealed at Sinai? One tradition holds that the Ten Commandments and the laws of Exodus 20–23 were all part of the Revelation. Other traditions say that all five books of the Torah were revealed at Sinai, or that *all* things that would *ever* be revealed to the Jewish people were revealed at Sinai, including all the interpretations of the sages.

For historical reasons we cannot accept the tradition that says that all mitzvot were revealed at Sinai. Various laws entered Israelite tradition in different periods.

For instance, according to Exod. 12:1–4, each family was to slaughter and consume the Pesaḥ lamb offering in its own locality. According to Deut. 16:1–8, however, each household was to bring the Pesaḥ offering to one central site where all Israelites would celebrate together. We learn from 2 Kings 22:3 that this Deuteronomic practice was not adopted until the reign of King Josiah (622 B.C.E.). Thus, some laws seem to have been introduced earlier in Israel's history than others.

There is no reason to believe that there were no other revelations after Sinai. Throughout the course of history, Israel developed forms of religious observances that were additional to existing laws or conflicted with them. These were included in the sacred tradition of Israel and represented in the laws of the Bible. The laws of many revelations were "telescoped" into one great revelation. This "telescoping" is a natural function of the mind. Thus the Bible attributes the revelations of many periods to Sinai. One law book may encompass laws from many decades. A book of baseball rules includes all current rules of the game.

To those unfamiliar with the history of the game, it might appear that the current index existed *always*. In reality, however, the various rules were introduced at various times in the history of the game. The book thus "telescopes" the rules. There is, however, one difference between the Torah and the book of laws of baseball. The baseball book eliminates "old" rules which have been changed and replaces them with "new" ones. This is not so in the Torah. The Torah, being sacred, retains all rules. No rules were allowed to be stricken or replaced. We therefore find duplicate rules and contradictory traditions in the Bible.

Each group of people, no matter how small, has its own code of conduct. Laws, therefore, must have existed in all societies throughout human history. We distinguish between laws and mitzvot: we regard *laws* as a general term, and *mitzvot* as only the laws that we understand to represent the will of God. Thus, Israel may have observed a law such as "You shall not murder" before the law became a *mitzvah*, part of the covenant obligations. Which *mitzvot* do we then attribute to revelation?

Take this example. In the latter part of Exodus and in 1 Kings we find laws concerning the building of the mishkan (portable sanctuary) and the Temple. Both texts describe the idea and the design of these structures as God-given. However, archeological excavations throughout the Middle East have unearthed the remains of numerous temples as well as texts describing them. Comparisons between the design of the Israelite sanctuaries and those of other ancient Near Eastern people, clearly show that the Israelites were using common ancient Near Eastern building practices in the construction of their own sanctuaries. We may therefore say that the physical design of the mishkan forms part of Israel's own contribution to the mitzvot. God's contribution may be seen in the event of the Exodus and the Sinai covenant in which Israel recognized God's presence and undertook to "house" this presence in their midst. The architectural designs for such a house, however, were adapted by Israel from their environment. Thus the mitzvot comprise both the Revelation experience (God's involvement in Israel's history) and also Israel's response to this experience. We have discussed slavery before. The institution and some of the practices involved in the purchase and deployment of slaves were part of Israel's contribution to the mitzvot concerning slaves. The uniquely enlightened laws concerning the humane treatment of slaves, however, may be identified as the revealed aspect of the mitzvot. The Israelites recognized God's presence in their own recent history and perceived that freedom and the individual worth of the person are values ordained by God. The book of Deuteronomy calls upon the Israelites to show compassion for the underprivileged in remembrance of the fact that they themselves have been slaves in Egypt. We may therefore surmise that the Exodus and the Revelation at Sinai contributed to the difference between Israel's laws of slavery and those of other Near Eastern people.

Many of the mitzvot reflecting high spiritual or ethical values are found not only in the Bible but also in other ancient Near Eastern literatures, some of which precede the Israelites by centuries. Among them are the laws about leaving the margins of the field for the poor (פֵּאָה) to gather.

In what sense then are such mitzvot revealed? There are at least two ways to view this issue. One might say that God spoke not only to Moses but also to Hammurapi.* After all God spoke to Adam

---

* The famous Babylonian king who lived in the eighteenth century B.C.E.

and to Noah, who were not Israelites. Also, we may say that the Israelites were enabled to recognize the merits of certain laws and practices of their neighbors and adopt these. Revelation gave them the insight to select these laws from among others which they rejected.

Here is an example. They accepted the law that says that when one causes somebody else economic damage he has to compensate his victim, but rejected the law what permitted a monetary fine to be paid in a case of murder. They modified those laws that could be changed for Israelite use, such as the laws of slavery.

The Rambam, in accordance with the thinking of the medieval Jewish philosophers, takes revelation to be a natural process of the human mind. God gave humans the capacity to discover the eternal truth present in the world and available for comprehension. When a person gains such insight—it may be viewed as a source of revelation. Thus revelation is both *human and divine* since God created the conditions for the discovery to take place.

Traditionally Jewish observance is not confined to the mitzvot that are explicitly ordained by the written Torah. (The Torah does not require the kindling of Sabbath or Hanukkah candles.) Jewish observance is based on halakhah ("law"). The halakhah is embodied in the "Oral Torah" (תּוֹרָה שֶׁבְּעַל פֶּה, "the oral instruction"). The Rabbis of the early Roman period claim that the halakhah was revealed as the Written Torah, by God at Sinai. But just as we do not accept the traditional belief that the entire five books of the Written Torah were spoken word-for-word to Moses, we do not share the traditions' understanding of the origin of the halakhah.

We understand revelation as an ongoing process and halakhah as emerging from revelations *and* from the Written Torah. There are indications that the five books of the written Torah were combined into one book in the fifth century B.C.E. The Torah was adopted as the "constitution" of the Judean community, but the specific applications to everyday life were not clearly defined. Consequently it became necessary to adapt the written Torah to a given situation. Thus the written Torah was never a complete system of law but rather a source book, a God-given guideline that required explanations by religious authority.

In order to explain the Written Torah one had to "seek" or "inquire" (לִדְרֹשׁ) into the text. In earlier times when one wanted to know God's will, one would approach a prophet and "seek" God's word. The prophet would give an answer—a revelation. At Sinai, although all people experienced the Revelation, laws had to be formalized by the prophet Moses.

From the Second Temple onward the Jews no longer relied on revelation but adopted a new form of revealed *midrash*. Instead of the prophet, the text of the written Torah was used to derive meaning from.

The text became fixed and standardized but people, times and needs change. Each change required adaptations and reinterpretations. These adaptations can be viewed not as human modification alone, but as revelation itself.

To the religious Jews the deliverance from Egypt was not the last significant event in history, all human events are a reflection of God's will, thus Jews see God's hand in the victory of the Maccabees, and although the Hanukkah holiday is not included in the Bible they have formulated the blessing over the kindling of the Hanukkah lights: "Blessed are you ... God ... who has commanded us to light the Hanukkah lamp." Halakhah changes when historical circumstances change. With the destruction of the Temple by the Romans, prayer and synagogue service took on a new importance. When gentiles regarded the wearing of a head covering as a sign of piety, Jews too adopted the practice of wearing a hat (or Kippa). Different Jewish communities developed different halakhot. Today, Eastern Jews are permitted to eat rice on Pesah, while Western Jews consider rice to be hametz.

Halakhah is not simply an explanation of the Written Torah, but often a revision of the plain sense of the Torah in the light of changing human understanding, or a new understanding of the world. We may therefore say that our new views result from revelation. We find revisions of old laws in the written Torah itself. Where in Exod. 21:2–4 a female slave is *not* set free after six years of slavery, in Deut. 15:12, both male and female slaves are emancipated after six years of service. We assume that the change resulted from a change in historical circumstances, a change in attitude, or both. As long as there is history, people who find God's presence in certain events* will come away with new revelations and new halakhot. Yom Ha'atzma'ut, Israel's independence day, is growing into an observance ordained by halakhah.

Torah in Exod. 35:3 prohibits the kindling of fire on Sabbath. Rabbinic literature goes on to discuss in detail this prohibition and the ways in which fire may be used—for instance, one may warm food over fire that was ignited earlier. The rabbis were able to relate these particulars of the halakhah to the Written Torah because they

---

* Not all events need be the manifestation of God's will or presence. Some see the *Shoah* (Holocaust) as a manifestation of God's *absence*.

believed that all of the Oral Torah is contained in the Written Torah and that it is possible to find the halakhah in the Written Torah provided one employs the proper methods of interpretation.

God has concealed the halakhah in the text leaving it to humans to disclose its hidden meaning. The means for discovering the "code," are the procedures of the *midrash*. For instance, the written Torah prohibits "boiling a kid in its mother's milk" three times.* This threefold repetition led the rabbis to take the law to imply more than its literal meaning. They went on to develop an entire system of separating dairy dishes (foods and utensils) from meat dishes. This halakhah is based on Jewish conduct that emerges from the experience of the Jewish people. Each halakhah, however, must be measured against the written Torah's basic principles. Just as the United States Supreme Court must measure each legislation against its understanding of the Constitution.

REVELATION

How much of the teacher's background material is relevant for the students? It is not suggested that revelation be treated as a "lesson" or "subject." The teacher will teach Exodus 19 and 20. We do know, however, that questions do arise in the classroom in connection with the events at Sinai and believe that the above summary of the essay by Dr. Greenstein will help the teacher in handling these questions. Remember however that other answers may be just as appropriate. "Did all the people really hear God speak?" We do not know. We do not have a videotape of the events.

All we have is a subjective retelling and explanation of the event, recorded long after it happened.

Biblical people believed some things were possible, although we may not believe that they are. If A believes that U.F.O.'s come from outer space, but B does not, A and B will describe the sighting of U.F.O.'s differently.

"Did the mountain tremble? Were the sounds of the shofar supernatural or was the sound caused by humans blowing the shofar?" Then, as now, people described things according to certain conventions. They do not have to be taken literally! (We say "the sun sets" although we know this is not true, literally.)

At Sinai God sent a message to the people. They were deeply impressed by the great deeds God had done for them and therefore open and willing to receive God's message. Had they not been receptive, revelation would not have been possible.

---

* Exod. 23:19, 34:26; Deut. 14:21.

Are we saying that only Jews have good mitzvot? Of course not. Many other nations have good moral and ethical laws. Jews also have laws which make those who keep them special, dedicated to God.

Was all halakhah revealed at Sinai? Most Conservative Jews believe that the halakhah continues to develop and change in response to changing needs of Jews in different generations and in different places. But the basic structure of Jewish observances is found in the written Torah. The essence is that we are a holy people who by our conduct should live holy lives. This is the thrust of the Torah's laws. The oral Torah helps us to observe these laws in our lives.

You may use the Constitution of the United States as an example (God-fearing people who view God as active in human events may claim that the Constitution too is God-given). New life situations demand changes in the law; the Supreme Court therefore adapts and interprets the constitutional law. For example, the Constitution does not deal with the segregation of schools. The Supreme Court, however, stated that segregation is not "constitutional" because the Constitution states that "all men were created equal" and therefore all deserve equal opportunities for education. Questions will depend on the sophistication and maturity of the students. You do not have to deal with problems which do not occur to your students.

❐ TEACHING PROCEDURE

You may choose to read one small segment at a time, instead of first reading the whole chapter. It is not imperative that you deal with each detail discussed here. Your students' interest should guide you.

The style of much of this chapter is "elevated" and poetic.

PREPARATION FOR REVELATION (19:1-13)

Read 19:1-2. What does the text achieve by placing the date first? (Compare it to the alternative: "After the Israelites had gone forth from the land of Egypt, they entered the wilderness of Sinai on the third new moon.")

It stresses the date.

What do we call the third month today?

According to Exodus 12 the Israelites left Egypt in the first month, which we call Nisan. Iyar would be the second month. The third month is Sivan.

What in 19:2 indicates that this is a known mountain?

The words "the" ("in front of *the* mountain") indicates that the mountain is known.

Look back to Exod. 3:12. At the burning bush Moses had been told by God that the people would worship at this mountain (Sinai and Horeb are the same). This fact may explain why Moses went up to God without being called (19:3). He seems to know that he is supposed to do so, and indeed God is expecting him.

(19:3–6) With what "review" information does God begin His speech to Moses and through him to the Israelites?

God sensitizes the people to the idea that it was God who had forged their recent history. God has shown His might to His people by smiting the Egyptians and bringing the people to Sinai speedily and safely (on eagle's wings).

Read 19:4–6. What special relationship between God and the Israelites does God describe here?

If the people will obey the laws which God will detail in the covenant between Him and His people, they in turn will become His very own treasured people. Although all the peoples of the world are God's, the Israelites shall become a holy* people, separated and consecrated to Him, "a kingdom of priests."

Examine the term "a kingdom of priests" more closely. Among any people, what is the relationship of priests to the rest of the people and to God?

Priests are a select group within a people who are dedicated to the service of their gods. There are certain laws and regulations that govern the lives of these priests. They have to be cultically pure to serve the gods.

How can the people of Israel serve the nations of the world?

All of Israel, by keeping God's mitzvot will become holy, as holy as *kohanim* are in other nations. All of Israel will be consecrated to God.

---

* For a discussion of the meaning of "holy," see *Genesis: A New Teacher's Guide*, 3rd ed., pp. 42–43.

Students may ask if every Israelite automatically became holy. The answer is that one became holy by keeping God's mitzvot. A "holy life" does not require withdrawal from life, but rather the hallowing of the actions of everyday life. Mitzvot are instrumental in turning everyday events, like eating and drinking (which animals do too) into "holy" occasions. Jews, by reciting berakhot like *Hamotzi* or *Birkat Hamazon* are indicating God's existence in providing sustenance to all His creatures. Laws and mitzvot touch on all areas of human life (property disputes, social welfare, health, marriage and much more).

Read 19:7. What message did Moses bring to the elders?

Moses assembled the elders and introduced them to God's proposition found in 19:3–6.

Read 19:8. What was the response of the people?

They agreed to do "whatever the Lord has spoken," although they did not as yet know what, specifically, they would be asked to do.

How do you feel about the Israelites' reaction: "All that the Lord has spoken we will do"?

(Open.)

Some may consider it risky for the Israelites to have agreed without seeing any "fine print." However, God had already made some laws known to Israel (Exodus 18) for which there was no precedent, so that by now they trusted God in the capacity of law giver.

God is building up their trust in Him both as law giver and savior.

Read 19:9–13. What is the purpose of God's appearing to the people in a thick cloud? Why didn't He continue to speak through Moses as He had done in 19:3–6?

The people doubted that God did indeed appear to Moses and spoke to him. God's public appearance in the cloud would teach the people that God does indeed speak to humans. They will trust Moses forever after.

THE PEOPLE'S RESPONSE (Optional Discussion)

This discussion is difficult and may be omitted.

Reread 19:8–9. How many times did Moses speak to the Lord? What did he say each time?

The text reports *twice* that "Moses brought back the people's words to the Lord" (once in 19:8b and once in 19:9b), yet the people gave Moses but *one* message, namely: "All that the Lord has spoken, we will do" (19:8a).

How might we explain the repetition?

(Open.)

Present the following possibilities and ask for reactions:

1. Some Bible scholars believe we have here two variants:
   a. A *private statement* to Moses (19:8b–9a). After hearing the reply of the people, God explains to Moses the purpose of the coming theophany (direct communication with God). According to 19:9, the people doubted that God spoke to Moses and that Moses was a prophet. The only way to clear that doubt was to have the people *listen* while God spoke to Moses.
   b. Right after Moses' report to God, God makes His *public statement,* telling the people how to prepare for the coming event but withholding the *purpose* of the theophany (19:9b).

2. The Rabbis also puzzled over the repetitions. They resolved it with a midrash. According to this midrash, there were two messages from the people to God.
   a. "Let us *hear* directly from the mouth of our own king."
   b. "It is our wish to *see* our king."

   God acceded to both demands and answered Moses (19:9):
   a. "I will come to you in a thick cloud in order that the people may *hear* when I speak with you."
   b. "The Lord will come down *in the sight* of all the people."

MOSES' DESCENT (19:14–25)

Read 19:14–15. What does Moses do?

Moses descends from the mountain and conveys God's message to the people.

What sort of role does Moses play in the communication between God and Israel?

He is the mediator—the prophet.

The text relates several "ups" and "downs" by Moses. This may be the text's way of emphasizing and stressing the importance of Moses as a mediator or prophet and interpreter of the Revelation.

Lesson 3 — Revelation at Sinai

Revelation in the Bible generally takes place through the medium of a prophet who interprets God's meaning for the community.

Read 19:16–20. What are God's heralds (messengers who precede Him and announce His arrival)?

> Thunder and lightning and a dense cloud, and a very loud blast of the horn. Then God Himself followed in fire, rendering the mountain smoking like a kiln and trembling violently.

Reread 19:19b–25. What earlier promise does God fulfill here (see 19:9)?

> God promised that the people would hear a dialog between God and Moses.

What is the content of this dialog?

> It is a simple dialog. God is calling Moses up to the mountain and then telling him to descend again to warn the people. Moses retorts that he had already warned the people not to approach the mountain. God, however, insists that he go down again and return with Aaron.

The content of the dialog is not important. The Israelites simply hear God giving instructions to Moses, and Moses responding. Why is it important for the Israelites to hear this dialog?

> The Israelites have to be convinced that such a dialog between God and a human *can take place.* The people will be able to trust Moses in his role as mediator-prophet.

Why does God demand that Moses descend the mountain before God pronounced the Decalog?

> (Open.) Suggestions:
> 1. So that people would not think that the Decalog comes from Moses.
> 2. So that all people, including Moses, would hear it together.
> 3. Lest Moses be considered somewhat more than human.

You may want to summarize this chapter with the following discussion:

What doubts of the people are dealt with in this chapter?

> (Open.) Suggestions: Is God really there? Does God really speak to Moses? Is Moses one of us (or is he semi-divine)?

According to some scholars, the theophany (direct communication with God) is not the Decalog itself but the dialog between Moses and God in 19:19b–24. The Decalog itself contains no dialog. It is an address by God. In Deuteronomy 5 we are told that Moses stood between God and the people to declare God's words to them because they were afraid.

The people are commanded to stay clear of the mountain, which will become holy as God descends upon it. That which is holy may not be approached by the "uninitiated"—here only Moses, Aaron, and Joshua (see Exod. 32:17) qualify. Should someone else touch the mountain he was to be be stoned or pierced through from afar—"no hand shall touch him" (19:13).

LESSON 4

The Decalog
Exodus 20

❐ IN PREPARATION FOR TEACHING

This chapter contains what is generally known as the "Ten Commandments." The expression in the Torah, however, is עֲשֶׂרֶת הַדְּבָרִים (Exod. 34:28, Deut. 4:13), which means "the ten sayings" or "the ten pronouncements," and not "the ten mitzvot" or "the ten commandments." Bible scholars use a word derived from Greek, Decalog, that means "the ten pronouncements."

The Decalog is the best known part of the whole Bible and the most "universal" part of the Torah. Teachers often teach their students that the ancient Israelites were the first to introduce laws to the world. This, of course, is not so. Some laws must have existed since the earliest societies of humankind (even a family has its own "laws"). We know of legal codes like the Hittite laws or the code of Hammurapi (eighteenth century B.C.E.) which preceded the biblical laws. The biblical laws do differ in many important ways from those preceding them and we shall deal with these aspects later in our study. The fact is that the Decalog serves as a starting point for all laws ever made in the western world. The Decalog is the core of the Sinai Revelation. Here God speaks at once to Israel and to the entire world, to the generations of the exodus and to all generations to come.

DIVISION OF THE DECALOG

The division of the Decalog into ten pronouncements can be done in several ways. Some students may be aware of the traditional way of dividing the Decalog into two sets of five pronouncements each, on two tablets. On "tablets of the law" which students may have seen in books or in the synagogue, the division of the first two pronouncements is as follows:

1. (20:2) "I the Lord am your God who brought you out of the land of Egypt, the house of bondage."
2. (20:3–6) "You shall have no other God beside me. You shall not make for yourself a sculptured image. . . ."

Modern Bible scholars suggest a different division, in which 20:2 is not one of the Ten Pronouncements but is instead a preamble or introduction, as shown below, p. 147.

According to this division, in the preamble God justifies His demand for adherence to his commandments: Because I, the Lord God and nobody else, have redeemed you from the land of Egypt, I have the right to bind you to Me in a covenant according to which: You shall have no other gods besides me; etc.

The second pronouncement, beginning with 20:4, states that even as you worship the one and only God, "You shall not make for yourself a sculptured image." That is, when you worship me, you do not need an *intermediary*.

It may be necessary at this point to say something about idol worship. The prophets, and later on the rabbis in their contempt for idols and their worship have depicted them as statues of wood or stone "who have eyes but cannot see, ears but cannot hear."* As a result, students may view idol worshipers as stupid, ignorant people who attribute divine powers to stone images. This, however, is a simplification of idol worship.

We know that the ancient Greeks, for instance, believed in living gods who dwelled on Mount Olympus, ate ambrosia and drank nectar, who loved or hated, who bore sons and fought battles in which they killed and were killed in turn. In spite of this belief in living gods, the ancient Greeks addressed stone images in their prayers, washed them, fed them and dressed them, since they believed that these images were intermediaries in which the spirit of the living gods would dwell when they were addressed by humans. The second pronouncement prohibits the making of such intermediaries (as the golden calf might have been), fearing that humans would soon substitute the image for God.

Later in the chapter the text is explicit: "You yourself saw that I spoke to you from the very heaven, with *Me* therefore, you shall not make any gods of silver . . ." (20:19–20).

---

* See Y. Kaufman, *The Religion of Israel,* translated and abridged by Moshe Greenberg (Chicago: University of Chicago Press, 1960), pp. 13–17.

The Decalog

(20:2)
"I the Lord am your God who brought you out of the land of Egypt, the house of bondage."

---

1. (20:3)
"You shall have no other gods beside Me."

2. (20:4–6)
"You shall not make for yourself a sculptured image. . . ."

3. (20:7)
"You shall not swear falsely by the name of the Lord your God. . . ."

4. (20:8–11)
"Remember the Sabbath day and keep it holy. . . ."

5. (20:12)
"Honor your father and your mother. . . ."

6. (20:13a)
"You shall not murder."

7. (20:13b)
"You shall not commit adultery."

8. (20:13c)
"You shall not steal."

9. (20:13d)
"You shall not bear false witness. . . ."

10. (20:14)
"You shall not covet your neighbor's house . . . or anything that is your neighbor's. . . ."

STRUCTURE OF THE DECALOG

The form of the Decalog is that of an address by God to each individual Israelite. Although by 20:7 the text switches to the third person when referring to God, the impression of an address continues throughout the Decalog, because of the use of the second person ("*You* shall not . . .").

Traditionally the Decalog is divided into two sets of five. Your students may notice that there is an imbalance between the two sets. The first five involve the phrase "The Lord your God"—the last five do not. In addition, the first five involve a motive clause (beginning with "for") or a result clause ("so that").

The second and fourth pronouncements are longer than the others. After the statement that "You shall not make for yourself a sculptured image" comes a long list of what one may not make a sculptured image of.

The same is true for the fourth pronouncement, prohibiting working on the Sabbath day. Some Bible scholars believe that these details were added to avoid any doubts and leave no occasion for dispute. The details cover all possibilities.

The first five Pronouncements are considered the more sacred since they pertain to relationships between a person and God (בֵּין אָדָם לַמָּקוֹם), while the second set of five pertains to relationships between one person and another (בֵּין אָדָם לַחֲבֵרוֹ). In each set of five there is an order of importance or severity (in the second set we begin with murder and end with coveting). Strictly speaking, the fifth pronouncement, "honor your father and your mother" should belong to the second set. We find that the Mekhiltah deals with this matter. (The Mekhiltah is a collection of halakhic midrashim on Exodus from the Tannaitic period, 200 C.E.). It states that parents are partners of God in the creation of children. The Bible often stresses the importance of the bonds and authority of the family unit, thus this pronouncement serves as a borderline case between the two sets.

❐ TEACHING PROCEDURE

ON THE IMPORTANCE OF LAWS IN GENERAL

Before dealing specifically with the Decalog you may want to spend part or all of a lesson introducing the students to the concept of law in general. Here are two possible strategies for pointing out the need for a system of laws (you may want to use either or both of these).

Lesson 4 — The Decalog

1. Bring several games to school. One should be a regular pack of playing cards, others should be games (like "Pit") with which students may not be familiar. Divide your class into groups (not more than five students in one group). Remove any instructions from the games, and then give each group a different game, one that those students have never played before.

The students who receive the regular playing cards know the value of the cards and will most likely be able to settle on some simple card game all can participate in. The other groups, playing games to which they have no instructions, will run into difficulties. They are going to make up rules as they go, only to change and discard them. Some players will become irritated and decide the game is no fun. At this point stop the games and discuss what happened. Why did one group do better than the others? You may now want to hand over the instructions and play another game. Students should come to the conclusion that rules and regulations make life a great deal easier. (They may also find it interesting that they were able to come up with a workable set of rules—if they did.)

2. Ask students to imagine themselves with a load of shipwrecked people on an island. What rules and laws would they think are essential to the well-being of the group (do not demand that they come up with ten each). They will most likely make up laws pertaining to relationships between people (like you shall not murder, steal, etc.). Keep a record of their rules or laws on the blackboard and then ask them to categorize them. See what areas they cover. Again, students should come to the conclusion that rules and regulations are necessary for individuals to co-exist.

ANALYSIS OF THE TEN PRONOUNCEMENTS

Preamble

In what way is 20:2 different in style from all the following verses (20:3–14)?

It is not a command, but a statement. It tells who God is, not what the people should or shouldn't do.

Pronouncements 1 (20:3) and 2 (20:4–6)

Read Pronouncements 1 and 2. What is the difference between these two pronouncements?

It is important to understand the difference between the worship of other gods, on the one hand, and, on the other, the worship of the God of Israel through the media of a sculptured image (see above, p. 146).

Read 20:19–20. What reason does God give for forbidding the making of sculptured images?

They are not necessary because God has spoken to the people directly, without an intermediary.

Some students may be disturbed by the statement that God "visits the guilt of fathers upon the children upon the third and upon the fourth generation." The Bible notices life's unfortunate reality. Children do indeed suffer for the sins of their parents.

The hatred of one generation may sow the seeds of war in a later generation. Similarly, the result of one generation's neglect and pollution of the environment may cause a great deal of suffering to future generations. It is, however, also important to explain that the Bible often reverses itself with the passing of time. The prophet Jeremiah says, "In those days they shall no longer say fathers have eaten sour grapes and children's teeth are blunted, but everyone shall die for his own sins: whoever eats sour grapes, his teeth shall be blunted" (Jer. 31:19–20)

The same sentiment is echoed by the prophet Ezekiel: "What do you mean by quoting this proverb upon the soil of Israel: Fathers eat sour grapes and their children's teeth are blunted? As I live, declares the Lord God—this proverb shall no longer be current among you in Israel. Consider, all lives are mine; the life of the fathers and the life of the son are both mine. The person who sins, only he shall die" (Ezek. 18:2–4).

It is important that students realize that Jews today do not live by the apparent meaning of what the Torah states literally, but by the ways our rabbis and teachers have interpreted or adapted what the Torah says to apply to us appropriately.

Pronouncement 3 (20:7)

"You shall not swear falsely by the name of God" refers to taking a false oath in court.

In courtrooms in the United States people take an oath to speak the truth. The President of the United States and other high elected officials take an oath on the Bible to fulfill their obligations. Taking a false oath in God's name indicates a lack of belief in God's power to punish, possibly even a doubt in His existence.

This pronouncement has been given also wider connotations. Thus, using God's name in an unnecessary berakhah has been included in this prohibition.

(Some Jews are of the opinion that writing "God" is similarly a violation of this pronouncement. However, Jewish law does not consider the English word "God" as a holy name of the God of Israel. Therefore, it is not necessary to write "G-d" in place of "God.")

Pronouncement 4 (20:8–11)

"Remember the Sabbath day and keep it holy . . . the seventh day is a Sabbath of the Lord your God."

The observance of the Lord's Sabbath is an act of honoring and emulating God. If you doubt that your students will ever study the book of Deuteronomy in school, it may be worthwhile to compare the fourth Pronouncement to that in Deuteronomy 5 where the rationale for keeping the Sabbath day is a social, moral one.*

Pronouncement 5 (20:12)

"Honor your father and your mother. . . ."

You may want to discuss with students different ways in which children can honor their parents. Point out that this obligation lasts throughout life. How might one honor a parent at different stages of life (e.g., as a young child, as a teenager, as an adult).

Pronouncement 6 (20:13a)

"You shall not murder" (*not* "You shall not kill").

You may want to discuss the difference between these two English words that have been used to translate the Hebrew תִּרְצָח. There are occasions when one might have to resort to killing, as in a case of self-defense or in the defense of an innocent victim and yet not be considered a murderer. Why one should not murder is obvious. This is the one crime which cannot be undone. Our respect for human life is based on the belief that all mankind was created in God's image (see Gen. 9:6). We respect the lives of others and our own lives too. We owe it to ourselves to keep our bodies healthy, clean.

* See *Genesis: A New Teacher's Guide*, 3rd ed., pp. 44–45.

Pronouncement 7 (20:13b)

"You shall not commit adultery."

"Adultery" denotes sexual relationships between a married woman and anyone who is not her husband.

The Bible upholds the sanctity of the family. (Children fare best within a family setup.) Since some students may come from broken homes, it may be important to add that when a couple finds it impossible to get along with one another, divorce is one solution recognized by the Bible.

Pronouncement 8 (20:13c)

"You shall not steal."

Stealing is probably the most common crime in our society. It runs the gamut from tax evasion and white collar crimes to armed robbery and holdups. Car thefts, gold chain snatching, and the stealing of credit cards can lead to more serious crimes, like lying under oath or even murder.

Pronouncement 9 (20:13d)

"You shall not bear false witness."

The intention is without doubt a legal one. Do not testify against another in court, falsely, or without enough evidence. As we are commanded not to use God's name falsely since this is a sin against God, here we are admonished not to sin against another person.

It may be possible to bring examples closer to our students' lives (they are not likely to be involved in a court case). To be a witness means having firsthand information, having been present at the scene, seen with one's own eyes, heard with one's own ears. We do, however, often judge people by "hearsay"—we heard a rumor, we are not quite certain of its truth but we pass it on as if we had been witnesses. Students may be willing to tell of situations where they themselves bore "false witness."

Pronouncement 10 (20:14)

"You shall not covet."

Everyone does feel jealousy at times. Few people have *never* envied the possessions of others—their homes, cars, clothes, gadgets. The Tenth Pronouncement, however, is not directed against such normal feelings, but against acts meant to transfer possession of those coveted goods into one's own possession. Teachers may want to relate occasions out of their own lives of how they dealt with jealousy. You may be able to teach that jealous people are often less able to enjoy the things they have, since there will always be those who have more. (One is rarely aware of those who have less.)

DIVIDING THE DECALOG INTO TWO SETS OF FIVE

The Ten Pronouncements are traditionally divided into two sets of five.

Give each student a sheet with the entire Decalog written out (see p. 147).

What are the differences between the two sets set of five?

(Open.)

This discussion should cover the differences in form and structure presented in the background material, pp. 145–48, above.

Some commentators say that the Ten Pronouncements are special because they represent the two basic categories into which all other laws fall: (1) laws pertaining to the relationship between a person and God (בֵּין אָדָם לַמָּקוֹם), and (2) laws relating to the relationship between one person and another (בֵּין אָדָם לַחֲבֵרוֹ).

List which of the pronouncements wound fall under each of these categories:

Between a person and God: Pronouncements 1–4.
Between one person and another: Pronouncements 5–10.

You have probably seen the Ten Pronouncements carved into two tablets of stone. Traditionally, it has been explained that first tablet (Pronouncements 1–5) pertain to the relationship between a person and God, while the second tablet (Pronouncements 6–10) pertain to the relationship between one person and another.

How is this different from our division?

Pronouncement 5 is out of place.

Can you think of some explanation for why this pronoucement in in the first tablet?

(Open.)

There is a traditional interpretation that states that parents are the partners of God in the creation of children. This helps to explain the placement of pronouncement 5 on the first tablet.

The Mekhiltah, for example, viewed this as a transition between the two categories. Why does the Bible values one's father and mother so highly? The answers may vary. By honoring one's parents one submits to authority. The authority of parents is akin to that of God. Also, the child's existence is tied in with that of parents, just as human existence is dependent on God.

If this is so, how would it affect our actions as children? as teenagers? as adults?

(Open.)

Look again at the arrangement of the pronouncements on the two tablets. In each column the pronouncements proceed from most important to least important. Explain.

First tablet: Having no other gods is most important.

Second tablet: Not murdering is more important than not coveting.

TRANSMITTING THE DECALOG

Many questions remain that cannot be fully answered from the text. Allow students to struggle with these questions:

How was the Decalog transmitted from God to the people?
How much did the people hear directly from God?
Did God speak with Moses—and the people overheard?
Did God speak to Moses who in turn transmitted His words to the people?

The Decalog is not a dialog but an address. The dialog between God and Moses (Exod. 19:20–24) proved that God could indeed contact humans. The people would therefore ever after believe Moses.

The following information from the Deuteronomy version of the Decalog may be helpful. In Deut. 5:4–5 we are told that God spoke to the people "face to face," yet Moses stood between God and the people "to declare God's words to you because you were afraid."

What is common to both versions is that the people heard God's voice and had no doubt that the laws were given by Him.*

---

* For a discussion of God's speaking, see *Genesis: A New Teacher's Guide*, 3rd ed., pp. 11–12.

CLOSING EXERCISE

A possible closing exercise is to give each pair of students an envelope with the Ten Pronouncements written out, each on an individual slip of paper. Ask them to make their own arrangement of the pronouncements. They should arrange them from most important to least important to them in their lives at present. They might also arrange them from hardest to keep to easiest to keep.

THE TEN PRONOUNCEMENTS AS A BASIS OF WESTERN LAW

The Ten Pronouncements serve as the basis of the whole law code of Western civilization. It is important to teach this.

It may be possible to visit a law office in the vicinity of the school and look at a lawyer's immense library, with the many shelves lined with hundreds of law books. Why does a lawyer need such a library, and what do the books contain? Basically these books contain cases that were actually tried in court, each of these cases makes for a "precedent," which may serve as guidance for future cases. How do laws come into being? Usually they result from real life experiences. Let us use the sixth pronouncement as an example. "You shall not murder." Such a law came into being as a result of certain events, namely: murder!

However, once the law was made and a penalty decided on, new cases came up which did not deal with plain brutal premeditated murder. For instance, cases of homicide occurred where one person caused another to lose his life unintentionally such as a house painter dropping a can of paint from a ladder and hitting a passerby, or killing a passerby while riding a horse that suddenly went wild. Many questions had to be asked about these two example cases. Was the ladder secure? Did the painter take reasonable precautions? Or was he careless? Did the rider know his horse to be moody and unpredictable or was this the first time the horse ever took off on a rampage?

In each instance the punishment had to be different. If premeditated murder was punished by death, surely the house painter did not deserve the death penalty. Nor did the horse rider, but in determining his punishment, it had to be considered whether the horse was known to be wild or was a first time offender.

You may now want to turn to a current day case. A person killed another while driving a car. Is the person who drove the car a murderer? What questions would have to be answered to decide this? Some possible questions:

1. What was the condition of the driver? (Was he drunk, under the influence of drugs, recklessly showing off, racing, speeding, etc.?)

2. What was the condition of the car? (brakes, lights, steering wheel, etc.)

3. What can we ascertain about the victim? (Was he drunk? careless? did he dash into the street? did he cross against the light? Or was he walking on the sidewalk?)

There will be no difficulty in realizing that the answers to the above questions (and to many other questions) will make a difference in the punishment (if any) meted out to the driver. The judge will not have to make up laws to apply to this case because in all likelihood a very similar case already took place somewhere, sometime in the past, and was recorded in the law books. The driver's lawyer will try to draw a parallel between his client's case and a previous case in which the driver was exonerated. The lawyer of the victim's family, on the other hand, may want to recall another case in which the victim's family received compensation for their loss.

All these laws are based on the sixth pronouncement ("You shall not murder"). They all reflect the basic idea that human life is precious and is to be kept inviolate. This pronouncement, part of the covenant between God and Israel made at Sinai, guides all cases that deal with the taking of life (murder or homicide).

The Torah itself, as well as the Oral Law (as later recorded in the Mishnah and the Talmud), deal with such case histories. When some people say that the Oral Law was given at Sinai, they do not mean this literally. They mean that all later laws included in the Mishnah and Talmud are based on the Ten Pronouncements. They are not new laws but rather interpretations of the Ten Pronouncements. In the same way all the laws in the law libraries in the Western World were given at Sinai.

UNIT FIVE

The Book of the Covenant

Exod. 21:1–24:18

LESSON 1

Setting Laws before People
Exod. 21:1

☐ IN PREPARATION FOR TEACHING

In this lesson we shall discuss the meaning of "setting rules before people." We know from Exodus 18 that the people did already have laws, rules, and a system of justice. As Moses explained to Jethro, people came to Moses "to inquire of God." "When they have a dispute," Moses explained, "they come before me, and I arbitrate between a man and his neighbor, and I make known the laws and teachings of God."

Thus, after a dispute had taken place, Moses would render judgment and restore order and harmony by relating the law to the people.

The practice was similar in the times of Hammurapi, a king in ancient Babylonia (c. 1792–50 B.C.E.) whose law code was discovered at the beginning of this century. The laws were carved on a tall stone monument set up in the temple of Marduk, and presided over by a statue of Hammurapi. The people (even the judges) were not familiar with the code and were not instructed in the law. Only retrospectively, after a court made its decision in a dispute could a citizen learn from a scribe what the code said.

Some Bible scholars note that the thousands of legal documents found in Mesopotamia and which describe the legal practices of the time, show little direct relationship to the code of Hammurapi. There seems to be a discrepancy between the desired, ideal condition and conditions as they existed in real life. Example: While the code of Hammurapi frees slaves after three years of slavery, we find no documents indicating that slaves were indeed freed.

In Exodus 21 the rules are to be *set before* the people. What this means is indicated in Exod. 24:3–7.

The rules are to be public knowledge. They are to be instruments of education. People will know their moral obligations before the occasion arrives. They will be able to avoid conflict in the first place. The conscience of the people has been sensitized in advance to what is right and wrong in a given situation. The rules will enable the people to become a holy nation, a kingdom of priests.

The rationale for introducing the Hammurapi code, which is more ancient than the Sinaitic laws, is the following: The laws of the Torah may sound primitive in many places. They were intended to lead an ancient Israelite society. In many ways the laws of Israel were similar to those of other ancient peoples who lived in the same geographic area. Jewish tradition has always adapted already existing laws to the changing life conditions of the people and to new circumstances, thus rendering them "timeless."

By comparing, as we go, the laws of the Torah to those of Hammurapi, we shall highlight the distinctive features of biblical law.

❐ TEACHING PROCEDURE

Without going into detail tell students that 21:1–27 is a list of specific laws. Then go back to 21:1 and ask:

What does "setting rules before people" mean?

(Open.)

Listen to some suggestions. Turn to Exod. 24:3–7. Have students read this section aloud.

24:3 Moses *repeated* to the people all the commands of the Lord.
24:4 Moses then *wrote* down all the commands of the Lord.
24:7 Then he took the record of the covenant and *read* it aloud to the people.

List the italicized words on the board.

We already know that the Israelite people had laws before the revelation at Sinai (Exodus 18). Compare justice before and after Sinai by asking the following three questions. (Make a chart on the board.)

1. Who knows the laws before Sinai, and who knows the laws after Sinai?

Before Sinai	After Sinai
The law is unknown. God reveals His will to Moses.	The law is common property.

2. What has to happen before a law is revealed before Sinai? after Sinai?

Before Sinai
There has to be a dispute, a conflict, otherwise there is no occasion to reveal the law.

After Sinai
The rules are publicly known. People know what is right or wrong before they act.

3. What is the purpose of the law before Sinai? after Sinai?

Before Sinai
Moses and the judges work to settle conflicts after they arise, to redress injustices.

After Sinai
The purpose is to teach everybody to live according to God's will. The law is the instrument by which the people are consecrated to God.

Tell students about King Hammurapi and his code (see above, p. 159). Hammurapi states that he wrote these laws by order of his god. These were good laws, meant to protect the weak from oppression. Explain where the code was kept and that there was a discrepancy between the code and reality. (Do not spend more than five minutes on this.) Then ask the following:

Are the laws of Hammurapi more like the laws of Israel before Sinai or after Sinai?

They are more like the laws before Sinai.

While the laws of Hammurapi are private, *retrospective* and concern themselves only with redress or restitution, the post-Sinaitic laws of Israel are public, *prospective and educative.* You may want to end your lesson with a reading of Deut. 6:1–9:

> And this is the instruction—the laws and the rules—that the Lord your God has commanded [me] to impart to you, to be observed in the land which you are about to cross into and occupy, so that you, your son, and your son's son may revere the Lord your God and follow, as long as you live, all His laws and commandments which I enjoin upon you, to the end that you may long endure. Do it, O Israel, willingly and faithfully, that it may go well with you, and that you may increase greatly [in] a land flowing with milk and honey, as the Lord, the God of your fathers, spoke to you. Hear O Israel! The Lord is our God, the Lord alone. You must love the Lord your God with all your heart and with all your soul and with all your might.

Take to heart these words with which I charge you this day. Impress them upon your children. Recite them when you stay at home and when you are away, when you lie down and when you get up. Bind them as a sign on your hand and let them serve as a symbol on your forehead. Inscribe them on the doorposts of your house and on your gates.

Exodus 21–23 are an example of how laws may have come into being. We find here many different single cases, as they may well have occurred in real life. As we read these cases we may learn a number of things about the society for which these laws were intended:

1. Laws reveal the basic concerns of a society. Exodus 21–23 reflect a simple agricultural society. (We shall not find laws here pertaining to real estate or traffic.)

2. Laws reflect some basic ideas about the nature of justice. Different societies or religions reflect different ideas of justice. (In some countries black people or women may not vote, or liquor is prohibited.)

3. In the study of any law one has to determine how to apply a law, which is a general statement, to any specific situation.

LESSON 2A

Redemption of Slaves
Exod. 21:2-11

☐ TEACHING PROCEDURE

THE MALE SLAVE (21:2-6)

Read 21:2-4 aloud. What do we learn about society it these verses?

We are dealing with a society where people own slaves.

Students may also note that this is a society in which women are treated differently than males.

(For a discussion of the institution of slavery in ancient Israelite society, see above, pp. 93-95.)

What is the idea of justice here?

A Hebrew slave is not to be sold into perpetual slavery.
His time of servitude is limited to six years.
Slavery is not a hopeless situation.

What happens when the master marries his male slave to one of his women slaves?

After six years he goes free. The wife and any children born of this union, however, remain as slaves in the master's house.

Your students may note that this principle of justice excludes women. This is an issue you shall return to at the end of this lesson.

Read 21:5-6. Under what circumstances does the slave forfeit his option to be redeemed?

1. When a slave declares that he loves his master.
2. When he declares that he loves his wife and children.

Although 21:5 fuses these two statements, separate the two issues. Write them on the board. Deal with the second statement first.

Why would the slave be willing to forfeit his chance for freedom in case 2?

He loves his family. He is attached to his wife and children.

Students will most probably consider the Torah unfair in the treatment of the slave. Let this anger be expressed.

How about the slave in case 1?

(Open.)

There will probably be less identification with a slave who professes to love his master to the extent of remaining in perpetual bondage than with the slave in case 2.

Let us try and understand: What motivates the slave in case 1?

(Open.)

Pretend you are the slave. What are the disadvantages of slavery?

(Open.) Suggestions:
You have to obey your master.
You may be punished.
You work very hard.
You cannot come and go as you please.

Strangely enough, however, some slaves might find advantages in slavery too. Can you think of any?

(Open.) Suggestions:

There is a kind of "security."
You don't have to make decisions.
Your master sees to your food and shelter.
You carry out orders but have no responsibility.

Imagine you are a slave! As freedom looms, what are some of your trepidations?

(Open.) Suggestions:
Will I be able to fend for myself?
Where will I live?
Where will I sleep the first night?
Will I make the right decisions?

What is the rule concerning the slave who professes to love his master or wife or children (or both)?

"His master shall take him before God. He shall be brought to the door or the doorpost, and his master shall pierce his ear with an awl; and he shall then remain his slave for life." (21:6)

What does this piercing of the ear symbolize?

The slave's permanent attachment to his master's house.

The slave was brought "before God," that is, presumably, before a judge, who represents God. It seems that God acts as a witness to the act.

How must a slave who is nailed to his master's door feel?

The slave is shamed.

It is degrading to be publicly nailed to the doorpost even if it does not hurt much. (As girls and women who have had this done for ornamental purposes know, piercing the ear is not very painful.)

In Babylonia an earring was inserted in the earlobe of a perpetual slave, marking the slave with his master's "brand" (just as cattle are branded nowadays).

This practice teaches us about the values of the Torah. What is the Torah's opinion of slavery and freedom?

The Torah values freedom and makes it shameful for a man to spurn it to remain a slave.

You may want to draw a parallel between a slave on the threshold of freedom and a modern-day prisoner who is freed after many years of imprisonment and who is concerned about his ability to "make it" as a free man.

Earlier we noted a difference between the way male and female slaves are treated in the Torah (above, p. 163). Let us see how these laws evolved.

Deut. 15:12–16 states:

> If a fellow Hebrew, *man or woman,* is sold to you, he shall serve you six years, and in the seventh year you shall set him free. When you set him free, do not let him go empty-handed. Furnish him out of the flock, threshing floor, and vat, with which the Lord your God has blessed you. Bear in mind that you were slaves in the land of Egypt and the Lord your God redeemed you, therefore I enjoin this commandment upon you today.

How does the law in Deuteronomy differ from the one in Exodus?

The book of Deuteronomy is a later book than the book of Exodus. It depicts a society more aware of the rights of women than Exodus is. In Deuteronomy both men and women go free after six years of servitude. The society of Deuteronomy is aware also of the plight of a slave who has just been freed. His master has to help support him in the initial days of his freedom, until he can fend for himself.

We read in Deut. 15:16–19:

> But if he [the slave] says to you, "I do not want to leave you," for he loves you and your household and is happy with you, you shall take an awl and put it through his ear into the door and he shall become your slave in perpetuity. Do the same with female slave.

Since in Deuteronomy the woman, too, is redeemed after six years, the slave-husband does not have to forfeit his own freedom on account of his family. Only if he professes to love his *master* does he have to submit to the degradation of having his ear pierced.

Why are the laws of slavery the first ones the Torah deals with?

Possibly because the laws of slavery in Deut. 15:15 are most directly related to the experience of the people of Israel.

THE FEMALE SLAVE (21:7–11)

This paragraph deals with a specific case. What is the purpose of this sale?

A man sold his minor (young) daughter for the express purpose of becoming the master's wife. (Inference from 21:8.)

What happens if the master then decides not to marry the young slave?

He has to give her family a chance to redeem her, or buy her back. He may not sell her to another person, treating her like an animal or a piece of furniture.

What is the law regarding a master who bought the young girl as a wife for his son?

He must treat her as if she were a free woman.

What is the law if the master does marry her, but then, in addition also marries another woman?

He may not neglect her. Should he deprive her of any of the rights she has as a wife, he has to free her.

What is the principle of justice in this specific case?

The status of the young slave woman is that of a wife. She has rights that may not be violated, or else she goes free.

As we see here, and as we shall note as we continue our study, the master's power over his slave is limited.

LESSON 3

Capital Offenses
Exod. 21:12–17

❐ IN PREPARATION FOR TEACHING

All societies abhor the murderers in their midst, and have found ways to deal with them: In some societies a killer could compensate the victim's relatives by paying them a sum of money.

The Bible, however, views murder as a sin against God, the giver of life, and not as a sin against the family of the victim, thus the family cannot forgive the killer.

In many ancient societies, including Israel, people believed that blood had to be avenged or the soul of the victim would find no peace. Many families became entangled in "blood feuds," the avenger being killed in turn by the family of the victim and so on and on. As we shall see, the Torah does not prohibit the "blood feud" altogether, but limits its scope considerably.

In some cultures (Babylonia, Greece) the murderer could find refuge in the sanctuary of one of the deities, the holiness of the altar protecting him, regardless of his guilt or innocence.

The Bible, however, makes a difference between the intentional killer and the one who kills by accident. (Example: a man uses an axe. The metal part flies off the handle and kills a bystander.)

❐ TEACHING PROCEDURE

MURDER (21:12–14)

Read 21:12–14 aloud. What is the difference between the two acts described?

Exod. 21:12 describes intentional killing.
Exod. 21:13 describes accidental killing.

What is the punishment in the case of intentional killing?

The death penalty.

Lesson 3 — Capital Offenses

What happens in the case of accidental killing?

There will be a sanctuary to which a person who committed manslaughter (killing without intention) could flee.

What is the principle of justice here?

Biblical law makes a difference between intentional and accidental killing (as does our law today).

The idea of a "sanctuary" is not unique to the Bible. What is unique, however, is that a difference is made as far as intention is concerned. A guilty person could not find protection in the sanctuary, even the holiness of God's own altar could not protect him. The holiness of the altar may protect the pagan from justice, but the Torah cannot conceive of holiness without justice. How much time you want to spend on the idea of the cities of refuge depends on you.

Eventually six cities of refuge were set aside for the accidental killer to flee to (aside from the altar). Your students may have many questions about these cities. Where were they? Who was to decide if the killer was guilty or not? You may want to direct your students to Deuteronomy where the subject is discussed in more detail:

> Then Moses set aside three cities on the east side of the Jordan, to which a manslayer could escape, one who unwittingly slew a fellow man without having been hostile to him in the past; he could flee to one of these cities and live: Bezer, in the wilderness in the Tableland belonging to the Reubenites; Ramot in Gilead, belonging to the Gadites and Golan, in Bashar, belonging to the Manassites. (Deut. 4:41–43)

These three cities are east of the river Jordan in what is now the Kingdom of Jordan. Later on three more cities of refuge on the west side of the Jordan river were allocated as cities of refuge:

> You shall set aside three cities in the land that the Lord your God has allotted to you, so that any manslayer may have a place to flee to. Now this is the case of the manslayer who may flee there and live. One who has killed another unwittingly, without having been his enemy in the past. For instance, a man goes with his neighbor into a grove to cut wood; as his hand swings the ax to cut down a tree, the ax-head flies off the handle and strikes the other so that he dies. That man shall flee to one of these cities and live. Otherwise, when the distance is great, the blood-avenger, pursuing the manslayer in hot anger, may overtake him and kill him; yet he did not incur the death penalty, since he had never been the other's enemy. That is why I command you: set aside three cities. And when the Lord your God enlarges your territory, as he swore to your fathers . . . then you shall

add three more towns to those three. . . . If, however, a man who is his neighbor's enemy lies in wait for him and sets upon him and strikes him a fatal blow and then flees to one of these towns, the elders of his town shall have him brought back from there and shall hand him over to the blood-avenger to be put to death. You must show him no pity. (Deut. 19:2–13)

You may also read in the book of Joshua:

The Lord said to Joshua: "Speak to the Israelites. Designate the cities of refuge—about which I commanded you through Moses—to which a manslayer who kills a person by mistake, unintentionally, may flee. They shall serve you as a refuge from the blood-avenger. He shall flee to one of those cities, present himself at the entrance of the city gate, and plead his case before the elders of that city; and they shall admit him into the city and give him a place in which to live among them. Should the blood-avenger pursue him, they shall not hand the manslayer over to him, since he killed the other person without intent, and had not been his enemy in the past. He shall live in that city until he can stand trial before the assembly, and remain there until the death of the High Priest who is in office at that time. Thereafter, the man slayer may go back to his home in his own town, to the town from which he fled."So they set aside Kedesh in Galilee, Shechem in Ephraim and Kiriat-Arba, that is, Hebron, in Judea. And across the Jordan, Bezer, Ramoth and Golan, for all the Israelites, to which anyone who killed a person unintentionally might flee, and not die by the hand of the blood-avenger before standing trial by the assembly. (Josh. 20:2–7)

Note that these texts give us information about who decides if it was murder or manslaughter and about the length of time one will have to spend in the city of refuge.

THE MISTREATMENT OF PARENTS (21:15, 17)

The Israelite family is the core of the nation. Hitting one's parents or abusing them is a mortal sin.

KIDNAPPING (21:16)

A kidnapper who sells his captive is condemned to death.

LESSON 4

Laws and Life
(Optional)

☐ IN PREPARATION FOR TEACHING

Whether you teach this section or not is at your discretion. It deals with the discrepancy between the *ideal* society that the laws attempt to achieve and *reality*. Laws, as we have mentioned, reveal the basic *concerns* of a society and its ideas about the *nature of justice*, but they do not reveal what life in that society is really like.

Anecdotes and stories, on the other hand, do tell us what society was like. Did one really executive people who killed intentionally at the very altar of God? (In contrast to other cultures where the holiness of the altar would protect the guilty?) The story of Joab (1 Kings 2:28–34) seems to indicate that it was indeed so.

☐ TEACHING PROCEDURE

You may want to bring a driving manual to class and read some of the instructions to the students.

What is the purpose of these laws?

The safety of drivers and pedestrians.

Now imagine that we put this driver's manual into a "time capsule" to be opened in the year 2500. Once the capsule is opened, what would people learn about us from the manual?

1. That we were a society concerned with traffic.
2. That one of our principles of justice was that drivers had to be aware of the rights of pedestrians and those of other drivers.

What would these people living in the year 2500 not know about our society?

They would not know if the laws were kept. They might believe that there were no traffic violations.

If we want the people of the future to view our traffic situation correctly, what would we have to add to the time capsule?

(Open.) Suggestions: A page from a daily newspaper; a police report of one day in traffic court.

We can see that stories and reports of real events tell more about what society is really like than do laws, which may or may not be actually observed and enforced.

By the same token, biblical stories tell us more about what biblical society was like than laws do.

It is useful in this regard to read the story of Joab, King David's general.

On his deathbed old King David said to his son Solomon, who was to reign after him:

> You know what Joab, son of Zeruiah, did to me, what he did to the two commanders of Israel's forces, Abner the son of Ner and Amasa, son of Jether. He killed them, shedding blood of war in peacetime, staining the girdle of his loins and the sandals on his feet with blood of war. So, act in accordance with your wisdom, and see that his white head does not go down to *sheol* [the grave] in peace. (1 Kings 2:5–7)

You do not have to go into detail. Just make sure that your students understand what David accuses Joab of having done. Then continue with the next paragraph. David is dead, Solomon is king.

> Joab fled to the Tent of the Lord and grasped the horns of the altar. ... Solomon was told that Joab had fled to the Tent of the Lord and that he was there by the altar. So Solomon sent Benaiah saying "Go and strike him down." Benaiah went to the Tent of the Lord and said to him "Thus says the king, come out!" "No," he replied. "I will die here." Benaiah reported back to the king that Joab had answered thus and thus, and the king said "Do just as he said; strike him down and bury him, and remove guilt from me and my father's house for the blood of the innocent that Jaob has shed. Thus the Lord will bring his blood guilt down upon his own head, because unbeknown to my father he struck down with the sword two men more righteous and honorable than he—Abner, son of Ner—and Amasa son of Jether, the army commander of Judea. May the guilt for their blood come down upon the head of Joab and his descendants forever, and may good fortune from the Lord be granted forever to David and his descendants, his house and his throne." (1 Kings 2:28–33)

LESSON 5

Bodily Assault
Exod. 21:18–27

☐ TEACHING PROCEDURE

FIGHTING (21:18–21, 26–27)

Read 21:18–21. What do these verses deal with?

21:18–20 deal with free men.
21:21 deals with slaves.

Who are the people involved?

As you ask the next several questions, use the answers to construct a chart on the board:

Two free men (21:18–19)	Master and slave (21:20–21)
1a. Two free men are fighting.	1b. A master beats his slave.

What tools are being used?

2a. One assaults another using a stone or *egrof*.*	2b. The master uses a rod.

Explain that a stone is a deadly weapon. The rod, on the other hand, was the accepted instrument by which slaves and children were chastised. (See Prov. 13:24, "He who spares the rod hates his son."

What does the one who wields the instrument in each case intend to do?

He intends to injure or kill (a deadly weapon is being used).	He intends to discipline (a rod is used).

---

* Bible scholars are not sure what the word אֶגְרֹף means in biblical Hebrew. It may mean a tool.

The law makes a distinction between the act (assault) and its consequences (injury or death). What are the consequences of the act in each case?

| 3a. The victim is injured but recovers. | 3b. The slave dies. | 3c. The slave recovers but dies later. |

What is the law in cases 3a and 3b?

Case 3a: The assailant pays for the cure and loss of income of the victim. (By implication, if he dies the assailant will pay the death penalty.)

Case 3b: This is a case of homicide. It must be determined whether it is intentional homicide (death penalty) or unintentional homicide (sanctuary).

In case 3c, were we to demand the death penalty for the master, what injustice might we commit?

It is possible that the victim died of causes unrelated to the assault (he might have died of of a disease).

Note that the law gives the assailant the benefit of the doubt and limits his liability. If the victim shows some degree of recovery, it is assumed that the later death is not necessarily the result of the assault.

Today it is easier to ascertain causes of death than it was in biblical times. If a person were to die of a heart attack following an assault, the defense might try to prove that the victim's condition would have caused his death at this time even if the assault had not taken place.

In the case of the slave, the master in a slave-owning society has the right to chastise his slave. He may not, however, use excessive force. If the slave does not die immediately and there is some doubt as to the cause of his death, the slave will not be avenged. The master did suffer a monetary loss at the death of his slave and will be given the benefit of the doubt.

Add the verdicts to the chart:

| 4a. Pays for cure and any loss of income. | 4b. Death or sanctuary. | 4c. Master goes free. |

As we have mentioned before, these laws read like cases that happened in real life. They do not cover all possibilities.

Lesson 5 — Bodily Assault

Here is a hypothetical case: Two free men fight using stones. One is wounded but does not die until later.

What is the law? If a free man dies later, is it the same law as when a slave dies later (3c)? Or is the responsibility of the assailant greater in the case of two free men fighting? If so, why?

> The assailant in the case of the two free men has greater responsibility. He had no right to assault another person, while the slave master had a right to discipline his slave. The assault was an illegal act. Furthermore, he used a stone—a deadly weapon—whereas the master used a standard instrument of chastisement.

Point out the ambiguity of the assailant's guilt as you did the ambiguity of the master's guilt earlier (3c). It is possible that the assault and the death are not related. Each case has to be judged on its own merits.

Read 21:26–27. What if the master maims his slave?

> He has to let him go free.

In other slave-owning societies (including this country before the Civil War) a master could treat his slave any way he saw fit. But in ancient Israel, the killer of a slave was considered a murderer. The Torah restricts the power of the master over his slave in other ways, too. Thus, the Israelite laws concerning slavery contain some revolutionary ideas.

THE PREGNANT WOMAN (21:22–23)

The purpose of this lesson is to establish a general principle from a particular case.

Read 21:22 aloud. Establish what happened and what the verdict is. Summarize the case on the board as follows:

Particular Case	**General Principles**
1. Two men fight.	
2. During the fight, a pregnant woman is pushed and miscarries.	
3. The man who pushed her is guilty.	

Now have your class discover the general principle.

Why is the man guilty?

> Because he caused the miscarriage.

Did he intend to harm the woman? If not, why is he nevertheless judged responsible?

> Because he was fighting. Fighting in public, where others may be endangered is an illegal act.

What, then, is the principle involved?

> When engaging in an illegal act, one is responsible for the consequences.

Now complete the second column of the chart:

Particular Case	General Principles
1. Two men fight.	1. Two people are engaged in a criminal act.
2. During the fight, a pregnant woman is pushed and miscarries.	2. As a result of a criminal act, an innocent bystander is harmed.
3. The man who pushed her is guilty.	3. The offender is responsible for the consequences of his act.

Find an example from our times. For instance: Two men, while robbing a store, break a child's arm.

What would the verdict be, according to the laws of Exodus?

> Guilty.

You have already learned in 21:12–13 that if a man kills another human being the penalty is death (or sanctuary). Now read 21:23. What do we learn from the fact that the killer of an unborn child may pay a fine while the killer of man, woman or child has to die (or flee to a sanctuary)?

> The unborn fetus is considered to be something less than life, not as valuable as a human being.

Because of this, the halakhah states that in the case of difficult labor, when the life of the mother is threatened, the fetus may be

Lesson 5 — Bodily Assault

destroyed in order to save the life of the mother. (This is in contrast to the teachings of the Catholic Church.)

What is meant in the text by "If however other damage ensues"?

It refers to the death of the mother.

What is the verdict if the mother dies?

The man who pushed her has committed an act of homicide.

LEX TALIONIS — LAW OF RETALIATION (21:23-27)

Read 21:23-25. How do you feel about these laws.

(Open.) Suggestion: They are primitive and barbaric.

Just imagine purposely blinding a man who, by shooting a dart, caused his friend to lose an eye. Or crushing someone's feet on purpose because he caused an accident. Surely these have to be considered "cruel and unusual punishments"!

Distribute to the students the laws of Hammurapi (p. 179), and read laws 196–201.

Who is the victim in each case?

In laws 196–98 it is a "seignior" (an aristocrat). In law 199 the victim is a commoner (a person of lower status).

What determines the punishments in these cases?

On the rank or status of the victim: If you harm an equal, you will suffer his fate. If you harm somebody from a lower class, you can pay a fine.

How do the laws of Exodus differ from those of Hammurapi?

Biblical law does not consider the status of the victim. All people are equal under the law.

Taken literally, the law demands justice—the punishment has to fit the crime. The punishment must be neither too harsh or too light. Granted, this justice is primitive.

In Latin this kind of equal justice is called *lex talionis*. The principle of the law is that life and limb have to be respected. All members of society know that violating others, and causing them bodily harm will have dire consequences. By the same token it is understood that "intentions" are taken into consideration (e.g., punishment for manslaughter is not the same as punishment for murder).

According to Hammurapi's code, if a man caused the death of a seignior's (aristocrat's) daughter, his own daughter will be executed (law 210)! But if he causes the death of the daughter of a commoner, a fine will suffice (law 212).

Some Bible scholars believe that the *lex talionis* was never taken literally in the Israelite community. The Bible never mentions official "mutilators," known to us from Babylonian sources, whose job it was to amputate limbs (this is still done in Saudi Arabia).

Nor does the Bible provide a list of alternatives (as in Babylonian law) in cases where the *lex talionis* could not be carried out in the prescribed manner. For instance, suppose a one-eyed man gouged out the eye of another person. If his remaining eye were to be destroyed, his punishment would exceed the crime. He caused someone partial blindness, but his punishment renders him totally bind. Therefore substitute punishments were considered.

These Bible scholars, in agreement with the Rabbis, believe that the *lex talionis* was never understood literally in Israel. Rather, monetary compensation was exacted instead. However, we have no legal documents to prove this point.

Lex Talionis — Law of Retaliation

From the Laws of Hammurapi
(Babylonia, Eighteenth Century B.C.E.)

195. If a son has struck his father, they shall cut off his hand.
196. If a seignior has destroyed the eye of a member of the aristocracy, they shall destroy his eye.
197. If he has broken another seignior's bone, they shall break his bone.
198. If he has destroyed the eye of a commoner or broken the bone of a commoner, he shall pay one mina of silver.
199. If he has destroyed the eye of a seignior's slave or broken the bone of a seignior's slave, he shall pay one-half his value.
200. If a seignior has knocked out a tooth of a seignior of his own rank, they shall knock out his tooth.
201. If he has knocked out a commoner's tooth, he shall pay one-third mina of silver
209. If a seignior struck another seignior's daughter and has caused her to have a miscarriage, he shall pay ten shekels of silver for her fetus.
210. If that woman has died, they shall put his daughter to death.
211. If by a blow he has caused a commoner's daughter to have a miscarriage, he shall pay five shekels of silver.
212. If that woman has died, he shall pay one-half mina of silver.
213. If he struck a seignior's female slave and has caused her to have a miscarriage, he shall pay two shekels of silver.
214. If that female slave has died, he shall pay one-third mina of silver.

LESSON 6

More Judicial Cases
Exod. 21:28–22:5

☐ TEACHING PROCEDURE

HOMICIDE BY BEASTS (21:28-32)

Read 21:28. What kind of society is depicted here?

A society of small farmers in which man and beast mix freely, the ox pulling the plough and bearing man's burdens.

There is a difference between homicide committed by a beast and homicide committed by a human? What aspect is not considered when dealing with animals?

In human affairs, as we have already learned, *intent* is of utmost importance. It makes the difference between murder and manslaughter. In regard to animals we do not raise the question of intent. An animal that kills a human is put to death. (See Gen. 9:5: "For your life blood, too, will I require a reckoning; of every beast will I require it.")

What happens to the flesh of the animal that kills a human?

The flesh is taboo. It may not be eaten. The ox is not only dangerous (that is why he has to die), it is also "tainted" (טָמֵא).

Read 21:29-31. How does this case differ from the one in 21:28?

In the earlier case, there was no indication that the owner of the ox was in any way aware of the fact that his ox might be dangerous. Thus he is not guilty of negligence. In the latter case, however, the master has been forewarned. He was negligent and shares the guilt of the animal.

How does the crime of negligence compare to that of murder?

21:30 indicates that negligence is regarded as a lesser offense. For in the case of negligence ransom is permitted. But it is never permitted in a case of murder.

Read 21:32. How does the law differ when the ox gores a slave?

The law permits the death penalty to be waived, the principle being that the life of the owner of the ox is valuable, too. He will pay thirty shekels as a ransom, the ox, of course, will be stoned and the carcass placed under taboo.

PROPERTY DAMAGE (21:33–36)

Read 21:33–34. What is the specific case?

A man digs a pit and fails to cover it. His neighbor's animal falls into the pit and dies.

Who is responsible? What is the punishment?

The one who dug the pit has to make restitution, but may keep the dead animal.

Why?

The owner of the ox has to be compensated for his loss. But he does not have to make a profit. The dead animal has some monetary value (skin, bones, meat) which may be used to defray the costs of a new ox.

What is the principle to be learned from this case?

When a person causes damages to his neighbor through negligence, he has to compensate him. The neighbor is entitled to exact compensation but not to profit.

Read 21:35. What happened?

An ox kills another ox. This is an accident. Both parties are victims who are bound together by a common misfortune. Thus they share the loss.

Read 21:36. What is the punishment?

The owner is guilty of negligence and has to replace the ox. He may, however, keep, use or sell the dead animal.

Make up some cases as they may occur in our society:

Suppose driver A rammed his car into B's car. It was already known that A's brakes were faulty (his repairman had repeatedly warned him). What happens if B's car is demolished?

Obviously A should be responsible for replacing B's car. But we may argue that A should be allowed to sell B's car for scrap. (Do not let the issue of insurance cloud the issue. You are interested in the principle of justice.)

Make up other cases. Make sure that they parallel one of the cases in the text (e.g., a dog bites a letter carrier).

THEFT (21:37, 22:2b-3)

Read 21:37 and 22:3. How does the law view theft in comparison to negligence?

> Theft is regarded as more severe. The thief does not only have to pay restitution but also punitive damages. He is severely punished.

What is the difference between negligence and theft?

> It is in the intention.

The punishment for stealing an ox is more severe than for that of stealing a sheep. Why?

Point out the function and value of an ox to a farmer in an ancient farming society. A man and his ox may have to spend many hours a day together. An ox was expensive. He pulled the plough and the cart that brought the harvest from the field. The farmer might be used to his particular ox. One animal may be better suited than another for a specific job. The loss of an ox might cause the farmer to miss the ploughing season. An ox was an economic asset.

Sheep, on the other hand, were cheaper. They were sheared once a year and a mother sheep would be milked by her owner. Sometimes a sheep would be slaughtered and consumed. Most of the time, however, the owner would not suffer unduly if he lost one of his sheep. Sheep did not work on the farm. It may also have been easier to steal a sheep. Stealing an ox took greater effort and therefore constituted a greater crime.

The Torah makes a difference between the case of a thief who sold or slaughtered a stolen animal and the case of a thief who still had the animal in his possession. Why?

> As long as the stolen animal was in the possession of the thief, there existed the chance that he would have a "change of heart" and return the animal. Not so once the animal was sold or slaughtered.

Consider this modern example: A person has pocketed an object in a department store, but has not yet left the store. The store's detective will not confront him unless he consummates the crime by leaving the store.

Read 22:2b. What happens if he can't afford to make restitution?
He is sold as a slave.

For how long does he serve?
The thief serves until he has worked off his debt.

This slave is really an indentured servant. See above, pp. 94–95.

TUNNELING (22:1-2a)

Read 22:1. What case are we dealing with?
A thief is caught while tunneling and is beaten to death by the owner of the property he is tunneling into.

What is the verdict?
There is no blood guilt in his case. The man who killed the thief is not guilty of murder.

Read 22:2a. How does this case differ from the previous one?
The thief was tunneling during the daytime. Apparently, the previous case deals with tunneling at night.

In the second case, what is the verdict?
There is blood guilt in that case. The owner of the property is guilty of murder.

Summarize these two cases and their verdicts.
They deal with what we call today "breaking and entering" or burglary. In the first case, a burglar digs a tunnel in order to enter a house *at night*. If the owner of the property catches him and kills him, there is no "bloodguilt," meaning the owner of the house is not guilty of murder. The death is considered justifiable homicide. If, however, the thief was killed during a *daytime* burglary, his death is not deemed justifiable and the owner of the house must be punished.

Why does the Torah make a difference between a nighttime robbery and one that takes place in the daytime?
A nighttime burglar knows that in all likelihood people are home. He knows that somebody might wake up and confront him, so he may be armed. The nighttime burglar knows that he faces serious risks, even loss of his life, and is willing to use force.

A daytime burglar, on the other hand, expects to find the house empty, since its inhabitants are working in the field or farm.

Thus, he doesn't expect a confrontation. He may not even be armed. He does not expect to risk his life.

At night, the owner of the house may be awakened from a sound sleep and be confused. Help is unlikely to be available. During the day, however, the owner of the house is alert and may be able to call for help. The Torah considers the owner who kills an intruder during the daytime as having used excessive force.

What is the principle of justice in this case?

A thief may not be killed unless he endangers lives in the performance of his criminal activity.

In modern times a distinction is made between armed and unarmed robbery. The armed robber, we assume, is willing to use his weapon if he considers it necessary.

A modern day example of use of excessive force: A man is observed stealing a bicycle in a garage. The owner pulls a gun and kills the thief. What would the verdict be? The owner is accused of using excessive force. If, however, the man entered the home bearing a gun, the owner would be exonerated.

PROPERTY LOSSES CAUSED BY NEGLIGENCE (22:4–5)

Read 22:4–5. Restate the cases in your own words.

1. A person allows his livestock to roam and eat the crops in his neighbor's field.

2. A person starts a fire and it gets out control. It spreads, so that damage is caused to a neighboring field.

In what way are the two cases similar?

Both are cases of negligence.

What is the verdict?

Both the owner of the livestock and the person who started the fire have to make restitution and pay damages. Since, however, it is assumed that no evil intentions were involved, no punishment is meted out.

LESSON 7

Safekeeping, Borrowing, and Hiring
Exod. 22:6–14

❐ **TEACHING PROCEDURE**

SAFEKEEPING OF OBJECTS (22:6-8)

Read 22:6-8. Restate the case in your own words.

A has left money or an object (e.g., a tool, a coat) with B's for safekeeping. The goods were subsequently stolen from B's home.

What happens if the thief is caught with the goods?

The thief pays double the value of the stolen object.

What happens if the thief is not apprehended? How far does B's responsibility extend?

B will have to establish that he did not misappropriate A's property. He will have to take an oath (in court), swearing that he did not steal the goods entrusted to him. He then will bear no further responsibility.

In biblical times an oath was sacred. When a person took an oath and swore by God, he would most likely speak the truth, since he believed that taking a false oath would result in punishment from God. In today's more secular society, an oath has lost some of its solemnity, and some people lie under oath.

What if A points out an object in B's house, claiming it is his property?

The court will decide who the true owner of the object is.

What might take place at such a court hearing?

Each party might have to identify the object (point out scratches, patches, or tears). One party may be able to bring evidence that he received or inherited the contested item.

What will happen to the one found lying?

Like the thief, he will have to pay double the value of the item.

Deception—lying under oath—is considered to be like theft. Truthfulness under oath is so important that it is the topic of one of the Ten Pronoucements: "You shall not swear falsely by the name of the Lord your God for the Lord will not clear one who swears falsely by His name" (Exod. 20:7).

SAFEKEEPING OF LIVESTOCK (22:9-12)

Read 22:9-12. What is left for safekeeping in this passage?

A left livestock (e.g., an ass, an ox, a sheep) in B's protective care.

What two cases are presented?

Case 1: The animal dies or is carried off in a raid, which B cannot prevent.

2. The animal is stolen from B's home.

In these cases, how far does B's responsibility extend?

Case 1: B takes an oath that he did not misappropriate the animal. Then he is not be responsible for making restitution.

Case 2. B must compensate A for his loss.

Why is B responsible in case 2 but not case 1?

In case 2, B is considered to have been negligent.

In 22:6-8 we learned that if B was given an object for safekeeping, he was not responsible in the case of theft. Here we find if B was given an animal for safekeeping, he is responsible in the case of theft.

How does a keeper of livestock differ from a keeper of goods?

(Open.)

Suppose you are going on vacation and leave your bike in your friend's garage, right next to his own bike. If it is stolen what is your friend's responsibility, according to the laws of Exodus?

The friend cannot be blamed. He safeguarded your bike in the same manner in which he safeguarded his own.

Now, imagine that you asked your neighbor to board your pet in your absence. What kind of instructions would you leave with him?

Instructions for feeding, grooming, exercise, etc.

According to Exod. 22:11 the keeper has to make restitutions in case of theft. Why?

If the neighbor accepts the responsibility of caring for a pet or other creature, his responsibility is greater than that of the neighbor who lets me put my bike in his garage.

The rabbis in the days of the Mishnah explained this distinction in the following way: The person willing to board an ox or an ass is likely to be paid for his efforts, while the keeper of a tool or money would do it as a favor. The paid keeper would bear greater responsibility than the volunteer. (Note that in the text there is no indication of whether or not the keeper is being paid.)

What if the animal is killed by a wild beast?

The keeper has to produce the carcass bearing the marks of the wild beast and need not make restitution. It is considered an act of *force majeure,* an "act of God," an event that is not preventable.

BORROWING AN ANIMAL (22:13-14a)

When a person borrows an animal and uses it to work with, to carry loads or plough a field, without the owner being present, the borrower is responsible in all cases of harm befalling the animal. If, however, the owner is present, the borrower is not responsible.

RENTING AN ANIMAL (22:14b)

If a man *rents* an animal for a price, the one who hired the animal is not responsible for harm befalling the animal, but he has to pay the rental fee.

In what way does the law treat the renter differently from the borrower?

When a person lets someone borrow his animal, the owner should be able to expect full protection in case of harm to the animal, since he is doing the borrower a favor.

When the owner rents his animal for a fee to another, however, he is not entitled to full protection because he stands to make a profit. Thus, he takes a calculated risk.

LESSON 8A

The Seduction of a Virgin
Exod. 22:15-16

❑ IN PREPARATION FOR TEACHING

In biblical times the father of a bride was entitled to receive a "bride price" from the intended husband. (Jacob had to work for seven years in Laban's household because he did not have the bride price for Rachel; see Genesis 29.)

In this section we deal with the seduction of a virgin for whom no bride price as yet has been paid. The father can no longer expect the bride price for a virgin (a larger amount than for a non-virgin). He has thus suffered a monetary loss that the seducer must compensate him for. He pays the bride price, even if the father refuses to let him marry his daughter.

A related law appears in Deut. 22:28-29, which deals with rape:

> If a man comes upon a virgin who is not engaged (for whom no bride price has been paid) and he seizes her and lies with her, and they are discovered, the man who lay with her shall pay the girl fifty shekels of silver (the bride price) and she shall be his wife. Because he has violated her, he can never have the right to divorce her.

It may appear surprising that a woman would want to marry a man who raped her. In ancient times the institution of marriage served to protect women. An unmarried or widowed woman (who had no sons) was at great disadvantage since she had nobody to protect her. A woman who had been raped would have a hard time finding a husband. Thus, the Torah assures the victim of rape protection for the rest of her life.

❑ TEACHING PROCEDURE

Read 22:15-16. In the case of seduction (two consenting adults), who was harmed?

The father—he lost the bride price.

How is he compensated?

He receives the full bride price.

The seducer may marry the girl, but must pay even if the father refuses to let him marry his daughter.

Introduce the laws from Deuteronomy regarding rape (see above).

Rape and seduction are not the same. Rape is a crime of violence perpetrated on a helpless victim, while in a case of seduction the woman consents to the act.

In the rape case (Deuteronomy) the man must marry the woman since he has rendered her undesirable to another man and unmarriageable (according to standards in biblical times). The seducer does not bear this onus since the woman shares the responsibility.

LESSON 8B

Prohibitions
Exod. 22:17–19

☐ IN PREPARATION FOR TEACHING

"You shall not tolerate a sorceress" (22:17). A sorceress, or a witch, is a person (most often a woman) who is believed to have special powers and "know-how" to influence events in the lives of other people. She may know special incantations (like "abracadabra" or "open sesame"). She may know how to brew magic potions or be in possession of a "magic wand" (or a "magic lamp" as in the Aladdin story).

In biblical times people believed that witches had magical powers but the Torah prohibited their use. Note that the Torah did not disclaim the power of Pharaoh's magicians, but claimed that God's powers were greater than theirs. Moses' rod never became a "magic wand." He could use it in the performance of miracles only when God gave him specific instructions.

We speak today of psychics and people who have E.S.P. (extrasensory perception). It is true that some people may have insights which we cannot explain. We would not, however, call them witches, since they do not claim to be able *to make things happen.*

There are those who do call themselves "witches" or "warlocks" and who run the gamut from plain swindlers to people with special insight.

☐ TEACHING PROCEDURE

THE SORCERESS (22:17)
Why does the Torah forbid witchcraft?

God reveals His will directly, or through the institutions set up by the Torah: the priests and prophets. Seeking God's counsel through the sorceress goes against God's will.

Sometimes when God refused to reveal His will to humans, they would go to the sorceress, thus trying to force God to reveal His will (e.g., the story of Saul and the witch of Ein-Dor; 1 Sam. 28:8–19).

BESTIALITY (22:18)

Bestiality is prohibited because it eliminates the difference between beasts and humans. You may want to deal with this issue in one or two sentences: Sexual acts with animals are forbidden.

SACRIFICING TO OTHER GODS (22:19)

The worship of other gods undermines the exclusive relationship between Israel and God ("You shall have no other gods beside me"; Exod. 20:2).

LESSON 8C

The Underprivileged
Exod. 22:20–26

❏ IN PREPARATION FOR TEACHING

The Torah prohibits taking interests on loans. This may come as a surprise to students since in our society almost everyone either pays or charges interest. We pay interest on the mortgage we take when we buy a house.

The biblical prohibition is applied to an agrarian society. Poor farmers often had to borrow funds to buy seeds or to sustain their families until the harvest was gathered. Exacting interest from these small farmers would have made their burden unbearable, possibly forcing them to sell their land or their children.

Today we are living in a mercantile society. Money is constantly borrowed for business and investments, few of us could buy houses if we were unable to borrow money for which we paid interest. It is, however, true that high interest rates are debilitating to the economy. In many European countries in the Middle Ages, Jews were kept out of many professions and were not allowed to own land. They were forced to become moneylenders, since Christians did not want to do it.

❏ TEACHING PROCEDURE

THE STRANGER, THE WIDOW, AND ORPHAN (22:20–23)

What do the stranger, the widow, and the orphan have in common?

> They have no protection. Strangers in ancient times did not have a consulate to protect them. Widows and ophans had no male to protect them.

INTEREST ON MONEY AND PLEDGES (22:24–26)

Read the verses. Why does the Bible prohibit the taking of interest on money lent?

Lesson 8C — The Underprivileged

Because in those days only the poor took loans. Interest might spell ruin for them.

What is the law in the case where a garment is given as a pledge?

It must be returned at night.

This admonition exemplifies the dire poverty of some people who owned only one coat which they would use for a cover at night.

IN CONCLUSION

Why are these laws grouped together (22:20–26)?

Because they deal with those who have no protection, the underprivileged. In freeing the Israelites from Egyptian bondage God had manifested his concern for the downtrodden. The weak enjoy God's special protection. Thus the Torah often reminds the Israelites to show concern for the powerless "because you were slaves in the land of Egypt." In all these there is a call for compassion (מִדַּת הָרַחֲמִים).

Who will punish the ones who disobey these laws?

God Himself. No court of law will be involved.

LESSON 9A

Duties to God
Exod. 22:27-30

❐ TEACHING PROCEDURE

Up to now we have learned about:

1. Laws, which if broken, will be punished by law.
2. Laws, which if broken, will be punished by God.

Read 22:27-30. What is different about these laws, compared to the preceding ones?

> Here we find a list of religious obligations. No punishments are mentioned. The laws are addressed to one's conscience, one's own knowledge of what is right or wrong.

12:27 states that one may not curse God or a chieftain (leader). It seems strange that God and a chieftain are grouped together in a single verse.

In what way does a chieftain resemble God?

> He is the legal authority.

(Some leaders then, as today, may not be the legal authority, but people who seized power against the will of the majority.)

What do 22:28-29 deal with?

> They admonish the people to deliver the tithe (10%) of the crops and the firstborn of the cattle to the Temple *promptly*. Part of these gifts were burned to God, the rest eaten by the priests. The priests who had no income of their own should not have to beg for what was rightly theirs.

What bearing does this law have on us, in today's society?

> We should pay our debts promptly. The person we owe money to may be in need of it.

What does 22:30 deal with?

The prohibition of eating flesh torn by beasts.

Why is such meat not to be eaten?

According to Deut. 14:21, priests were to refrain from eating the flesh of animals killed by beasts or that of animals that died of natural causes. Eating such meat made one ritually impure.

Only the flesh of animals which had been slaughtered, their blood poured on the altar (symbolically returned to its source) was to be eaten by the priests. Eating flesh of animals torn by beasts made one ritually impure. Priests who were on constant call could not risk impurity. Since all of Israel was to be a "kingdom of priests and a holy nation" the prohibition was extended to all the people of Israel.

LESSON 9B

Moral Laws
Exod. 23:1-9

☐ TEACHING PROCEDURE

RUMORS (23:1)

The Torah continues with laws directed to one's conscience, moral obligations.

Why is it forbidden to carry false rumors?

Innocent people might be maligned and consequently suffer.

Can you cite examples?

(Open.)

Few of us spread false rumors on purpose, yet we often pass on rumors without checking them out first as to accuracy.

Why do we do this?

It is probably human to want to gain some recognition by passing on bits of information to others. It is an "attention getter."

THE MALICIOUS WITNESS (23:2-3)

What two things is the witness warned about?

1. Siding with the rich.
2. Siding with the poor.

That one might not side in a dispute with the rich and mighty may seem obvious. More subtle is the prohibition against siding with the poor just because he happens to be poor.

What is the principle involved?

In all cases justice must prevail, regardless of the economic status of the plaintiffs.

THE ENEMY'S ANIMAL (23:4-5)

On first reading students may say these verses deal with concern for the suffering animals צַעַר בַּעֲלֵי חַיִּים. On close reading, however, one discovers that these verses deal with consideration for one's enemy. An ox or ass is not necessarily better off working for his original master than working for a new one.

Similarly, when one helps raise an enemy's fallen animal, one acts out of consideration for the enemy (although also the animal benefits in this case).

What is the principle?

It may be our natural inclination to be vindictive toward our enemy. However, we are instructed to curb our natural instincts and help our enemy instead.

How would this principle apply in today's society?

(Open.)

Example: We should help our enemy pull his car out of the mud. Hostility and vindictiveness are to be limited.

Read 23:6-9.

Briefly discuss.

LESSON 10A

Laws Related to Time and Seasons
Exod. 23:10–19

THE SEVENTH YEAR (23:10)

This is the first mention of the special status of every seventh year (elsewhere called שְׁמִיטָה).

What is the law?

In the seventh year the land shall lie fallow and whatever grows wild shall be eaten by the needy and by the beasts of the field.

Why?

1. So that the land will restore its strength and recoup the minerals that the plants sapped during the preceding six years (an ecological concern).
2. So that the poor may glean whatever grows wild (a social concern).

THE SABBATH DAY (23:12)

Why is the law of Shabbat repeated here?

Because Shabbat also is a holiday determined by time.

THE THREE PILGRIM FESTIVALS (22:13–19)

Read 22:13.

The verses that follow deal with three agricultural holidays (שְׁלֹשׁ רְגָלִים). The Canaanites celebrated holidays similar to these. Thus, we are admonished in 23:13 to "make no mention of the names of other gods." This will ensure that there is no misunderstanding. These agricultural holidays are not the ones celebrated by the Canaanites—they now have new meanings, related specifically to the life of the Israelites.

Read 22:14–17. What are the three festivals mentioned here?

1. The Festival of Matzot = Pesaḥ (פֶּסַח)
2. The Festival of the Harvest = Shavuot (שָׁבוּעוֹת)
3. The Festival of Ingathering = Sukkot (סֻכּוֹת)

Lesson 10A — Laws Related to Time and Seasons

How shall the festivals be celebrated in the future?

By the males appearing at God's Temple, bearing gifts.

Read 23:18.

As we have already discussed in Exodus 12, all sacrifices were accompanied by unleavened bread (מַצּוֹת).

In addition, the unedible, hard fat of the animal should not be left lying until morning. In the detailed laws of the sacrifices, we are told that this fat must be burnt as sacrifice to God.

Read 23:19.

The practice of boiling a kid goat in milk was common among the pagan people of biblical times. Israelites are forbidden to engage in this practice.

This prohibition is believed to be rooted in the prohibition of mixing life and death. We do not kill an animal and boil it in the milk that was intended to sustain it in life.

LESSON 10B

The Epilogue
Exod. 23:20–33

❑ IN PREPARATION FOR TEACHING

23:27–28 deal with driving out all the inhabitants of Canaan. Some of your students no doubt will be upset by this section, finding it cruel and unfeeling (as indeed it is). It is thus important to put the conquest of Canaan in a historical context.

The history of the human race is not a peaceful one. All through history one people has replaced another, one people conquering others and dispossessing them. Thus Babylonia was taken over by Persia and Persia in turn by Greece. By the same token the United States was populated by Europeans who dispossessed the native Indians. No people ever apologized for their conquests, to the contrary, they commemorated them in song and poetry. The Torah views the conquest of Canaan not as the heroic deed of Israel's forces, but as a religious obligation, a necessarily to safeguard Israel's sacred destiny.

The borders of the land of Israel, "from the Sea of Reeds [Egypt] to the Euphrates [Babylonia]," that the Torah foresees here were never realized. A conquering people usually does not conquer a land in one swoop, but little by little. The reason given here, however, is that the people of Israel are as yet not numerous enough to cultivate *all* the land. There is a danger that abandoned land will "become desolate, and that wild beasts multiply to your hurt."

❑ TEACHING PROCEDURE

Read 23:20–33. What is the passage about?

The passage deals with the relationship between God's indwelling with the people and their faithfulness to his laws. If the people observe the laws, they will feel God's presence in their midst. If they obey the angel (who in this passage is synonymous with God) "I [God] will be an enemy to your enemies and a foe to your foes."

We also find a warning. "When my angel goes before you and brings you to the Amorites, the Hittites, the Perizzites, the Canaanites, the Hivites and the Jebusites and I annihilate them, . . . you shall not bow down to their gods in worship."

Why is the admonition repeated here?

Pagans believed that gods had territorial powers. As the Israelites were to stop being desert dwellers and become farmers who till the soil of Canaan, the Torah foresees temptation. The people might want to adopt the gods of the local inhabitants—gods of rain and of fertility.

By what means does God assure the people that they do not need the local gods?

> By promising God's bounty: "You shall serve the Lord your God, and *He* will bless your bread and your water."

Why will God drive out the inhabitants of the land before the Israelites?

> Because they and their gods constitute a threat to Israel. (23:33)

LESSON 11

Ratifying the Covenant
Exod. 24:1–18

❏ IN PREPARATION FOR TEACHING

These verses present a problem as far as chronology is concerned: in 24:1–2 Moses is commanded to "come up to the Lord" the actual ascent to take place only in 24:14 after the ceremony has taken place.

The first two verses of the chapter seem to give Moses directives to be fulfilled once the covenant has been accepted and ratified by the people.

On Mount Sinai Moses will receive the stone tablets (לוּחוֹת הַבְּרִית) documenting the covenant between God and His people (24:12).

The ceremony itself begins with 24:3: "Moses went and repeated to the people all the commands of the Lord, and all the rules; and all the people answered with one voice, saying, 'All the things that the Lord has commanded we will do!'" Thus the people accepted the covenant.

Moses acted early in the morning, indicating his eagerness and willingness to ratify the covenant. Moses set up an altar with twelve pillars, one for each tribe. The young people (probably the firstborn sons, who in later times would be replaced by the *kohanim*) brought sacrifices. Then Moses sealed the covenant with blood, half being poured before God on the altar and half dashed on the people, thus symbolizing the mutual agreement between the two parties.

Then Moses, Aaron and Aaron's two eldest sons Nadab and Avihu and seventy people of Israel (the number seventy signifying a multitude) partially ascended the mountain where a second revelation took place. The people saw manifestations of the God of Israel (this does not mean they actually saw God Himself) and symbolically "broke bread with God" as one did when a covenant was sealed.

After appointing Aaron and Hur in charge of "legal matters," Moses ascended the mountain, God manifested Himself by a cloud and consuming fire, and Moses remained on the mountain forty days and forty nights.

UNIT SIX

The Mishkan
Exod. 25:1–31:17

LESSON 1

The Mishkan
Exod. 25:1–9

❐ INTRODUCTION

In Exod. 24:12 God instructs Moses, "Come up to Me at the mountain and wait there, and I will give you the stone tablets." Yet Moses does not receive the tablets of the law until Exod. 31:18. Instead of being given the tablets and descending, Moses receives a large body of instructions pertaining to the building of the mishkan (the portable sanctuary). (Some Bible scholars view these instructions as a second, cultic revelation, standing along side the Decalog.)

Why is there a need for a mishkan? The people of Israel have two conflicting ideas about God. On the one hand He is God the Creator, universal and omnipresent. On the other He has a special relationship to Israel, to whom He has given a special set of laws and among whom He will dwell in the special place they are to build for him.

How are we to handle this paradox? The mishkan has to be understood as fulfilling human, rather than divine needs. All ancient people envisioned their deities as connected with certain locations. The God of Israel had appeared to them at Sinai, and there He had made His presence felt, yet now they were to move on, leaving Sinai behind them. How could they be assured of God's presence in their midst on their long trek to Canaan?

In response to their need God commands His people to build the mishkan, a place where He can dwell with them, and through which they will be able to achieve a degree of closeness to Him. The mishkan can be understood as a portable Mount Sinai, to be carried along as they go.

The instructions regarding the building of the mishkan are found in Exodus 25–31, and describe: (1) the wooden structure, which is divided into two sections (the Holy and the Holy of Holies), (2) the outer court, (3) the furnishings of the wooden structure and of the outer court. It should be noted that the term *mishkan* is used in two different ways: it may describe the whole complex, or it may refer only to the wooden structure.

These chapters describe also the garments of the *kohanim* and the ritual that Aaron is to perform.

Great emphasis is put on the importance of following the instructions to the smallest detail.

Exodus 35–40 describe the actual building of the mishkan. The order of the construction is different from the order given in the instructions. The actual construction began with the wooden structure, rather than with the Holy Ark and the cherubim, and other furnishings. This stands to reason, since the Ark and the cherubim cannot stand in the open. (Probably, since different people fulfilled different tasks, the various tasks were performed simultaneously.)

You cannot expect your students to read and figure out what the mishkan looked like. It is suggested that the teacher present the content to the students and minimize their reading.

We have no exact knowledge of what the mishkan looked like. We are told that Moses was shown exactly what to build, but we do not have the model he was shown. Any attempt to depict the mishkan or its furnishings must rely on some imagination. The standard books about the mishkan must be used with caution. Although many of their illustrations and diagrams do mirror the *peshat* of the Exodus text, others follow later interpretations (e.g., the racks on the table for the show bread).

The illustrations included in this volume are based on the standard illustrations, but do not incorporate obvious later influences. For example, later interpretations depict the cherubim as a winged boy and a winged girl crouching on the ark. The cherubim appearing here (p. 239) reflect the carvings and pictures of cherubim found in the Ancient Near East, namely, a mythical animal with a head of a man, a body of a lion, and wings of an eagle.

Some Bible scholars doubt that the mishkan was built in the desert. They believe it depicts the structure King David built for the ark when he first brought it to Jerusalem. This is for your information and does not have to be taught.

❐ TEACHING THIS UNIT

Because this section is extremely detailed and technical, it does not lend itself to a close classroom reading. Instead, teach the contents of the material by presenting the basic points frontally, using diagrams and small sections of text as examples. You will have to determine how much detail to examine, based on the nature of your own class.

Lesson 1 — The Mishkan

The lessons about the various parts of the mishkan do not follow the sequence found in Exodus. A general understanding of the overall structure of the mishkan is helpful before learning about the details of the furnishings. Distribute copies of the diagrams (pp. 224–51), or make overhead projector overlays. Direct students to the appropriate verses where they can find descriptions of the various items in the diagrams (e.g., ark, cherubim, *kaporet*, table, menorah).

The following are the underlying principles of this section. They should be familiar to your students by the time your presentation is complete:

1. The mishkan "recreated" Sinai for the Israelites. At Sinai the Israelites had felt God's presence among them. The mishkan would be a portable reminder of that time and feeling.

2. The mishkan was a portable structure. It was designed so that it could be set up, taken apart, and set up once again as the Israelites traveled through the desert.

3. The mishkan was holy. Some areas were more holy than others. Each area was taboo, or unapproachable to the uninitiated.

4. The degree of holiness of objects or areas within the mishkan were in direct relationship to the value of the material of which they were constructed. For example, the Holy of Holies was the most holy area since it housed the cherubim and the ark (God's throne); it was therefore made mostly of pure gold had a costly, woven curtain. The Holy was made of less expensive materials: mostly gold-plated wood, and a simpler, embroidered curtain. In the outer court even less costly materials, mostly silver and copper, were used.

5. Being in the proximity of holy places or holy objects was dangerous. Only Aaron could enter the Holy, which he did twice a day. He alone was safe in the presence of *kedushah* (holiness) because he had been anointed. Contact with *kedushah* would be fatal to anyone not qualified..

6. Mixed materials "conduct" *kedushah* (holiness). Fabrics of a single material do not let the *kedushah* pass, and therefore serve as insulation to protect people from the power of *kedushah*.

❒ **TEACHING PROCEDURE**

Look back at Exod. 24:12. Why did God call Moses up to Sinai?

According to the text, to receive the tablets of the law.

What would you expect Exodus 25 to be about?

Moses receiving the tablets.

Read 25:1-9. What do you find instead?

The people are to build a portable sanctuary (mishkan).

According to 25:8, why is is a mishkan needed?

So that God can dwell with His people.

Students may say that God is everywhere, and He needs no place for Himself. You may want to explain the difficulties the Israelites faced in the worship of an invisible God.

How would an Egyptian feel close to his god?

He had statues and idols he could hold and fondle.

When were the Israelites certain of God's presence?

When He appeared to them at Sinai. Experience taught them that God did dwell on Sinai. Now, however, they were to leave Him behind.

How were they to be sure that He was to dwell with them?

By building a mishkan.

Does God need a mishkan?

No.

He had manifested Himself to Moses and to Pharaoh in Egypt. At the Sea of Reeds at Marah and Rephidim, God's presence guided them on their exodus from Egypt as a pillar of cloud by day and a pillar of fire by night. Obviously God is not subject to place and time. The mishkan is to serve the human needs of Israel, not those of God.

Where were the Israelites to get the gold and other precious materials to build the mishkan?

Upon the departure from Egypt the Israelites, by God's order, carried with them gold and silver objects and costly garments.

Now they shall have the opportunity to use this wealth, not for themselves but in honor of God. The gifts are listed in descending order according to value: from gold to silver to copper.

LESSON 2A

The Mishkan Complex
Exodus 25, 26, and 27

For this lesson use figs. 1–7, 12 (pp. 224–37, 246–47).

The whole complex (figs. 7, 12) consisted of a wooden structure surrounded by a large enclosure.

THE WOODEN STRUCTURE (26:1–30)

The wooden structure (מִשְׁכָּן; see fig. 1.B) was made of wooden planks (26:5) covered with gold. Each plank had two tenons, or prongs, at the bottom. These were inserted into two silver sockets (silver being stronger than gold) to hold the planks upright (26:17) (fig. 3). Each two planks were held together by "rings" (26:24) (fig. 3) and each wall of twenty planks (for the long walls) or six planks (for the short wall) were held together by means of wooden bars overlaid with gold. These planks were to form three walls, the fourth to be covered by a screen made of colored wool, yarns and twisted linen, embroidered (26:36) and suspended on five poles.

The structure was as yet open at the top (fig. 4), but was to be covered by an intricately woven cover (26:1–6) made of twisted linen and blue, purple and crimson wool yarn with a design of cherubim "worked," or woven into it. This cover was to be made of two parts, each part consisting of five strips of cloth horizontally sewn together (fig. 5). The two parts were to be connected by fifty blue wood buttons attached to fifty golden clasps.

This cover, placed over the gold planks from the outside, would serve as a ceiling of the structure (fig. 6). One would, however, not be able to see the ceiling from the outside since it would be covered by two pieces of five strips each of goat hair held together by copper clasps and on top of the goat hair cover would come another cover of ram's skins and dolphin skins (fig. 12). Thus, only the leather cover would be seen from the outside. (Here you may want to explain why the ceiling was שַׁעַטְנֵז but the roof was made of one material; see above, pp. 207, 219–20.)

The wooden structure was divided into two parts: the Holy of Holies (fig. 1.C), and the Holy (fig. 1.D). The Holy of Holies

(קֹדֶשׁ הַקֳּדָשִׁים) was a cube. It measured ten cubits (fifteen feet) wide, ten cubits high and ten cubits long. The Holy (הַקֹּדֶשׁ) was a double cube. It measured ten cubits wide, ten cubits high and twenty cubits long.

The two areas were separated by a curtain (פָּרֹכֶת; see fig. 1.H). This *parokhet* was intricately woven of the most costly materials: blue, purple, and crimson wool yarns and fine twisted linen (שָׁעְטְנֵז) with a design of cherubim worked into it. The *parokhet* would hang on four posts of acacia wood overlaid with gold and set in four silver sockets (26:32). It would separate the Holy of Holies from the Holy.

THE OUTER COURT (27:9–19)

The outer court or surrounding enclosure (חָצֵר; see fig. 1.A) was made by suspending five twisted linen hangings (fig. 2.A) on wooden posts (fig. 2.B). The wood was acacia wood found in the arid Sinai (by and large the tree trunks of the acacia tree were thin and bent, and it must have been difficult to find straight, broad acacia planks).

Each post would be placed in a copper socket (fig. 2.C) for support and the material would be connected to the posts by means of bands and hooks of silver. The entrance to the outer court would be curtained by a screen (מָסָךְ, see fig. 1.E.) made of colored yarns and fine linen.

The whole complex, both the wooden structure and the outer court could be taken apart and moved from one location to the next.

LESSON 2B

The Ark and the Cherubim
Exod. 25:10–22

For this lesson use fig. 8 (pp. 238–39).

THE ARK OF THE PACT (25:10–16)

The Ark of the Pact (אֲרוֹן הַבְּרִית; see fig. 8.B) was to hold the tablets of the Pact (לְחוֹת הַבְּרִית), which God would give Moses. The Ark and the cherubim were the only objects in the Holy of Holies. Your students may assume that the Ark looked like the familiar ark in the synagogue: an upright closet-shaped structure. In 25:10 we learn that the Ark was two and one-half cubits long, one and one-half cubits wide and one and one-half cubits high, thus it was an elongated box (coffin-shaped). Such a structure was easier to carry than an upright closet. It too was made of acacia wood and overlaid with pure gold. Four rings were attached to its short sides, two on each side, and two poles were inserted into the rings. The Ark was carried by these poles which were left permanently in 'the rings (26:15).

The Ark was open on top. Moses was instructed to make a cover (כַּפֹּרֶת), a slab of pure gold two and one-half cubits by one and one-half cubits and to make two gold cherubim at the two ends of the cover facing one another.

The cover and the cherubim were to be made of one piece. "There," God tells Moses, "I will meet with you and I will impart to you—from above the cover, from between the two cherubim that are on top of the Pact—all that I will command you concerning the Israelite people" (25:22).

We know from other parts of the Bible that the cherubim served as a seat for God whenever He chose to indwell with His people (1 Sam. 4:4). Figuratively, the Ark with the cherubim served as a throne for God. The invisible presence "sits" on the cherubim, His "feet" resting on the ark. (In Babylonia treaties between tribes or nations were kept for safekeeping under the idols' feet in the temples. Here too, in a symbolic sense, the tablets of the Pact would be placed under God's "feet").

Throughout Israelite history the Ark often led the people into war. God was invisibly riding into battle ahead of his people. In the synagogue today, as we open the ark, we still use the ancient call to God to fight our battles for us: קוּמָה ה׳ וְיָפֻצוּ אֹיְבֶיךָ וְיָנֻסוּ מְשַׂנְאֶיךָ מִפָּנֶיךָ "Advance, O Lord! May Your enemies be scattered, and may Your foes flee before You" (Num. 10:35).

THE CHERUBIM (25:17–22)

The cherubim (כְּרוּבִים; see fig. 8.A). were mythical animals with a head of man, a body of a lion, and wings of an eagle. Their purpose was to serve God as His throne or his chariot. Pure gold was to be used for overlaying the Ark and making the cover and the cherubim (Exod. 25:10). The Ark was to be placed in the Holy of Holies. It seems that the poles holding the *parokhet* did not permit the removal of the Ark unless the mishkan was dismantled. Nobody could enter the Holy of Holies except Moses, who would there talk with God. In later history, the High Priest would enter the Holy of Holies only once a year, on Yom Kippur.

We shall note that as we move from the *kaporet* and cherubim, the materials used for making the mishkan become less costly. Like a stone causing ripples when thrown into a pond, the further we move from the center, the less holy the area and the less costly the materials used.

LESSON 3

The Furnishings in the Holy
Exod. 25:23–40, 30:1–10

For this lesson use figs. 9 and 10 (pp. 240–43).

In the Holy stood three articles: a table, a menorah (or lampstand), and a small altar for burning pure incense.

THE TABLE (25:23–30)

Like the Ark, the table (שֻׁלְחָן; see fig. 9.B) was to be made of acacia wood overlaid with pure gold. Two cubits long, one cubit wide and one and one-half cubits high with a gold molding around the top. Four rings were to be attached to the four legs of the table as holders for the two poles to carry it by.

Lev. 24:5–9 describes the purpose of the table: twelve loaves of bread (לֶחֶם הַפָּנִים) were to be placed on the table every Sabbath day in two rows; six loaves to a row. With each bread frankincense was to be placed as a token offering. The loaves were replaced by fresh ones on the Sabbath. The old loaves were to be consumed by Aaron and his sons.

THE MENORAH (25:31–40)

The lampstand (מְנוֹרָה; see fig. 9.A) was to have "six branches issue from its side: three branches from one side . . . and three from the other side . . . on each branch there will be three cups shaped like almond blossoms." The lampstand was to be made of one single piece of hammered pure gold. On each branch, and also on the centerpiece, a "lamp" or small dish would be placed (seven in all). The lamps would hold pure olive oil and wicks. (Before the invention of wax candles, candles consisted of wicks placed in oil). The lamps were removable for cleaning purposes.

Today in the synagogue we light a light in front of ark, which is reminiscent of the menorah in the Holy. We call it "the eternal light" (נֵר תָּמִיד). This light burns day and night.

Although in modern Hebrew the word *tamid* means "nonstopping," "continuous," "always," in biblical Hebrew the word *tamid* means "recurring at regular intervals," (The *tamid* offering, for example, was brought daily, not continuously.) Aaron would light the menorah at twilight, and clean the lamps in the morning. Thus, the menorah was lit at night only. (See also 1 Sam. 3:3: "The lamp of God had not yet gone out.")

THE INCENSE ALTAR (30:1-10)

The incense altar (מִזְבַּח הַקְּטֹרֶת; see fig. 10) was placed in the Holy, in front of the *parokhet*.

The altar was to be one cubit long, one cubit wide and two cubits high (two perfect cubes attached to one another), with four "horns" at the four corners. Two gold rings were to be attached at opposite legs as holders for the poles with which to carry the altar. Aaron would burn incense at the altar twice a day: in the evening when he lit the lamps and in the morning when he cleaned the lamps.

LESSON 4A

Priestly Garments
Exodus 28

For this lesson use figs. 13–14 (pp. 248–51).

AARON'S GARMENTS

When officiating in the Holy, Aaron was to wear an *ephod*, a breastpiece, a robe, a fringed tunic, a headdress, and a sash (28:4), as well as a frontlet (28:36).

The Ephod (28:6–14)

The *ephod* (הָאֵפֹד; fig. 13.B) was to be made of gold, of blue, purple and crimson yarns, and of fine twisted linen worked into designs. It was to have two shoulder pieces attached. On these shoulder straps two lapis lazuli stones (semiprecious stones) would be placed (fig. 13.E). Engraved on the stones would be the names of the twelve tribes, six names on each stone. These were to be a constant reminder to God that He was to be concerned with His people Israel.

The Breastpiece (28:15–30)

Over the *ephod* Aaron would wear the breastpiece (חֹשֶׁן; see figs. 13.C and 14), which was made of gold, blue, purple, and crimson yarns and twisted linen. The breastpiece was folded (doubled) to make a square. On it was to be set four rows of three semiprecious stones. These stones were to be framed with gold. Each stone would be engraved with the name of one of the tribes of Israel (one for Reuben, one for Simeon, etc.). The breastpiece would be held in place by a cord of blue (fig. 14.C).

These stones were to be called the "Urim and Thummim" (אוּרִים וְתֻמִּים). In many places in the Bible we find that when the king wanted to "inquire of the Lord" (for instance, to ask whether to go to war or to refrain from war), the Urim and Thummim indicated which of the two alternatives was correct. Inquiries were designed to elicit "yes" or "no" answers. Josephus, a Jewish historian in the second century C.E., writes that the answer was decided by the "shining of the stones." The six *urim* would shine for one answer, the six *tummim* for the other.

Others believe the stones were used like dice, and cast down like lots. The last to use the Urim and Thummim was King David. After that the word of God was conveyed to the people through the prophets.

It may be of interest to students that the Urim and Thummim appear in the emblem of Yale University.

The Robe of the Ephod (28:31–35)

Underneath the *ephod* Aaron would wear a robe (מְעִיל הָאֵפֹד; see fig. 13.A) of pure blue, its hem decorated with gold bells and pomegranates made of yarn (fig. 13.D). Aaron was to wear it while officiating so that the sound of the bells would be heard. Aaron had to approach God as one would approach a king. One does not come into the presence of a king unannounced. (Remember the Esther story: she, although queen, was not to come before the king unless she was invited.) To approach the Holy unannounced was fraught with danger. (See 28:35: "that he may not die.")

Headdress and Frontlet (28:36–38, 39b)

Aaron would also wear a fine linen headdress (מִצְנֶפֶת; see fig. 13.F) and a pure gold frontlet (צִיץ; see fig. 13.G)—a band worn on the forehead. Engraved on the frontlet would be the words "Holy to the Lord." It would be suspended on a blue cord, resting on the headdress. "It shall be on Aaron's forehead, that Aaron may take away any sin arising from the Holy things that the Israelites consecrate ... to win acceptance for them before the Lord" (28:38).

Other Garments

In addition, Aaron would wear a tunic (כְּתֹנֶת) of linen and a sash (אַבְנֵט) of embroidered work. Underneath all these garments he would wear linen breeches (pants).

Just as the materials and ornaments inside the tent itself were more valuable and elaborate than those of the outer court, so was Aaron's garb for service inside the Holy more elaborate than the simple, linen *ephod* he wore when making offerings in the public, outer court.

THE GARMENTS OF AARON'S SONS (28:40–43)

Aaron's sons would assist him at the sacrificial altar. They would be provided with tunics and headdresses made of fine linen, and also with embroidered sashes. They would wear linen breeches (pants) covering them from the hips to the thighs as they approached the altar. (In some ancient cultures priests performed their sacrificial duties to their gods in the nude. Israelite priests were not to approach the altar naked (see Exod. 20:23).

LESSON 4B

The Service

As Aaron officiates inside the Holy, his actions, together with his clothes, form a cultic whole. All senses of the divine were to be served symbolically. The incense provided a fragrance for God's nose as though God were a human king. The people are concerned with God's "comfort," and since humans did not know how to please God, they did it in the best way they knew, namely, in the way they would treat a human king. God's sense of sight, like human sight, would presumabley be satisfied by the light of the menorah. The bells announced the human presence "to God's ears." The show bread was presented "for God's tastebuds" and the breastplate was a visual aid "reminding" God of His covenant with the twelve tribes.

LESSON 5

Holiness and What It Means

There was mortal danger attached to *kedushah* (holiness). Nobody but Aaron and Moses could enter the Holy. Nobody else could look at the menorah, the table, and the incense altar. Aaron had to announce himself by means of the bells on his robe "that he may not die." He wore a frontlet of pure gold on his forehead in case the Israelites inadvertently brought a blemished offering.

To do anything that was not in accord with the regulations was punishable by death (e.g., Lev. 10:1–3). For a person to come closer to holy places or holy things than his status entitled him was dangerous. Many stories in the Bible testify to this (e.g., 1 Sam. 6:19, 2 Sam. 6:6–8). Intention was not considered. We may best liken it to high tension electricity: touching the source is lethal. One's morality—whether one was good or evil—does not enter the picture. Anybody who touches the wire will die, indiscriminately.

Mixed materials (כִּלְאַיִם, שַׁעַטְנֵז) like wool yarn mixed with linen, were not created in the six days of creation. They are not "natural." We find that the *parokhet*, the curtain between the Holy of Holies and the Holy was made of mixed materials, as was the ceiling of the Holy and Aaron's *ephod*.

Mixed materials are good conductors of *kedushah*, just as metal is a good conductor of electricity. Mixed materials let *kedushah* flow back and forth. Thus, *kedushah* flowed through the *parokhet* into the Holy, and some *kedushah* would leak through the outer curtain of the mishkan into the outer court. Aaron was safe, even though he wore mixed materials, because he had been anointed with the prescribed perfumed oil that prepared him for the service. (Similarly, the furnishings were anointed with the same oil, to prepare them for use.) Mixed materials were "unnatural," forbidden to humans, appropriate only to the service of God.

Materials made of only one material, however, blocked the holiness from leaking out. Thus the ceiling of the mishkan was covered from the outside by a cover of goat hair and that in turn by covers of skin.

When the mishkan was about to be moved, Aaron would place individual wrappers of goat hair and skins over the Ark and over each piece of furniture and each utensil used in the Holy (Numbers 4). Only then could the Levites safely approach the objects and carry them away by the poles. (One can compare this to radioactive material, which is safe to transport only when encased in a block of lead from which no leakage can occur. We know of the difficulty we encounter in our efforts to get rid of radioactive material.)

LESSON 6

Articles in the Outer Court
Exod. 27:1–8; 30:17–22

For this lesson use figs. 7, 11, and 12 (pp. 236–37, 244–47).

THE ALTAR (27:1–8)

The measurements of the altar (מִזְבַּח הָעֹלָה; see fig. 7.L, 11, and 12.B) were: five cubits long, five cubits square, and three cubits high. The altar, too, was portable. It was made of wood overlaid with copper, much cheaper material than the gold of the incense altar. While the furnishings inside the tent could not be touched, approached or even seen by anybody but Aaron, the sacrificial altar could be seen by all of Israel, but only Aaron and his sons could approach and touch it. Aaron, when officiating at the sacrificial altar would not wear his clothing of mixed materials but a plain linen garment. Note that the altar would have a horn on each of its four corners.

All the utensils used in connection with the altar (e.g., the pails for the removal of ashes, the basins, the flesh hooks) were to be made of copper.

THE LAVER (30:17–22)

Between the altar and the wooden structure was to be placed a laver, or big basin (כִּיּוֹר; see figs. 7.K, 12.C). The laver would contain water for Aaron and his sons to wash their hands and feet before they approached the altar. Aaron would also wash with water from the laver before entering the Holy.

LESSON 7

Building the Mishkan
Exod. 31:1-17, 40:1-16

COMMISSIONING THE WORK (31:1-11)

God informed Moses that He had singled out Bezalel to supervise the construction of the mishkan and all its furnishing, as well as the garments for Aaron and his sons. God had endowed Bezalel "with a divine spirit of skill, ability and knowledge in every kind of craft to design the work of the mishkan" (31:3).

(It may be of interest to students that the Jerusalem museum and school of fine arts is named after Bezalel.)

ERECTING AND CONSECRATING THE MISHKAN (40:1-16)

Once erected, the entire mishkan complex, including all its furnishings, had to be anointed with sacred oil before it could be used for the service of God. Similarly, Aaron, his sons, and all their garments had to be anointed.

This "oil" was not heavy or greasy. It was a perfume made by mixing prescribed quantities of spices: myrrh, cinnamon, aromatic cane, cassia and some olive oil. Laymen were prohibited from using the sacred perfume (30:37).

(Today we use the oil—"attar"—of spices and certain flowers, such as roses and jasmine, to make perfumes.)

The perfumed oil was sprinkled over everything that was to be consecrated to God—the ark, the incense altar, the lampstand, the table, the wooden structure and its coverings, the sacrificial altar, and the laver. Aaron and his his sons were washed with water from the laver. They were then dressed in their special garments, and anointed with the perfume.

The perfumed oil served to purify Aaron and his sons, as well as all the objects, insulating them from any subsequent ritual pollution. This single act of anointing would serve the priesthood throughout the ages. Priests in generations to come would not need to be anointed.

PROHIBITING WORK ON THE SABBATH (31:12–17)

This prohibition has appeared before (Exod. 20:7–11). It is repeated here because God fears that in the people's zeal to build the mishkan ("dwelling place") for God, the people might assume that this sacred task would supersede the sacredness of the Sabbath day. Therefore, the people are now reminded of the fourth Pronouncement.

THE MISHKAN

The Mishkan: Overview
Figure 1

This diagram depicts structures of the mishkan complex.

Hebrew	Label	English
חָצֵר	A	Outer court
הַמִּשְׁכָּן	B	The Mishkan (wooden structure)
קֹדֶשׁ הַקֳּדָשִׁים	C	The Holy of Holies
הַקֹּדֶשׁ	D	The Holy
מָסָךְ	E	Outer screen
עַמּוּד	F	Pole
קְלָעִים	G	Hangings
פָּרֹכֶת	H	Parokhet, curtain dividing The Holy from The Holy of Holies

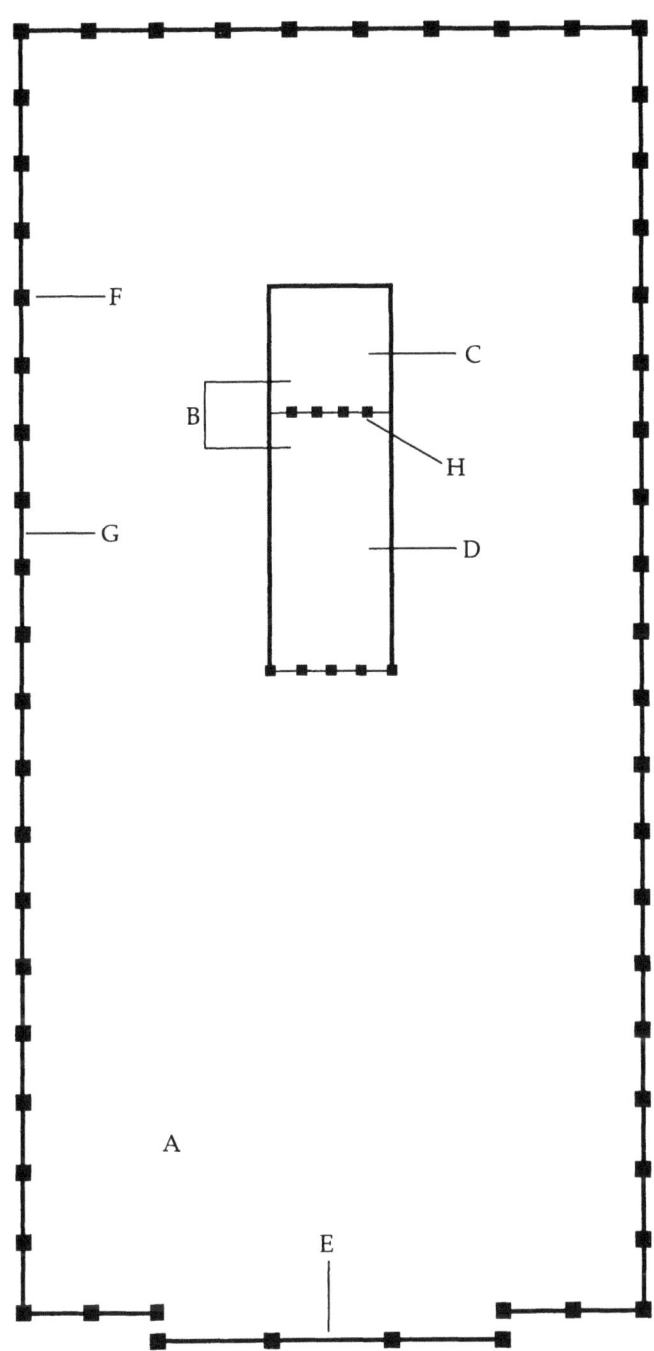

THE MISHKAN

The Outer Court
Figure 2

The enclosure of the outer court (חָצֵר) would be dismantled in preparation for moving to a new location. The materials used here (linen and copper) were less costly than those used in the wooden structure.

קְלָעִים (שֵׁשׁ מָשְׁזָר)   **A**   Hangings (fine linen)

עַמּוּדִים (עֵץ)   **B**   Poles (wood)

אֲדָנִים (נְחֹשֶׁת)   **C**   Sockets (copper)

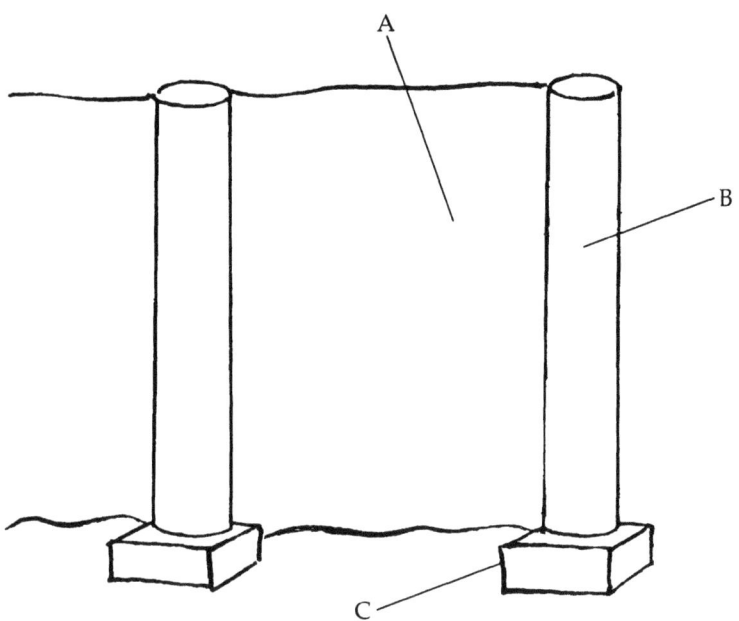

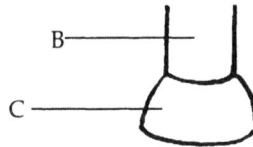

The poles may have been round, as above, or they may have been flat or square.

The sockets may have been square, as above, or round.

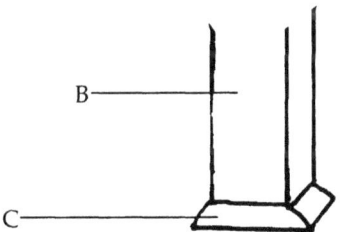

THE MISHKAN

Building the Wooden Structure
Figure 3

The planks of the wooden structure (מִשְׁכָּן) were held upright by means of prongs inserted into sockets. Each pair of adjacent planks was held together by a ringed bracket. Bars along the outside of the planks and a bar through the center of the planks made the planks into a rigid wall. The materials used for the wooden structure were more precious than those used for the outer court.

קְרָשִׁים (עֲצֵי שִׁטִּים מְצֻפִּים זָהָב)	A	Planks (acacia wood overlayed with gold)
טַבָּעוֹת (זָהָב)	B	Ringed brackets (gold)
אֲדָנִים (כֶּסֶף)	C	Sockets (silver)
בְּרִיחִים (עֲצֵי שִׁטִּים מְצֻפִּים זָהָב)	D	Bars (acacia wood overlayed with gold)
יָדוֹת (כֶּסֶף)	E	Tenons, prongs (silver)

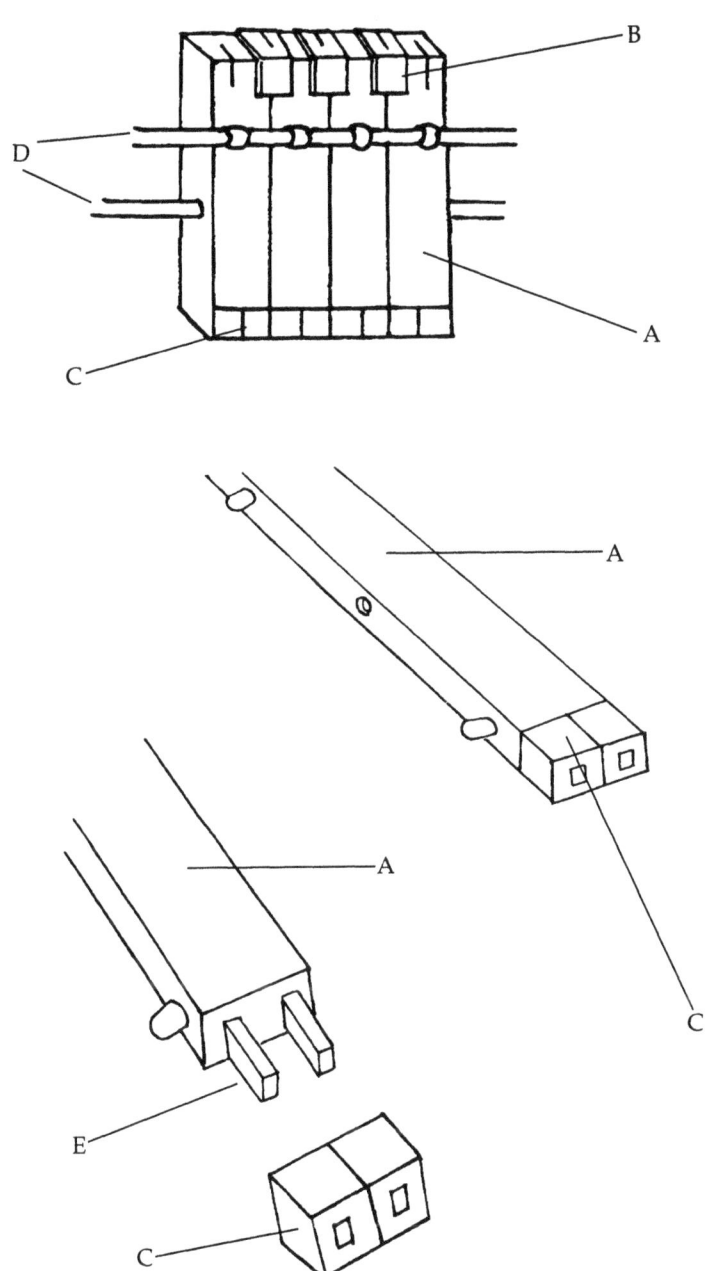

THE MISHKAN

The Wooden Structure
Figure 4

The wooden structure consisted of three walls and a screen.

קְרָשִׁים A Planks

טַבָּעוֹת B Ringed brackets

אֲדָנִים C Sockets

בְּרִיחִים D Bars

מָסָךְ (מַעֲשֵׂה רֹקֵם) E Screen (embroidered)

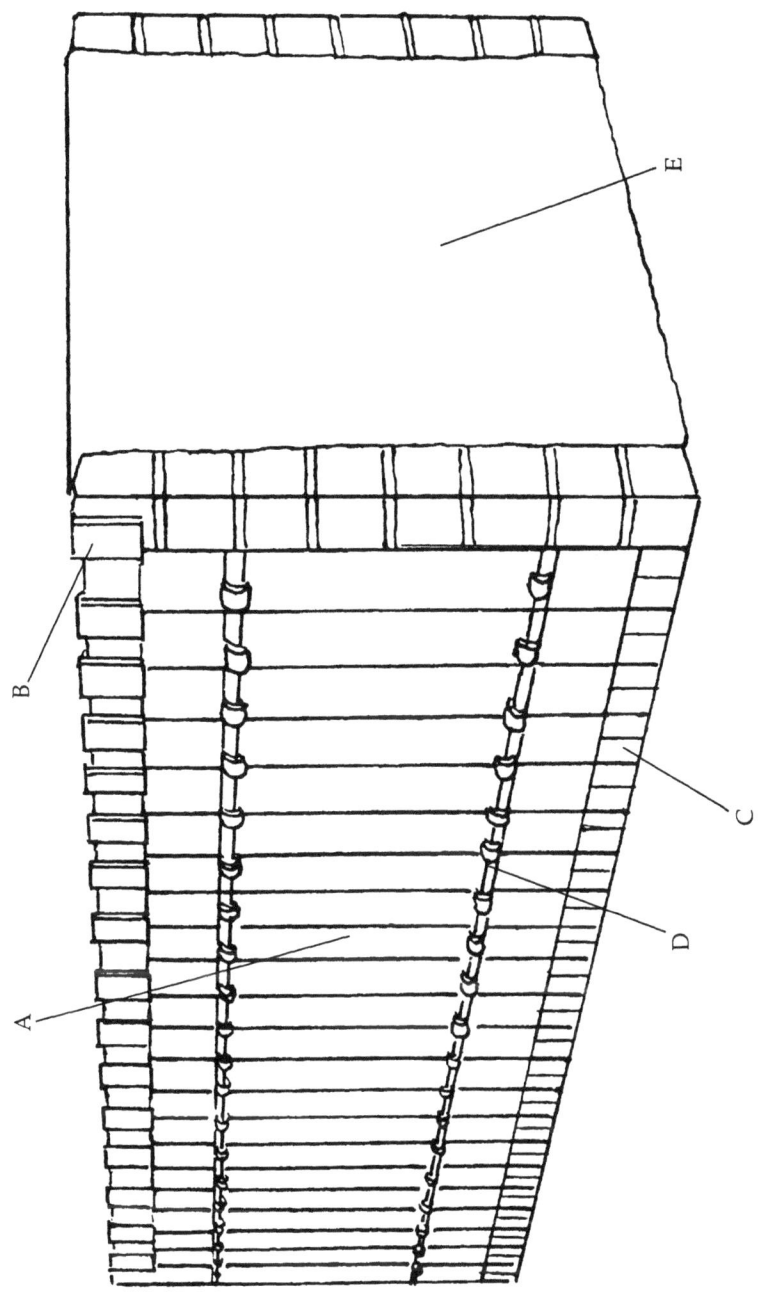

THE MISHKAN

Ceiling and Cover
Figure 5

Five intricate strips of fine linen, blue, crimson, and purple yarn with a design of cherubim worked into them were sewn together and joined to another identical set of five strips by fifty gold clasps and wool loops. Together they formed the ceiling and inner cover of the wooden structure.

יְרִיעוֹת (מַעֲשֵׂה חֹשֵׁב)   A   Strips of cloth (woven)

לֻלָאוֹת (תְּכֵלֶת)   B   Loops (blue wool)

קְרָסִים (זָהָב)   C   Clasps (gold)

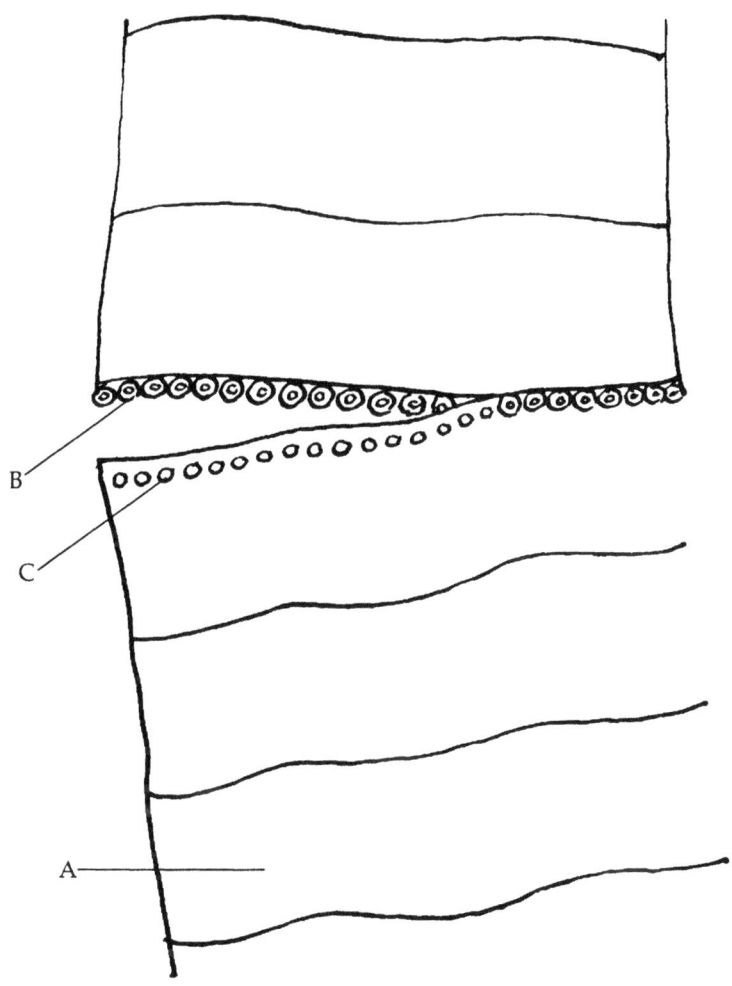

THE MISHKAN

The Covered Wooden Structure
Figure 6

> The wooden structure was covered with the intricate woven cloth covering. This cover, made of mixed materials, was not seen from the outside since it was covered by three separate covers (not shown), each of a single material (goats' hair, ram skins, and dolphin skins).

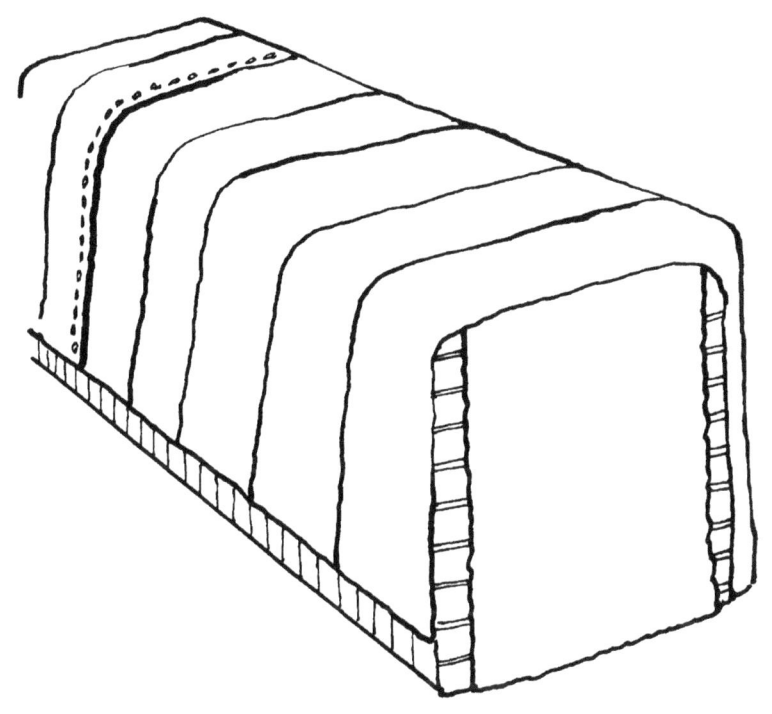

THE MISHKAN

The Furnished Mishkan
Figure 7

This diagram depicts the entire furnished mishkan complex.

חָצֵר	A	Outer court
הַמִּשְׁכָּן	B	The Mishkan (wooden structure)
קֹדֶשׁ הַקֳּדָשִׁים	C	The Holy of Holies
הַקֹּדֶשׁ	D	The Holy
אֲרוֹן הַבְּרִית	E	Ark of the Pact
מִזְבַּח הַקְּטֹרֶת	F	Incense Altar
שֻׁלְחָן	G	Table
פָּרֹכֶת (שַׁעַטְנֵז)	H	Parokhet, inner curtain (mixed materials)
מְנוֹרָה (זָהָב טָהוֹר)	I	Lampstand (pure gold)
מָסָךְ	J	Screen
כִּיּוֹר	K	Laver, basin
מִזְבַּח הָעֹלָה	L	Sacrificial altar

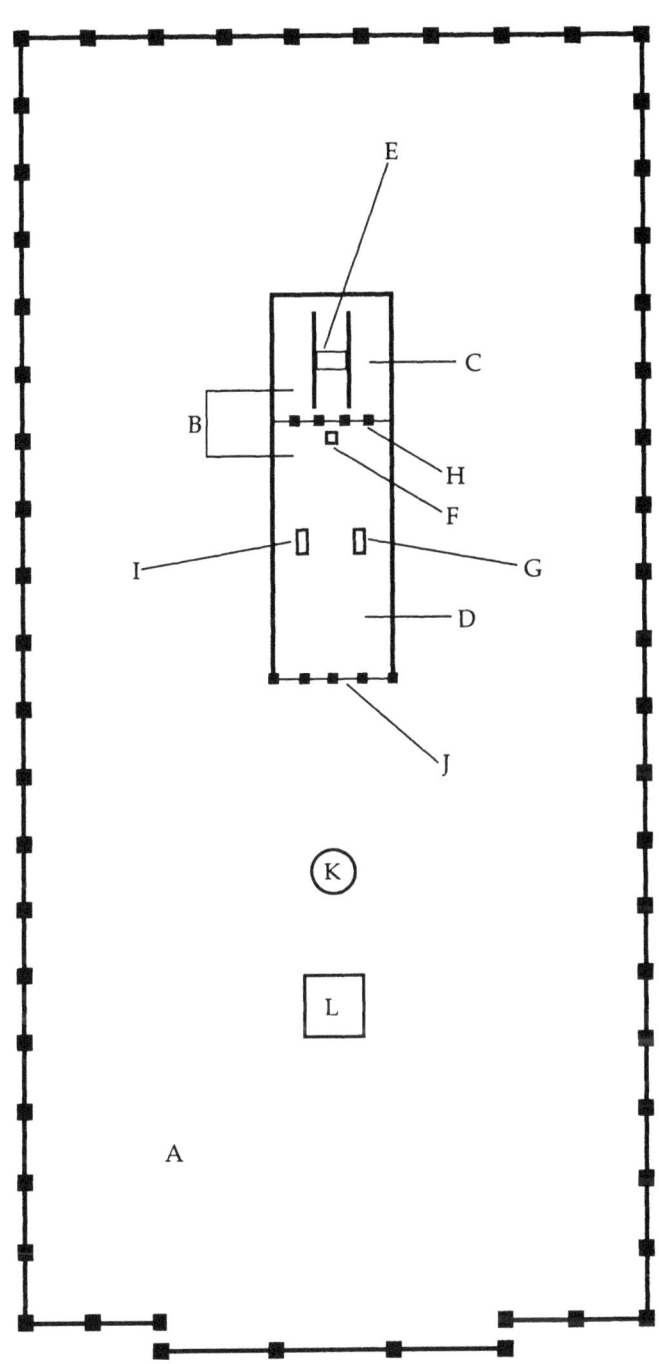

THE MISHKAN

Ark and Cherubim
Figure 8

A pure gold cover rested upon the Ark of the Pact. The cover consisted of two cherubim facing one another upon a solid slab. The poles of the Ark could not be removed from their rings. The Ark was the only furnishing of the Holy of Holies and could not be removed without dismantling the structure. Since the Ark and the cherubim represented God's throne, only the most costly of materials were used.

אֲרוֹן הַבְּרִית (עֲצֵי שִׁטִּים מְצֻפִּים זָהָב)	A	Ark of the Pact (acacia wood overlayed with gold)
כְּרוּבִים (זָהָב טָהוֹר)	B	Cherubim (pure gold)
כַּפֹּרֶת (זָהָב טָהוֹר)	C	Kaporet, slab covering the Ark (pure gold)
זֵר (זָהָב טָהוֹר)	D	molding (pure gold)
בַּדִּים (עֲצֵי שִׁטִּים מְצֻפִּים זָהָב)	E	Poles (acacia wood overlayed with gold)

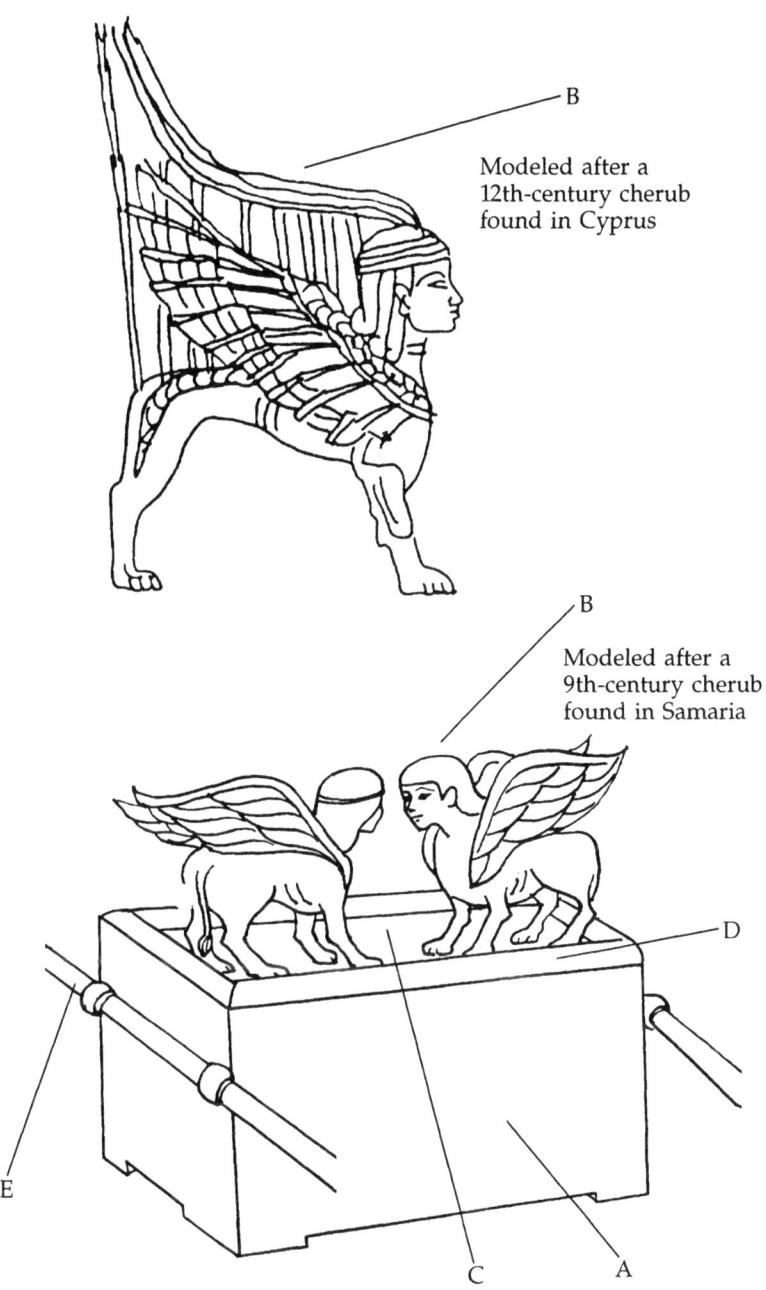

Modeled after a 12th-century cherub found in Cyprus

Modeled after a 9th-century cherub found in Samaria

THE MISHKAN

Menorah and Table
Figure 9

The lampstand and the table were placed in The Holy, together with the incense altar. The lampstand was kindled every evening and cleaned every morning. The table held the showbread (לָחֶם פָּנִים), which was replaced every Friday with fresh loaves. The old loaves were eaten by Aaron and his sons.

מְנוֹרָה (זָהָב טָהוֹר)   **A**   Lampstand (pure gold)

שֻׁלְחָן (עֲצֵי שִׁטִּים מְצֻפִּים זָהָב)   **B**   Table (acacia wood overlayed with gold)

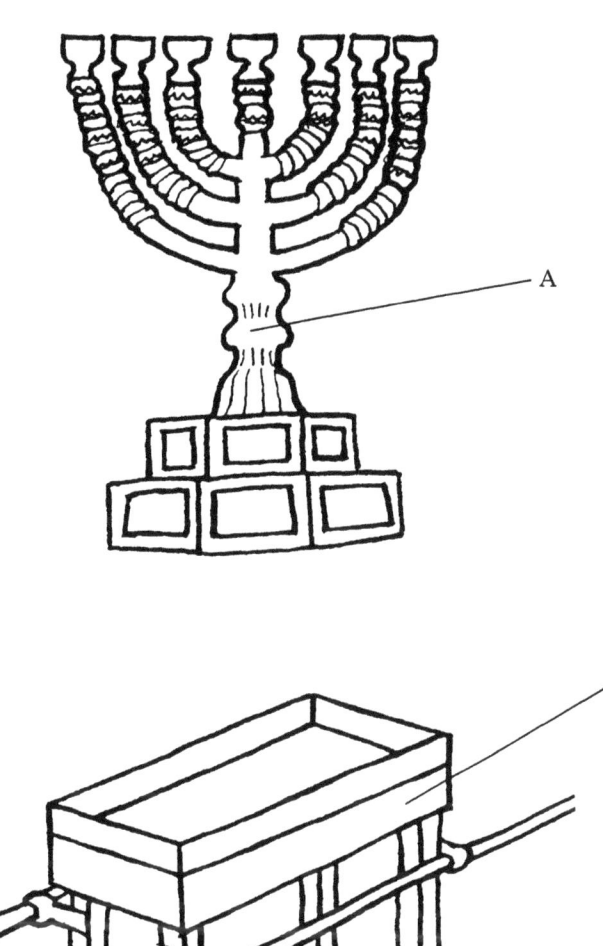

THE MISHKAN

Incense Altar
Figure 10

The incense altar (מִזְבַּח הַקְּטֹרֶת), made of acacia wood overlayed with gold, was used for burning incense within The Holy. Aaron would burn incense every morning when he cleaned the lamps.

טַבָּעוֹת (זָהָב) **A** Rings (gold)

בַּדִּים **B** Poles

קַרְנַיִם (זָהָב) **C** Horns (gold)

זֵר (זָהָב) **D** Molding (gold)

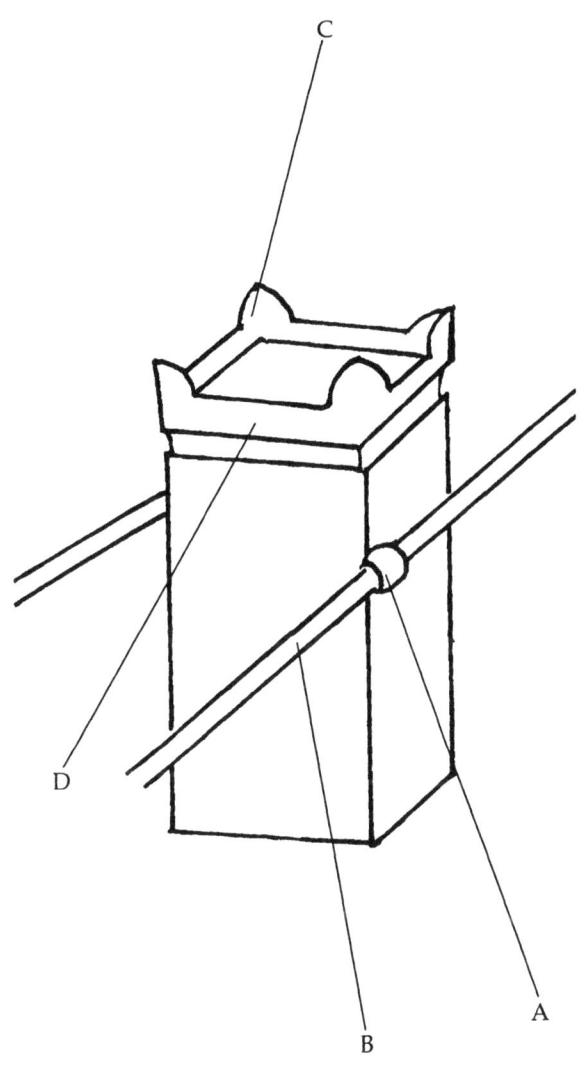

THE MISHKAN

Sacrificial Altar
Figure 11

The sacrificial altar (מִזְבַּח הָעֹלָה), made of wood overlayed with copper, stood in the outer court. All Israelites were permitted to see it but not to approach it.

קַרְנַיִם	A	Horns (copper)
מִכְבָּר (מַעֲשֵׂה רֶשֶׁת נְחֹשֶׁת)	B	Grating (copper meshwork)
טַבָּעוֹת (נְחֹשֶׁת)	C	Rings (copper)
בַּדִּים	D	Poles

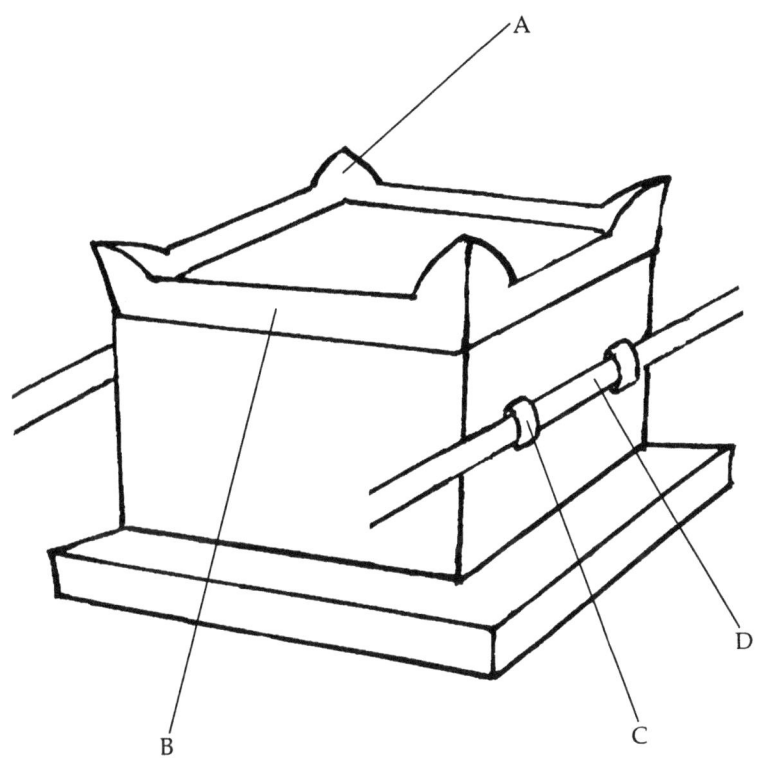

THE MISHKAN

The Completed Mishkan
Figure 12

The wooden structure was covered with goats' hair and skin covers, which overhang the front and the back. The screen at the opening is suspended on five poles. The laver would hold water for Aaron and his sons to wash with before performing their ritual duties.

הַמִּשְׁכָּן	A	The wooden structure
מִזְבַּח הָעֹלָה	B	Sacrificial altar
כִּיּוֹר (נְחֹשֶׁת)	C	Laver, basin (copper)

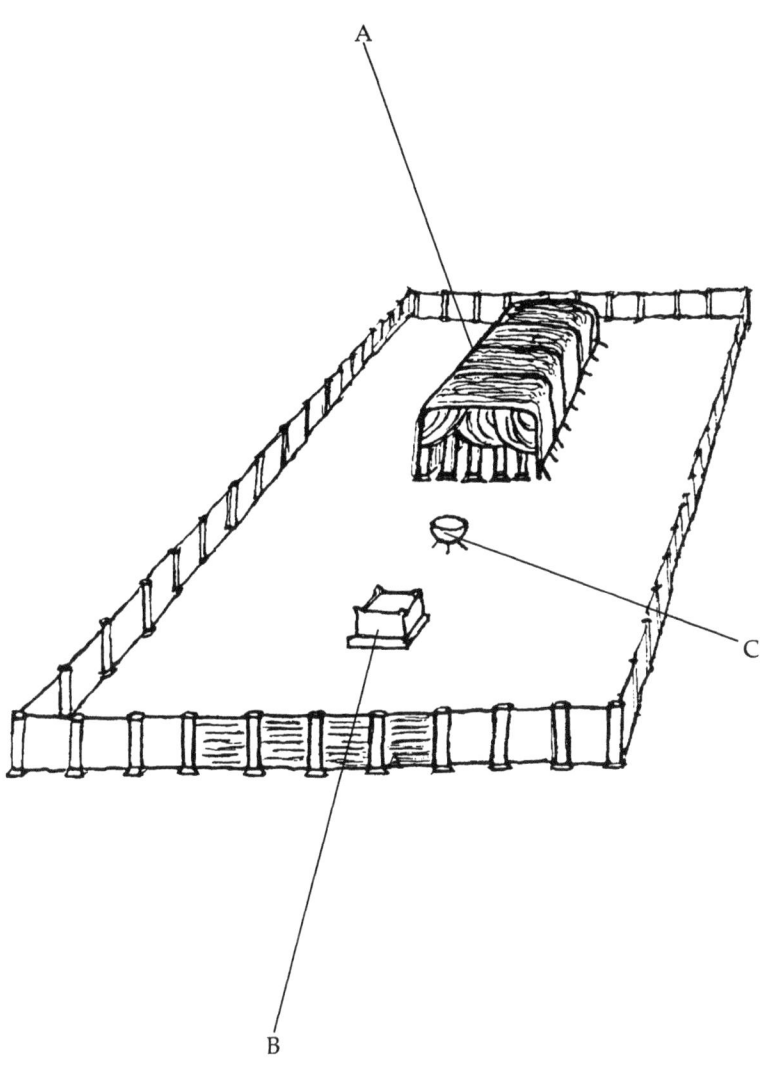

THE MISHKAN

Aaron's Garments
Figure 13

When Aaron would perform his ritual duties in The Holy, he would wear garments of mixed materials. Each of the onyx stones was engraved with the names of six tribes of Israel. The frontlet, worn over the forehead, was engraved with the words "Holy to the Lord." Aaron also wore breeches (not shown) underneath his clothes. When officiating at the sacrificial altar, Aaron would wear instead a plain linen gown.

מְעִיל תְּכֵלֶת   **A**   A blue robe

אֵפֹד   **B**   Ephod

חֹשֶׁן   **C**   Breastpiece

פַּעֲמוֹנִים וְרִמּוֹנִים   **D**   Bells and pomegranates

אַבְנֵי שֹׁהַם   **E**   Onyx stones

מִצְנֶפֶת   **F**   Turban, headdress

צִיץ   **G**   Frontlet

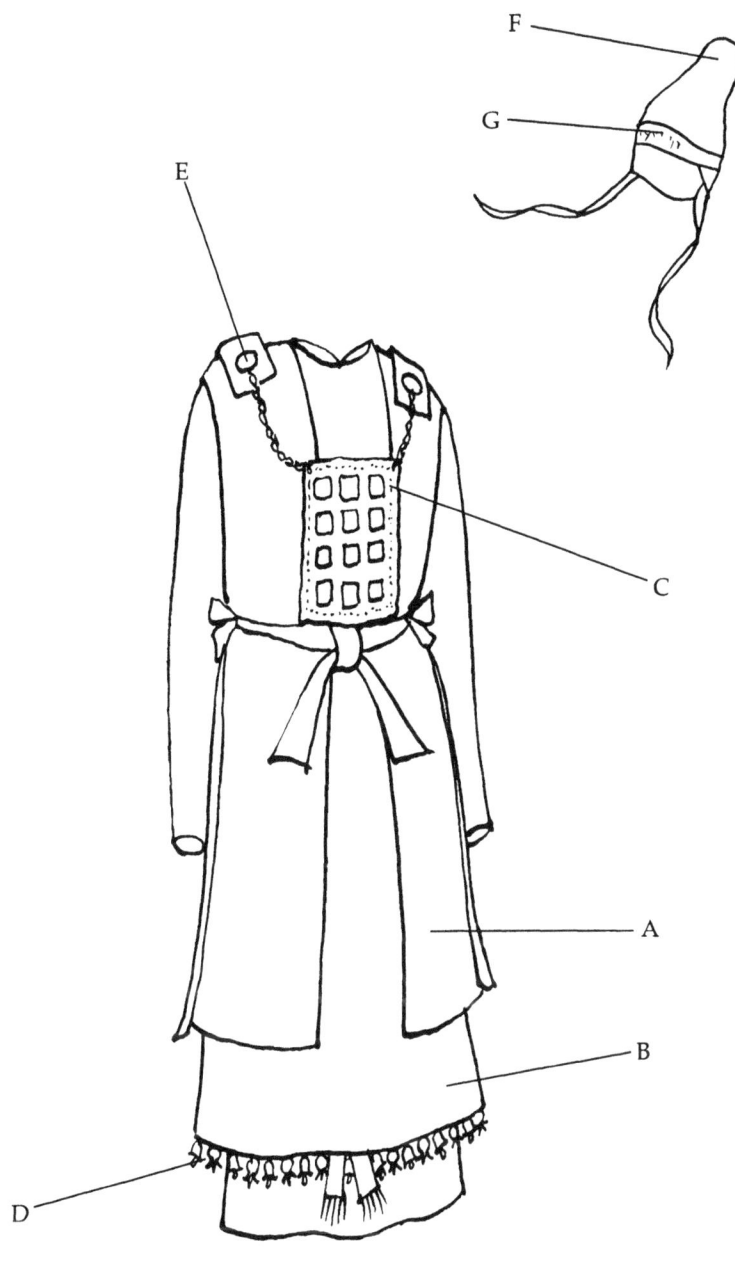

THE MISHKAN

Breastpiece of Decision
Figure 14

Aaron would wear the breastpiece of decision (חֹשֶׁן הַמִּשְׁפָּט) when he would perform his ritual duties in The Holy. On it were mounted twelve semiprecious stones, representing the twelve tribes of Israel. The mounted stones, called Urim and Thummim (אוּרִים וְתֻמִּים), were used inquire of God. It is not certain how God made His will known through these stones.

חֹשֶׁן	A	Breastpiece
	B	Piece of material to be folded under the breastpiece
	C	Ribbons, to tie the breastpiece to the ephod
אוּרִים וְתֻמִּים	D	Urim and Thummim, mounted stones
עֲבֹתֹת זָהָב, שַׁרְשְׁרוֹת זָהָב	E	Braided gold chains

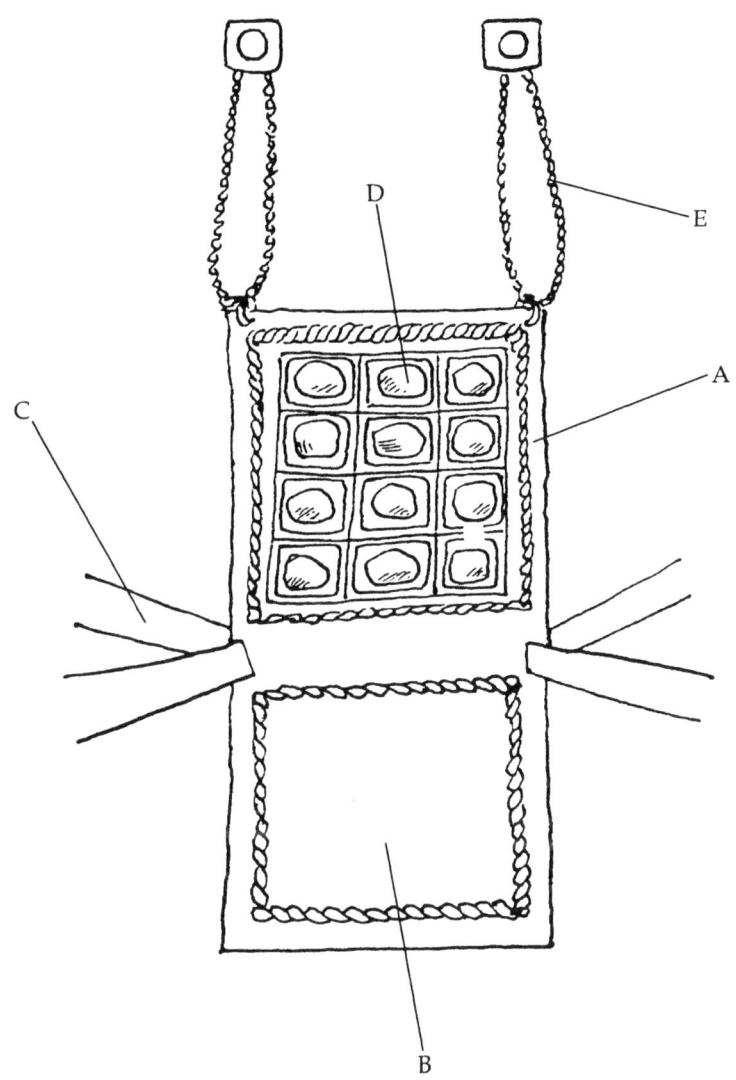

UNIT SEVEN

Rebellion and Reconciliation

Exod. 31:18–34:35

LESSON 1

Receiving the Tablets of the Pact
Exod. 31:18

☐ IN PREPARATION FOR TEACHING

Finally, Moses receives the two tablets of the pact testifying to the covenant between God and His people. The tablets are inscribed "by the finger of God." This statement does not have to be taken literally. Just as God's "strong hand and outstretched arm" was understood by us metaphorically to stand for God's strength and protection, the "finger of God" is also a metaphor. It represents our belief that the Ten Pronouncements are an expression of God's will.

☐ TEACHING PROCEDURE

Turn back to Exod. 24:12. Why did God originally call Moses to climb Mount Sinai?

To receive the Ten Pronouncements, carved on two tablets of stone.

What happened instead?

God instructed Moses regarding the building and consecration of the mishkan.

Read 31:18. What finally happens?

God finally presents Moses with the two stone tablets of the Pact.

How, according to the text, were these tablets inscribed?

"With the finger of God."

We have seen before that metaphors are used to describe divine actions. Can you think of any examples?

God took the Israelites out of Egypt "with a strong hand and an outstretched arm."

How can we understand the metaphor of God's "hand" and "arm"?

They stand for God's power and might.

How might we understand the metaphor of God's inscribing the tablets with His finger?

The Ten Pronouncement express God's will.

LESSON 2

The Golden Calf
Exod. 32:1–6

☐ IN PREPARATION FOR TEACHING

The image of the bull played an important role in the religion and the art of the Ancient Near East. We find frequent scultures and pictures of gods riding or standing on bulls.

There are two episodes in the Bible relating to the making of images of bulls. One is here in Exodus; the other is found in 1 Kings 12. (The term "calf" seems to be a derogatory term used in the Bible to refer to these bulls.)

We may have to digress and deal with some historical facts: Saul was to become the first king of the United Kingdom of Israel. David, who became king after Saul, greatly enlarged and strengthened the kingdom, which he left after his death to his son Solomon. Solomon would be the last king of the United Kingdom, since his son, Rehoboam, lacked the political ability to hold the tribes together.

Ten tribes of Israel broke away from Rehoboam and the tribe of Judah. Under the leadership of Jeroboam, they fortified Shechem in the hill country of Ephraim and made it the capital of the northern kingdom, called Israel. Only the tribe of Judah remained loyal to the house of David. Since Jeroboam did not want his people to go south to Jerusalem (in the land of Judah) to worship at the Temple, he made two golden calves, or bulls, and placed them in the northern kingdom, in Bethel and Dan.

The making of the calves was seen as a great sin, which would eventually bring Jeroboam to "utter annihilation from the face of the earth" (1 Kings 13:14). Obviously, this account originates in Judah. It is interesting to note that the two prophets of the Northern Kingdom who lived at the time, Elijah and Elisha, who were outraged at the prevalent worship of foreign gods in Israel, did not criticize the bulls at Dan and Bethel.

It is possible that these prophets viewed the bulls as performing the function the cherubim served at the Temple, namely, serving as a seat or pedestal for God.

In the Exodus story, it is possible that Aaron viewed the calf in the same manner. It must be remembered that the cherubim were secreted away in the Holy of Holies and were not accessible to the people. The calves or bulls, on the other hand, were openly displayed in the court and could be seen, touched, and kissed by anyone.

In Exod. 32:25–29 the Levites purge the people from their sins. Thus we have Aaron on one side and the Levites on the other. In the later history of the people, the priests in Jerusalem were Levites, while those in the Northern Kingdom were Aaronites. It seems, therefore, that the Golden Calf story as we find it is a version as told in Judah (the good Levites versus bad Aaron). This point need not be taught.

Aaron is never punished for making the calf, possibly because he had not intended to make a god, but only a platform or a seat for God. Yet Moses accuses him of bringing sin upon the people, and according to Deut. 9:20 Moses says: "Moreover, the Lord was angry enough with Aaron to have destroyed him, so I interceded for Aaron at that time."

This is the first time the Lord punishes the people. In all previous cases of rebellion they had been forgiven, since they had not yet been covenanted to God. We shall find that in post-Sinaitic rebellions the people shall be held responsible for their deeds.

❒ TEACHING PROCEDURE

Begin with a series of questions:

How much time had elapsed since Moses left the people?

Forty days and forty nights.

The number "forty" indicates "a long time" and does not have to be taken literally. Students will remember that the flood too lasted forty days. The Israelites would wander in the desert for forty years. "Forty" seems to be a number associated with an act of "cleansing."

What are the people worried about?

(Open.) Suggestions: That Moses would not return. They wonder how Moses could be alive. Who would feed him? If he were dead, how would God contact them? Who would be their intermediary?

Lesson 2 — The Golden Calf

Are their worries justified?

(Open.)

What were the people unaware of?

(Open.) Suggestions: That God could communicate with them if he so wanted. That God could provide for Moses in ways unknown to humans.

What are the people demanding now?

A god to replace Moses and serve as an intermediacy.

Why does Aaron acquiesce to their demands?

(Open.) Suggestions: He is afraid of the people. He lacks Moses' access to God. He does not possess Moses' personality.

Aaron might have intended to build a substitute for a cherub, a platform for God, not a foreign idol.

What might Aaron have hoped for as he demanded the people's gold earrings?

(Open.) Suggestion: That the people would loath to part with them, for these were the objects they received in compensation for their years of slavery.

Did the people act as he might have expected?

No, Aaron had miscalculated. The people contributed with enthusiasm and generosity.

If Aaron had indeed hoped that the people would realize that the calf was a platform for the God of Israel only, how did this hope fare?

It was not fulfilled. The people declared that the calf was the god who had taken them out of Egypt.

How did Aaron try to save the situation?

He declared that on the morrow a holiday to God would be celebrated.

What happened during the celebration?

The holiday soon disintegrated into a pagan one.

Heavy drinking and dancing were part of pagan celebrations.

LESSON 3

Moses Stands Up for His People
Exod. 32:7–14

❒ IN PREPARATION FOR TEACHING

At Sinai Moses had become a prophet. The Bible depicts different kinds of prophets. Some congregated in groups and prophesied in ecstasy (e.g., 1 Sam. 10:10–12). Some were "seers" who predicted the future.

The great prophets of Israel, however, acted on their own in the service of God. They fulfilled a dual role. On the one hand, they brought God's message and admonition to the people, and on the other they protected the people from God's blazing anger, and begged God for mercy and forgiveness. Thus they were intermediaries between God and His people. (Abraham too became a prophet when he begged for the people of Sodom and Gemorrah; see Genesis 18.)

Prophets were not popular people. Elijah, Jeremiah and others were shunned and persecuted. Moses and Jeremiah initially refused to act on God's behalf. Jonah tried to run away from God, to no avail.

Moses is traditionally considered the greatest of all prophets. Deut. 34:10 declares: וְלֹא קָם נָבִיא עוֹד בְּיִשְׂרָאֵל כְּמֹשֶׁה, "Never again did there arise in Israel a prophet like Moses." It is likely that the present story is the reason for Moses' reputation.

❒ TEACHING PROCEDURE

On the top of Mount Sinai the all-knowing God is aware of the situation in camp. Moses of course is not.

Read 32:7–9. How does God refer to the Israelites?

As *your* [Moses'] people.

Lesson 3 — Moses Stands Up for His People

What does this tell us about God?

That he renounces them. In his anger God disassociates himself from the Israelites.

How does Moses react to this?

He asks God to be forgiving: "Let not your anger blaze against *Your people*."

What is Moses actually saying?

He reminds God that Israel is His, *God's*, people and not Moses'.

Students may recognize a familiar scene. The "good" child is "my son" or "my daughter," the "bad" one is the other parent's!

Read 32:10. What does God plan to do?

Destroy the people.

What role would Moses play in this plan?

He would, like Abraham, become the father of a great nation.

Some students may suggest that annihilating the people and starting afresh with Moses as a patriarch would constitute a breach of God's promise to Abraham. But it would simply delay the fulfillment of the promise by a few hundred years. God has infinite time; it is we humans, with our prescribed life span, who are in a hurry. That is why we say, for example, in the Kaddish: וְיַמְלִיךְ מַלְכוּתֵהּ בְּחַיֵּיכוֹן וּבְיוֹמֵיכוֹן וּבְחַיֵּי דְכָל בֵּית יִשְׂרָאֵל, בַּעֲגָלָא וּבִזְמַן קָרִיב "May He cause His kingdom to reign during our lifetime and that of the House of Israel, speedily and soon."

What is the image you see when you read God's proclamation to Moses, "Let me be—that my anger may blaze forth"?

Moses is restraining God. It is as if God said: "Leave me alone!" "Don't hold me back!" "Let go of my arm!"

Moses, however, being a prophet, does not let God be (nor does God want him to).

What are some of Moses' arguments?

1. He turns the tables on God. "These are *your* people, not mine, and it is *you*, not me, who delivered them from the land of Egypt" (compare to 32:7). Thus, the people are God's responsibility.

2. Moses invokes *kiddush hashem* (aggrandizing God's name). What would happen to God's reputation among the other

peoples if the Israelites were to be annihilated in the desert? The lesson of the ten plagues for all peoples will come to naught.

3. Moses invokes *zekhut avot* (the merits of the Patriachs). God had promised Abraham, Isaac, and Jacob to make them as numerous as the stars of heaven. Would He break this promise?

How does God react to Moses' pleading?

The Lord heeded His prophet and renounced the punishment He had planned to bring upon His people.

Here, as in story of Abraham's plea for the people of Sodom (Genesis 18), God involves His prophet in His plan. God wants to be moved to forgive His people. That is the kind of God He is.

LESSON 4

Confrontation with the People
Exod. 32:15–30

❐ TEACHING PROCEDURE

In 24:13 we had been told that Joshua had gone part of the way up the mountain with Moses. Upon receiving the tablets of the law, Moses descended from the top of the mountain and joined Joshua.

Read 32:15–17. As Moses and Joshua approached the camp and heard the noises coming from the crowd, what did Joshua assume?

> Joshua assumed that the people had been attacked by an enemy and were engaged in battle.

Read 32:18. What did Moses tell Joshua?

> That it was the sound of song, not war.

Moses knows, since God had told him what had taken place in his absence. (One's hearing is keener when one knows what to expect.)

What kind of song can be mistaken for the sound of war?

> A loud, rough song.

Read 32:19–20. What does Moses do upon seeing the calf?

> Enraged, he hurls the tablets from his hand, shattering them. He burns the calf and grinds it to powder. He strews the powder upon the water, which he then makes the people drink.

Read 32:21. What does Moses say to Aaron?

> Moses accuses Aaron of bringing a great sin upon the Israelites.

Read 32:22–24. How does Aaron justify his actions?

> He explains that the people are "bent on evil" and that under pressure he had "hurled [the gold] into the fire and out came this calf."

What do you think of Aaron's excuse?

(Open.) Suggestion: It is a lame excuse indeed.

Read 32:25–29. Moses knows that the people have to be purged. At his cry "whoever is for the Lord come here" what takes place?

His own tribe, the Levites, rally to him and at his command kill all those who had worshiped the golden calf.

LESSON 5A

Pleading for Mercy
Exod. 32:30–33:6

◻ IN PREPARATION FOR TEACHING

With the breaking of the tablets of the pact, the covenant had been terminated. Moses goes back to the Lord to beg for full forgiveness. In contrast to God's plan to do away with the people and start again with Moses, Moses proclaims, "Now, if you forgive their sin [well and good], but if not, erase me too from the record which You have written." Thus, Moses wishes to tie his lot in with that of the people. Moses informs God that if the people are to be erased from this "book of life," he, Moses, wishes his name to be erased, too.

This "record" or "book" which God is writing may not be new to your students; it is a common motif in the High Holy Day liturgy. In the וּנְתַנֶּה תֹּקֶף prayer we find the notion that God keeps a book or scroll in which the fates of humans are recorded: who is to live and who is to die, who is to live a happy life and who is to suffer.

God grants Moses partial forgiveness. He sends him back to the people and tells him to lead them on. However, He also tells Moses that from now on an angel, and not He Himself, would lead the people.

The reason why God would not indwell with them (33:3) is that the Israelites, being a stiff-necked people, are bound to sin again. Should God dwell in their midst He would surely destroy them. The Lord is about to remove His presence for the protection of the people. (This implies the cancellation of the building of the mishkan.)

◻ TEACHING PROCEDURE

Have students read the section and retell the story in their own words. Help them get the sequence straight, ask questions as you go, and explain difficulties.

Does God fully forgive the people?

No. He shall not go in their midst. An angel will go instead of him.

Why?

As a measure of self-protection, lest He destroy them.

If God is not going to indwell with the people, what orders of God are in effect canceled?

All the instructions for building the mishkan.

Read 33:5 carefully. What in this verse still gives Moses hope?

God offers to reconsider. His decision is not final.

What condition does God put on His reconsidering?

The people are to remove the finery they had donned in preparation for the Revelation.

Why?

They are not to wear their golden ornaments throughout their journey since these are a reminder of the golden calf. The people must humbly await God's decision.

LESSON 5B

The Tent of Meeting
Exod. 33:7–11

☐ TEACHING PROCEDURE

Now that the camp had become polluted by the presence of the golden calf, how can Moses still meet with God?

> Moses pitches his own tent outside the camp, as a temporary meeting place with God.

How would God's presence manifest itself?

> God's presence would manifest in the form of a pillar of cloud at the entrance of the tent whenever the Lord would speak with Moses.

When this happened, what would the people do?

> All the people would rise and bow low in respect and humility.

LESSON 6

God's Essence
Exod. 32:12–34:9

☐ IN PREPARATION FOR TEACHING

Moses is intent on receiving God's complete forgiveness, having Him Himself dwell with the Israelites and lead them to the Promised Land. Moses wrests from God the revelation of His essence, since only the knowledge of God's nature will enable him to successfully appeal to God to rescind His verdict. In our daily dealings with people, our insight into their characters and personalities direct us in the way we deal with them. We present our requests and demands in different manners to different people. We may try to flatter the egos of those we consider vain. When we deal with people we consider fair we may try to appeal to their sense of justice.

God acquiesces to all of Moses' requests. The Lord will go in the lead and lighten Moses' burden. He will also reveal His essence to Moses. Mankind, however, is unable to perceive God's full presence (symbolically: His face). Humans can only understand God's partial essence (symbolized by His back). God would protect Moses from the intensity of the impact of His full presence by shielding him with His hand. Moses will see God's back, but His face may not be seen.

Moses is to carve two tablets of stone, resembling the first set, and to present himself on Mount Sinai. As promised, God reveals Himself to Moses. "The Lord! The Lord! A God compassionate and gracious, slow to anger, abounding in kindness and faithfulness, extending kindness to the thousandth generation, forgiving iniquity, transgression, and sin. Yet He does not remit all punishment, but visits the iniquity of fathers upon children and children's children upon the third and fourth generation.

What in the present situation should Moses know about God so he can win approval for His people? Although God had threatened to annihilate the people, and although the punishment is well-deserved, God may be moved to judge compassionately, with חֶסֶד. God is a loving God.

This does not, however, mean that humans have license to do whatever their hearts desire. God does not remit all transgressions, but visits the iniquity of fathers upon children (see above, p. 150). Moses uses his newfound knowledge in his dealing with God. He hastens to bow low to the ground in homage: "Pardon our iniquity and our sin, and take us for your own," he pleads.

☐ TEACHING PROCEDURE

What is it that Moses wants to learn about God?

His essence or nature—what kind of God He is.

Why?

Because only if Moses knows what God stands for will he know how to please Him.

Since God does not have a "front" and "back," what does God's back symbolize?

Seeing people from the back, we do not fully perceive them, we get a vague impression only. By the same token humans can never fully know and perceive God. They can understand some, but by no means all His attributes.

What are some of God's attributes Moses comes to know?

He is compassionate, gracious, slow to anger, abounding in kindness and faithfulness. Extending kindness to the thousandth generation. Forgiving iniquity, transgression and sin. Yet He does not remit all punishment but visits the iniquity of fathers upon children upon the third and fourth generation.

How do you feel about this God?

(Open.) This is a God one can "live with."

How does Moses immediately use his newly found knowledge?

He asks Him to forgive Israel's transgression. And, of course, he succeeds.

LESSON 7

Renewing the Covenant
Exod. 34:10–28

☐ IN PREPARATION FOR TEACHING

Before receiving the second set of tablets from God's hand, Moses receives ten instructions. These instructions are a variation of those given in Exodus 23. The covenant made at Sinai had been broken by the people and thus made invalid. A new covenant had to be made.

1. (34:11–16) As the people take possession of the land of Canaan they are prohibited from making covenants with the people of Canaan "lest they be a snare in your midst" (34:12). The golden calf episode has made it clear that the people are not strong enough to uphold their own beliefs and their specific identity when living among the pagans. Surely they will assume the way of life of their neighbors.

2. (34:17) The people are admonished not to make for themselves molten gods, as they had just recently done.

3. (34:18) The repetition of the observance of the Passover feast.

4. (34:19) The repetition of the observance of redeeming the firstborn.

5. (34:21) The observance of the Sabbath.

6. (34:22) The observance of the holiday of Shavuot.

7. (34:23) The command to appear three times a year "before God." (In later times this was understood to mean that all males had to present themselves on the three Pilgrim Festivals at the Temple of Jerusalem.)

8. (34:25) Prohibition of offering any sacrifice accompanied by anything leavened (see Exod. 12:8), and the admonition not to leave any of the Passover sacrifice lying until morning (whatever is not consumed has to be burned; see Exod. 12:10).

9. (34:26a) The choice first fruits (בִּכּוּרִים) are to be brought to the house of the Lord during the period from Shavuot to Sukkot.

10. (34:26b) The repetition of the prohibition of boiling a kid in its mother's milk.

LESSON 8

The Radiant Face
Exod. 34:29–35

☐ IN PREPARATION FOR TEACHING

"So Moses came down from Mount Sinai bearing the two tablets of the pact, Moses was not aware that the skin of his face was radiant, since he had spoken with Him" (34:29).

In the ancient Near East, gods were perceived as radiating light. Their faces were so radiant that one could not see the faces themselves due to the aura emanating from them.

The Israelites too believed that God radiated light. Moses had been so close to God that although he saw only God's back, his face picked up some of the radiance.

LESSON 9

The Mishkan Is Complete
Exodus 40:17–38

☐ TEACHING PROCEDURE

Moses had the mishkan built and anointed the priests, just as God had commanded him.

Scan the conclusion of Exodus, focusing on the following verses:

"In the first month of the second year, on the first of the month the tabernacle was set up" (40:17).

"The cloud covered the Tent of meeting and the Presence of the Lord filled the tabernacle" (40:34).

"When the cloud lifted from the tabernacle, the Israelites would set out on their various journeys, but if the cloud did not lift, they would not set out until such time as it did lift. For over the mishkan a cloud of the Lord rested by day, and fire would appear in it by night, in the view of all the house of Israel throughout their journey" (40:36–38).

For most of a year the Israelites had camped at the foot of Mount Sinai and had worked at the construction of the mishkan, a portable "Sinai" that enabled them to keep God's presence in their midst wherever they went. In the final verse we read that the cloud of God rested over the mishkan. The Israelites, at times rebellious and unfaithful, had been forgiven. Their ordeals are far from over. There will be many years of wandering before they enter the Promised Land. But the Israelites can look forward throughout to God's presence in their midst and His guidance.

חֲזַק חֲזַק וְנִתְחַזֵּק!

APPENDIX

Understanding the Sinai Revelation

Edward L. Greenstein

APPENDIX

Understanding the Sinai Revelation
Edward L. Greenstein

◻ THE PROBLEM

To discuss the meaning of God's revelation to the people Israel at Mount Sinai is not easy. It is not only because we do not fully understand what the Torah says about the Sinai event, but because we have trouble believing in the Sinai event as Exodus tells it. The Bible tells us that this is what happened. The Torah's assertive tone and straightforward style confront us with a choice: accept or else. But we do not always believe what the Bible reports in its literal sense. Nor, as we shall see below, should we. We should learn to read the biblical text not as a literal accounting of historical fact—which we have no way of testing—but as an expression of our ancient Israelite forbears in which we find enduring religious truth. Just as we do not take Genesis 1 as a literal, "scientific" account of the formation of the world but seek to understand the religious or philosophical ideas that the story conveys, so we may seek to understand the religious message that the revelation story relates without accepting the literal truth of the story.

The problem here is especially hard because the Sinai event is presented not as a prehistoric act of God, like the Creation, to which no person was witness, but as an event in the lives of the Israelites. This event is filled with more significance than any other in Jewish history. It was this event that fashioned the people Israel into a nation. At Sinai Israel entered into a bond or covenant (*brit*) with God. Whatever else might differentiate Jews from each other, it is our common affirmation of the *brit* that binds us to one another. At many points of Jewish history we have developed into diverse and scattered communities with different customs, languages, and attitudes. Yet even as we grow along separate lines, we continue to hold together, to feel kinship and responsibility for one another, to a large

---

Edward L. Greenstein is Professor of Bible at The Jewish Theological Seminary of America.

degree on account of our mutual bond, the *brit* that was first established at Sinai.

It is crucial, therefore, that we accept the idea of a covenant, that there be a reason to affirm the people Israel and assert our own membership in it. Without Sinai, the formation of the people Israel could be viewed as a mere accident of human history, a chance development that could—if we allowed it—be undone as it was done, in the natural course of human events. We need to be convinced that the Sinai event is essentially a real, *spiritual* one and not a routine historical occurrence.

But the biblical description of what happened at Sinai contains many physical trappings that tend to undermine our belief in the event: God's appearance as fire in the midst of smoke, God's speaking in a human voice amid thunder and lightning. Yet, in truth, our difficulty is not so much in accepting these physical descriptions. We could attribute these to a more primitive, anthropomorphic understanding of God by the Israelites. Rather, the main difficulty we have in understanding the Sinai event is a more general, theological problem: "How is revelation possible?" How can God speak to us? And not only individually, but to a large group of us simultaneously? Can such divine communication be experienced as we experience the voice of another person, by our senses?

In other words, our understanding of what actually happened at Sinai is restricted by our personal beliefs about what possibly *could* have happened. A person who does not believe in a God who communicates with people at all cannot believe that such a God communicated with the Israelites at Mount Sinai. Each of us has a different notion of what God is and is not. Very likely, a person will change his or her idea of God from time to time. Then, we must be open to a variety of possible understandings about what the Sinai event means. It follows that we will understand the Sinai event somewhat differently from our ancestors, who experienced it according to their own conceptual framework (see further below) and recorded in the Bible their own impressions of what had occurred. It also follows that teachers and students may have differing notions about what God and revelation mean.

Since there are many different ways to explain God's Revelation to the people Israel at Mount Sinai, we should remain flexible in seeing the rightness of each one according to divergent beliefs about God. Nevertheless, there are certain basic differences between the way our ancestors in the biblical period described the Sinai event and the way historically-oriented students of the Bible today understand it. It will be important for us to deal with these differences now.

☐ THE BIBLICAL UNDERSTANDING

At the outset, we must bear in mind that the Torah's description of what happened at Sinai is not the same as an eyewitness account. What we know of what happened at Sinai comes to us through the *experience* of the Israelites. There is no direct record of that experience, nor could there be. Once the experience is over, once it becomes past, one can only try to explain it, that is, to identify what one experienced as the "facts" of what happened and to come up with an explanation—to make sense—of the "facts." The account in Exodus 19–20 (and Deuteronomy 4–5) is one attempt to describe that experience at Sinai. It is necessarily limited by what the Israelites understood to have happened. Just as we see things according to our abilities and habits of noticing and understanding, the ancient Israelites saw according to the limits of their perception. The Israelites were a product of their times as we are of ours. While we, for example, tend to perceive natural phenomena as the product of impersonal forces, the Israelites saw these phenomena as direct manifestations of God's will, each a deliberate act of God.

The ancient Israelites describe their experiences differently from the way we would because for one thing, they experienced things differently to begin with. But this is not all. The Torah's description of the Sinai event is not only an explanation, or interpretation, rather than a transcription of the experience. It is a report of the Sinai experience that had been passed on among the Israelites for at least a few generations before it was written down in something like its present form. This means that the story was changed as it was told and retold from parent to child to grandchild.

In the first place we *select* out of the various aspects and details of the event only certain striking aspects and details to store in our memories. We don't remember everything; and to a large degree we are affected in what we select by our past experiences, our present concerns, our expectations of the future, and other factors, to remember certain things and not others. (Think of what in particular you remember of a book you've read recently, a film or sports event you've seen, a song you've heard, etc.)

(We should perhaps mention here, before going on, that we are speaking of the biblical account of the Sinai event as one that was produced by the Israelites rather than, as the tradition would have it, by God through Moses. We do, however, attribute the content of the Torah to revelation. But we shall discuss below the share that the Israelites had in shaping the form and substance of the revelation.)

In the process of telling what happened another kind of change takes place. The teller elaborates on some aspects, perhaps adding new explanatory insights, perhaps adding decorative touches here and there. We know from experience that in different cultures, different aspects will be elaborated in particular ways. You will recall, for example, that when the Bible describes how an Israelite hero came to find his wife, the hero or his agent often meet the woman at a well (Abraham's servant and Rebecca, Jacob and Rachel, Moses and Zippora). A well was a common meeting place, so stories about meetings would often use the well as their scene. The memory of the event is expanded according to traditional methods of elaboration. Each time a story is retold, the same processes are liable to occur. Thus, the Torah's report of the Sinai event is not only an interpretation of experience; it is a remodeled memory of the interpretation. In fact, our own interpretation of the Torah is also a remodeling of the explanation.

To sum up our conclusions so far: The biblical account of the Sinai revelation is a mixture of the Israelite's *perception* of their experience and their *transmission* of that perception. Both processes have the effect of distancing us from the event itself.

Now that we are aware of the difference between what may have happened at Sinai and what the Torah explains happened at Sinai, let us turn to the Torah's description itself. First, it is clear that the Torah presents the revelation as a historical event. In the very first two verses (Exod. 19:1–2) we are told the time and place of the event. We are also told that the revelation has distinct parts to it. In the first part, only Moses speaks with God, on the mountain. Moses will serve as the intermediary in the revelation of God to Israel. In this first encounter the relationship between God and Israel is revealed. God has shown his favor to the people Israel in history, by bringing them out of Egypt. The people Israel is, therefore, special and must fulfill certain obligations as their contribution to the relationship.

In the second encounter God appears to the entire people Israel and speaks to them from the heavens (Exod. 20:22). What captures our imagination most, of course, is that the Torah describes God's appearance in physical terms. Although the Israelites do not claim to have seen God directly, as a physical being with a specific form, they claim that God's appearance was accompanied by certain phenomena that could be seen or heard.

The Lord comes down from the heavens toward the summit of Mount Sinai. As God descends, the Israelites are said to witness thunder and lightning. God surrounds himself with a cloud. God himself appears in the form of a smoking fire, radiating light from within the cloud. To the sound of the thunder is added the sound of shofar blasts. The people tremble at such a sight, and so does the mountain. Then Moses addresses God, who responds "with voice" (*bekol*).

Now this *description* of the appearance of God occurs elsewhere in the Bible. You will recall that when God makes the covenant (*brit*) with Abraham (in Genesis 15), God passes through the segments of the animals that Abraham had cut in half in the form of fire and smoke. In Exodus 3 God appears to Moses at the bush on Mount Sinai in the form of a fire. When Israel went out of Egypt they were guided by a pillar of fire by night and a pillar of fog by day. It was a convention among the Israelites (like meetings at wells) that God would appear before them in the form of fire (and smoke) and/or fog. We need not believe that God literally, physically appeared in fire and fog. We may understand this as one of the ways in which the Israelites were used to conceive of God's presence. And in forming this conception the Israelites were influenced by the current notions of how the divine presence might look (just as we have been influenced by Christian art to think of cherubim as chubby toddlers with angels' wings).

We should not get caught up in whether God actually resembled fire in a physical way. Rather, we ought to consider what *ideas* about God the Torah implies by likening God's presence to fire. Following the lead of the midrash, we may ask: What are the qualities of fire that are comparable to God? Fire is real, present, and perceptible. It can be seen and felt. The closer we are, the brighter it appears. The nearer we are, the warmer it feels. And yet, fire has no concrete, permanent, or fixed form. It has color, but it is transparent. When one is near, it provides warmth. But if one comes too near, one comes to harm. These are qualities that are also attributable to God. Although God has no concrete, fixed form, God is real, present, perceptible, effective. It is good to come near to God, to worship and emulate God, but not to come too close.

When we return to the other physical descriptions of God's appearance at Sinai, we find that these, too, reflect ways in which the Israelites had yearned to experience the reality of God. The Israelites' perceptions, like ours, are conditioned by the surrounding cultural influences and conventions. Being of a certain time and place, the Israelites shared much of their imagery and even many of their religious conceptions with the neighboring cultures of the ancient Near East. Thus, although the Israelites did not believe in the many gods of nature that their neighbors worshipped, they ascribed to the God of Israel the powers and qualities that the pagan gods possessed. It is not surprising, then, that the Bible often describes the God of Israel in terms that other ancient Near Eastern peoples would use to depict their gods.

God, we believe, has innumerable aspects. But we cannot apprehend God in all of these—or even several of these—aspects at one time. Our minds automatically organize what we perceive into structures or patterns. When we listen to a song, we organize the notes into a pattern, a melody we can identify. We sort out the tones into a melodic line and an accompanying harmony. We're trained by our past experiences of music and induced by the structure of our minds to make this distinction. And so, nearly all of us could listen to a song and agree on what is melody and what is accompaniment. Similarly, when we look at an object against a background, we organize the various lines and colors before us into patterns representing distinct objects. Our vision distinguishes the tree in front of the building from the building itself. We see according to particular patterns of perception.

We experience God, too, according to learned habits and patterns of the mind, patterns that help us organize certain aspects of God's behavior toward us and the rest of the world. We assemble God's nurturing and guiding us, God's compassion and discipline for us, into an image of God as parent. Our tradition, therefore, speaks of God as *avinu* "our father" (though many classical images of God would be better served by the term "mother"). God is not literally our parent, but we may speak of God as such in order to evoke with a single metaphor one of the many images of God that we wish to express. The term for such a metaphorical image is a "model." Thus, one of the models of God that we employ in order to speak about God is "father," another is "king," another is "redeemer," another is "shepherd," another is "potter," another is "rock," another is "lion," etc.

One of the most common biblical models for relating to God is that of storm or rain god. In this model the Israelites organized those aspects of God in which God manifests his powers as the provider of wind and rain. Rain was the chief source of water, and consequently of life, in Eretz Israel. Therefore, the Israelites felt dependent on God for rain perhaps more than for anything else. In order to express this in words, the Israelites adopted the imagery of a storm or rain god from neighboring peoples and applied the model of storm god to the Lord. This image abounds in the Bible, particularly in the poetry of the Psalms. Thus, taking Psalm 18 (2 Samuel 22) as an example, God is described as riding through the skies on a winged sphinx (cherub), bellowing thunder, snorting fire, and casting out lightning bolts like arrows. As far as we may be able to tell, when the Israelites experienced a rain storm, they actually perceived God riding through the skies, providing life-giving rain.

In addition to "fire" the description of God's appearance on Mount Sinai reflects the biblical model of God as giver of rain, as "storm." That is, when the Israelites experienced God at Sinai and/or recounted their experience of God, they experienced God through the model of a storm god. God descends from the heavens amid thunder and lightning. Typically, even the mountain shakes in response to the storm. (Compare, for example, Psalms 29 and 114, in which nature responds physically to God's presence.) In addition, the radiance surrounding God's presence is also familiar from ancient Near Eastern imagery as the aura (Hebrew: *kavod*) that emanates from the face of the god.

There remains now one more aspect of God's appearance at Sinai that needs to be explained: the blasts of the shofar being sounded as God descends from the heavens (compare Psalm 47:6). Commonly, storm gods in the ancient Near East are thought of as warriors. The model of storm god in its fullness includes elements of war imagery. Thus, the storm god rides on a chariot of clouds; he wields and throws down lightning bolts like spears or arrows. The shofar blasts represent the sounding of the trumpets that signal the battle charge. The association derives from real life, as armies would sound the shofar when charging into battle. The Israelites, then, employing this model, perceived God as a warrior (compare Exodus 15, in which God is called *ish milḥamah*, "man of war") who would lead them in battle, or fight for them personally (see Exod. 14:14, 25).

To sum up what we have concluded so far: The Israelites experienced the presence of God, an experience they remembered later as having occurred at Mount Sinai. But in perceiving God, they structured their experience through models of God: as fire, storm and warrior. The Israelites used the language of these models to speak of God. Today we experience God according to different models and we employ different imagery and literary conventions, according to our own cultural influences. (Think of how our way of talking has been shaped by movies, songs, computer technology.)

Allowing for different models of God, how are we to understand the Torah's assertion that He spoke to the people Israel "with voice," that is, with a voice that could be heard by all those assembled? It is nearly certain that the Torah means God spoke with a human voice. This may be gathered from the story of the boy Samuel who served as assistant to the aging priest Eli at Shiloh (1 Samuel 3). God called to Samuel by name during the night. God's calling must have resembled a human voice because Samuel mistook it three times for the voice of Eli. The Israelites believed that God is creator of the world, possessing a mind and will, breaking the regularities of nature with miracles, capable of appearing on earth in human form (as in Genesis 18). For the Israelites, God could naturally speak with a human voice, if he chose to. Perhaps the Israelites could only conceive of God speaking in a human voice. But how are we—who may or may not believe that God speaks with a human voice—to understand God's communication with the Israelites?

This question brings us to the need to define our own beliefs about what we mean by "God" and how we understand revelation.

◻ OUR OWN UNDERSTANDING

As we said above, our understanding of God's revelation to the people Israel at Mount Sinai is a combination of what the Bible reports as having happened and our own ideas about what *could* have happened. Our understanding of the Sinai event is limited by our beliefs about God and the process by which God communicates to people.

What do we mean by "God"? We all know that we cannot define God. There are numerous ideas about what God is like. Since we cannot see God directly, we cannot describe God physically. And because God has an uncountable number of aspects, we can never perceive God wholly, in God's entirety. But this does not mean that God is completely unknowable. We cannot perceive a person, even one whom we know very well, in his or her entirety. It is true that we may be able to describe a friend's appearance, but even then we will not be giving a complete description because our friend has different appearances on different occasions. This is what we mean by such expressions as "a new look," etc. Since we can describe a friend's appearance only partially and inadequately, how much more difficult would it be to try to describe God, who hasn't even a physical appearance!

This is already said in the second commandment. If we were to try to represent God with a physical likeness, we would be grossly distorting God's character or personality, which has innumerable aspects, by identifying it with a concrete, static image.

Moreover, returning to our friend, we would not be able to offer anything that even approaches a complete accounting of his or her qualities. One's personality is composed of many and various aspects. No one person could know another in all of his or her aspects. Thus, if there can be no adequate description of a person, all the more can there be no adequate description of God.

We come to know some aspects of God by noting God's behavior toward the world and toward us—in a similar way to that by which we come to know a person, through observing his or her behavior, including what he or she says to us.

We are particularly interested at this point in our discussion with what we learn about God, or believe concerning God, with regard to the communication of God to people, that is, revelation. It should be borne in mind that what I am presenting here expresses *one* view of God and revelation, not by any means the only understanding of these concepts. Even within Conservative Judaism, there are several answers to our questions. But I hope that the ideas offered here will find some consensus among many Jews, will be compatible with the approaches taken within the other Melton Bible materials, and will be amenable to discussion with our students.

The aspect of God that is perhaps most important to our concept of revelation is that God has a personality. That is, God is like a person in certain ways. Thus, God "sees," "hears," and "remembers." God is aware of our behavior. This basic belief finds expression in the famous teaching in Pirkei Avot (2:1):

> Keep your mind on three things and you will not come into the hands of transgression. Know what is above you: a watching eye, a hearing ear, and all your actions are written in a book.

In addition, God has a will and the power to carry out what God plans. In terms of communicating with people, God wills revelation. God initiates the revelation (see Exod. 19:3). Revelation, then, is not an accident. Nor is it the same as an "inspiration" or "discovery" that comes to you as a product of your own mind alone.

Revelation is an act of God that conveys a message to a person or a group of persons. Just as God is in some ways similar to a person, so is revelation similar to the communication between one person and another *via* language or any other means. In other words, there is a SENDER of the MESSAGE and a RECEIVER of the MESSAGE:

SENDER ⟶ MESSAGE ⟶ RECEIVER

In this simple outline, SENDER = God, MESSAGE = revelation, and RECEIVER = person(s). In traditional Jewish terms, God = SENDER = *metzavveh* "the one who commands," the revelation = MESSAGE = *mitzvah* "the command," and the Jew = RECEIVER = the *metzuvveh* "the one commanded."

However, further examination of revelation leads us to realize that our outline is much too simple and does not properly describe what we understand as revelation. Revelation is more complicated. For example, the diagram tells us nothing about *how* revelation takes place.

We have spoken briefly about God, the "sender" in the revelation. But revelation also requires a "receiver," in this case, a person. There is a famous philosophical teaser that asks: If a tree fell in the forest and there was no one there to hear it fall, did it make a sound? Certainly the tree's fall would create vibrations in the air which would be picked up by a properly functioning ear, if one were within range. But we could argue that the air vibrations themselves do not constitute "sound." Similarly, there can be no communication without a receiver. In the case of revelation, there must be a person to receive the message; otherwise, there is no message. Revelation is more like a meeting of two persons. Without both parties present, there is no meeting.

What are the characteristics of the "receiver," the person, in the revelation experience? For one thing, only a person who believes in the possibility of revelation can experience revelation. This means that the person must recognize that there exists a "sender," a God who reveals himself to a person. The person who may experience revelation must be trained or sensitized to acknowledge God's presence in the world. Such a person holds a view of the world that allows divine intention behind the events he or she observes. It is a way of looking at the world and the events in it. The events fit into patterns, and the patterns point to God. Revelation is an interpretation of experience as the act of God.

From biblical times to the present, Jewish tradition has understood all events on two levels: the human or worldly and the divine. That is, events can be understood on both levels *simultaneously*, not one way or the other. The Bible is itself aware of both levels. An excellent illustration is provided by the story of Joseph and his brothers. As the story is first presented, Joseph is brought down to Egypt as the result of his brothers' reaction to his behavior. The brothers wanted to be rid of him because they were jealous that their father, Jacob/Israel, loved Joseph more than them; and because Joseph antagonized them by bearing tales about them and by telling them of his dreams, which implied that Joseph would be lord to his brothers. This part of the story explains Joseph's descent to Egypt as the result of family relations and motivations that we can readily appreciate from our own experiences.

When Joseph in Egypt finally reveals his identity to his brothers, the brothers remember their past cruelty to young Joseph and fear that Joseph will take vengeance on them. However, Joseph sets aside the human level of the action, the observable, human causes for his descent to Egypt. He declares that, in actuality, it was God who arranged his descent to Egypt in order to store up grain and provide food for Jacob/Israel's family in Canaan during the drought.

Thus, Joseph does not deny the human chain of events that led to his enslavement in Egypt. But he adds to this explanation a divine dimension: God was controlling the entire chain of events. God was working behind the scenes. One who recognizes only the human level of the course of events, views history as a pointless series of causes and effects. But one who, in addition, sees history as being guided in a direction (e.g., to get Joseph down to Egypt), toward a purpose (e.g., to provide food for Jacob's clan), toward a destiny (e.g., to form the Israelite people), may see a divine dimension to history.

The Israelites told their own history with just such a religious attitude. They saw behind the survival of the Patriarchs and their families—in the face of personal danger, famines, inter-tribal hostilities—the blessings of divine protection; behind the Exodus from Egypt, redemption by God; behind the formation of the Israelites into a people, the covenant presented to them by God. Being able to interpret history as the plan of God was necessary to the Israelites' being able to experience the revelation at Mount Sinai.

That the Torah understood this attitude as a prerequisite to a revelation experience can be inferred from the very beginning of the account of the Sinai event. Before God speaks to all the Israelites directly, God has Moses sensitize the people to understanding their recent history as the mighty acts of God for the Israelites. Moses is first to instruct the people, in the name of God: "You have seen that which I have done to Egypt; I bore you up on the wings of eagles, and I brought you to Me" (Exod. 19:4). Once the people have been trained to see behind events to the divine level, to witness God's presence in history, then they can experience revelation.

In fact, the very acts of God in history, once understood as such, constitute revelations of God. For revelations need not be "messages" similar to our own verbal messages. Just as we get to know a person through what the person *does*, we get to know God through what God does. As the great Medieval Spanish Jewish philosopher, Maimonides, has said: "All attributes ascribed to God are attributes of his acts." But it seems to be true that a person must be able to recognize the divine revelation in events, in acts, before that person can "hear" the "word" of God's revelation.

The "receiver" in the revelation, the person, must be ready to view an event as a revelation experience. Thus, if two people were standing at Mount Sinai, one of whom had learned to see God's presence and the other of whom had not, only the sensitized person would have experienced the revelation. Only that person would have "heard" God's "voice" at Sinai; the other would have heard either meaningless noise or nothing at all. The "voice" that speaks from Sinai is heard by the heart, not the ear (or a tape recorder!).

The situation is similar to having two cameras photographing an event. Both take a picture of the event, opening their shutters and exposing the film to light. But despite the fact that the film in both cameras was exposed to light, no picture will emerge unless the film is developed. Without development, the film will remain blank, without an image. Likewise, the person without religious sensibility may be exposed to the same event as the religious person; but without a religious attitude, without "development," that person will notice nothing remarkable in those events. The religiously sensitized person may experience the events as revelation. We might say that the religious person is equipped, like a Polaroid camera, to develop the picture; the non-religious person is not so equipped and must await development.

Now there is one other characteristic of the "receiver" of revelation that is important to consider. It is that no two "receivers" are quite alike. They each have different personalities, different past experiences, different bodies of knowledge, different abilities of perception and comprehension, different opinions about the world. Therefore, it is possible that different people experiencing the same event as a revelation may yet have somewhat different experiences of it. Their reports of what happened will differ.

A good example of such a difference is brought out in the Talmud (Ḥagigah 13b). The rabbis wanted to explain a difficulty: Both the prophets Isaiah and Ezekiel had a vision of God sitting among his heavenly attendants. Why is it that Isaiah's description (Isaiah 6) is brief and spare while Ezekiel's description (Ezekiel 1) is elaborate and detailed? The explanation: "All that Ezekiel saw, Isaiah saw. [But] what is Ezekiel like? Like a villager who [came to the capital and] saw the king. And what is Isaiah like? Like a capital resident who saw the king." Ezekiel was experiencing something novel. He reflected his excitement in his account. Isaiah was experiencing something routine and expressed himself with great reserve. In other words, the rabbis are implying that Ezekiel and Isaiah both witnessed the same revelation (on different occasions), but on account of their different backgrounds and personalities, they received different impressions and/or related different impressions of their experience.

The rabbis also believed that different people have different depths of spiritual perception. That is, owing to varying degrees of knowledge, of insight, of sensitivity to the divine, different people "see" more or better in a revelation experience. Thus, the rabbis liken Moses, the prophet with the keenest and most penetrating vision, to one who views the divine through a clear mirror, while the other prophets view the divine as though through a dull mirror (Yevamot 49b).

❐ WHAT IS REVELATION?

Revelation is an experience in which God conveys a message to those who are trained to experience revelation but who may have different impressions of it, depending on their individual backgrounds and personalities. This process may be likened somewhat to viewing a film. In order to view the film, there must be a projectionist (God) who will show it. In addition. there must be viewers (people) who will see it. These viewers must be both *capable* of seeing and hearing and *attentive* to the film (just as people must be sensitized and attentive to experience revelation).

When various people view the same film, they will probably differ in what they noticed and understood of it. There will be agreement on certain aspects of the film—its characters, its topic perhaps, its plot perhaps. But people will come away with different notions about what "message" the film conveyed, what impressions it made. Viewers who are more experienced or learned in the history of film and/or in its style and subject will experience more than the others. Likewise, the more religiously sensitized a person is, the more he or she will experience in revelation. And different people will have different impressions about what the revelation conveyed.

This analogy leads us to consider to what extent the *content* of revelation is like the film. In our example the physical film is completely independent and separable from the projectionist and from the viewer. But we have seen that the film does not have a life of its own. It does not exist (except as a long strip of celluloid) until it is projected. Moreover, it does not exist until it is seen by the viewers. But the "message" of the film depends, to some degree, on the conditions under which it is presented (how dark the room is, how comfortable, how quiet, etc.) and even more on the nature of the audience. For each viewer the message will vary, as we have explained above.

Thus, revelation is not a clearly defined "message," as it was shown in the over-simplified diagram above. The "message" cannot be separated from the "sender," on the one hand, whose behavior is a component of the "message" itself. And it cannot be separated from the "receiver," on the other hand, whose personality contributes to shaping the message. Revelation, then, is a *process* between the "sender" and the "receiver" that may not be separated from either. But how much does God contribute to revelation, and in what way? And how much does the receiving person contribute, and in what way?

Within the Jewish community today, there are, as I have said, a variety of views concerning the nature of revelation. Knowing about some of these perspectives will help us understand why the question cannot receive a simple answer.

There are those who continue to understand revelation as being more or less like our simple model, in which God spoke in clear words and the Israelites heard them as spoken. This view is related in the Talmud (Bava Batra 15a) concerning how the Torah was written: God dictated, and Moses wrote down what God said word for word.

This view of word-by-word revelation, though traditional and perhaps so understood by the Israelites, is difficult to accept when we consider the positive results of modern study of the Bible. Careful study of the language of the Torah indicates that different parts of the Torah are written in different styles and even in different dialects or stages of the Hebrew language. We have reason to believe, therefore, that the Israelites recorded their impressions of the revelation in their own language, not some timeless divine tongue.

(While Jewish tradition once regarded the Hebrew of the Torah as God's special language, the discovery of other ancient languages spoken in Canaan shows that Hebrew was a local Canaanite dialect—or dialects—not a unique language. In fact, the Bible itself refers to Hebrew as "the language of Canaan" (Isa. 19:18). We may regard the Hebrew language as sacred not because God spoke in this language, but because the Israelites recorded God's revelations in the Bible in Hebrew. The Bible is not sacred because Hebrew is sacred; Hebrew is sacred because it is the language of the sacred Bible.)

If the biblical record of revelation is not word-for-word the "message" of God, then how should it be understood? Perhaps the words of the Torah are a paraphrase of God's speech to the Israelites. That is, after God had spoken to the Israelites, they recorded what God had said in their own language, using their own words and their own style. Such a view still assumes that God spoke in *words*, in human language.

This understanding of revelation and the nature of God is too literal. It is true that the Bible—and we—speak of God as a person, with eyes, ears, hands, etc. But we speak of God this way because we have no other way to talk about God. There is, as we have said, a degree to which God's actions resemble those of a person. But although God is in some ways *like* a person, we do not claim that God *is* a person. We do not claim that God actually possesses eyes like ours, ears like ours, a mouth like ours. Thus, if God does not possess the same physical organs of speech that we possess, we cannot say that God's *words* are the same as ours.

Perhaps comparing God's communication to people to a message consisting of words is the clearest way that we—and the Bible—can explain that God conveys a message to people, but we do not take this model literally. In the words of Maimonides, God's speaking is a metaphor.

❐ TWO MODELS OF REVELATION

I would like to suggest that revelation might be understood in one, or both, of the following two ways.

In the first, I compare revelation to music. When a person experiences God's presence in an event it may be somewhat like listening to music. There must be some agency to produce the music. This agency is God acting in history. The Exodus from Egypt, the deliverance of the Israelites from bondage, is for Israel God's greatest act. It is great "music" for all Israel to hear. But one who has been trained to listen to music and one who is attentive to it does not merely *hear* notes. One is moved by the music, affected by it. The listener experiences something new and different. The music in a sense conveys a "message," but that "message" will be interpreted differently by various listeners. Yet, the clearer, the bolder the music, the more each listener will agree on what "message" the music conveys. In this case, individual differences will not matter so much, and an entire audience may share a similar understanding of the music.

Likewise, all Israel interpreted, or learned to interpret, the Exodus as a clear and bold message from God: "I am the Lord your God who brought you out of the land of Egypt, from the house of bondage."

Additionally, an attentive listener not only hears and interprets the music. He or she also *responds* to it. One is so moved that one's behavior is completely transformed by that experience. The experience demands actions, changes in behavior, special behavior. Out of the experience emerge "commands," mitzvot carried out in the listeners' responses to the music/revelation. Similarly, the Exodus, climaxed by the assemblage of all Israel at the holy mountain, Sinai, was the most special of all experiences. In it the people Israel together saw the very presence of God in their history and "heard" the commands of God to them. These commands we may understand not as a one-sided message from God, but as an interaction between God's acts in history and the responses of Israel. If Israel had been composed of different people, living in a different place and in a different time, the "music" would not have "sounded" exactly the same or had the same effect. Hence, we today sometimes interpret the mitzvot a bit differently from the way the ancient Israelites did. (We shall return to this topic below.)

Now because the revelation, including the mitzvot, results from an interaction between God and Israel, it is impossible to pry apart God's contribution to the experience from the people Israel's contribution to it. It would seem that the Israelites themselves attributed the entire revelation and its "message" to God. God appeared, and God spoke. The Torah does not recognize, as we do, that without Israel's sensibility to "see," God would not be "seen." And without Israel's sensibility to "hear," God would not be "heard." But although we may understand the *process* of revelation differently from the way our Israelite forbears represent it in the Torah, this does not prevent us from accepting the revelation and finding in it a meaning for us. We can believe in the revelation itself, even though we may explain it differently.

After all, the Israelites believed that the sun literally crosses the sky while the earth remains stationary. We do not believe that the sun literally crosses the sky. We believe the earth rotates. Nevertheless, we agree with the Israelites that the sun appears to rise and set. We agree on what we see. We only disagree on how it happens.

Now we have used the model of the experience of listening to and being moved by music in order to understand the process of revelation more clearly. However, I believe that another model is necessary in order to explain revelation. Revelation is not so much like one or the other of these models but rather like *each* of them in certain respects.

This second model compares revelation to illumination, to light. God's presence may be likened to a source of light. Seeing things in the presence of God is like seeing them illumined, enabling one to observe that which could not otherwise be observed. For example, the eye can see objects under infrared light that the eye could not otherwise see. The objects may have been there all along, but only under this special light could we become aware of their existence.

Without God, there would be no light; but without a person present there would be no seeing. A person brings to this "seeing" his or her own keenness of vision, intelligence, abilities to understand or interpret that which may be "seen." Thus, different persons may vary in what they see or in how they interpret what they see. (Recall the comparison of Moses and the other prophets.) For example, some pictures are more straightforward in their reference than others and can be easily interpreted. Other are more ambiguous and are open to a variety of interpretations. Some people can see more in a picture, owing to keener vision, intelligence, etc. And each person will, to some extent, see what he or she has been trained to see through cultural conditioning, personal background, and the like. Thus, an observer such as Sherlock Holmes may notice many significant aspects to an object that the rest of us might overlook. On the other hand, some images are so clear and straightforward that each member of a group of viewers would come away with the same understanding of what they had seen.

The comparisons with the Sinai event are by now obvious. Once Israel had been trained to interpret the Exodus from Egypt as God acting in history, they were enabled to "see" their relationship with God as special. They could apply their intelligence and cultural concerns, their ways of proper living, in the "light" of God's presence and God's behavior in order to adopt the mitzvot, the acts they were expected to perform. By employing this model, the mitzvot may be understood as Israel's response to God's presence. But this response is a combination of human understanding of how people should live *and* the additional, special "light" that is thrown on human experience by God's acting in history. The people Israel, experiencing God's acts on their behalf in the Exodus events, viewed their obligations to God, to each other, and to other peoples in the "light" of God's presence.

Why is it advantageous to describe revelation by two models rather than one or the other? Am I not complicating the matter? Two models are useful because there is, as we have seen, an aspect of revelation in which the person is impressed by some stimulus in the world to be struck, affected by it, moved by it. This is similar to the effect of music upon a sensitive and attentive listener. But there is another aspect of revelation in which the person is enabled to see a pattern in events one could not see before; to see old things in a new light; to see new, previously "hidden" things that were not before visible. This is similar to the effect of seeing with the aid of a special light. The experience of revelation is not entirely like either of the models, being different in many respects and therefore unique. It is in a category by itself.

The Sinai revelation, as we have said, was, as it is reported in the Torah, an experience shared by all Israel. Israel responded as one, achieving a consensus on what their relationship to God is and what obligations are bound up with this relationship.

◻ WHAT WAS REVEALED?

What, then, is the *content* or meaning of the Sinai revelation? One thing that was almost certainly at the center of the Sinai event was the special relationship between God and Israel that was formalized as the covenant, the *brit*. The events involved in the Exodus were clear signs to Israel that God was acting to deliver them to freedom. Moreover, Israel understood that God's great favor to them was not arbitrary or without purpose. Rather, God brought Israel to Sinai, the holy mountain, in order to reveal the purpose: Israel will accept the Lord as God; God will remain the guardian of Israel. Israel will then receive a special status vis-à-vis God: they will be a "kingdom of priests." This seems to mean that just as the priests of a nation have learned the special ways of serving God and are entrusted with instructing the rest of the people in the proper service of God, so will Israel serve as the "priests" to the other nations, teaching them the proper service of God.

In order to carry out this sacred function, Israel must agree to observe a number of rules of behavior—the mitzvot—that will guide Israel's life and will lead Israel, and ultimately humankind, to the proper service of God. The observance of the mitzvot is the obligation that Israel willingly accepts in return for God's acts of favor to Israel and for God's continuing guardianship of Israel.

Which mitzvot were revealed at Sinai? The tradition that is represented in the Torah seems to hold that the Ten Commandments and the laws that follow in Exodus 20–23 were all part of the Sinai revelation itself. There developed another tradition among the Jews that the entire five books of the Torah were revealed at Sinai. According to an opinion expressed in the midrash (Shemot Rabba, Yitro 28), *all* things that would *ever* be revealed to the Jewish people were revealed at Sinai, including the prophecies of Israel's prophets and the interpretations of the sages in later generations. There is even a midrash that all the Torah was revealed to humankind by the time of Abraham and that Moses merely taught these laws to the Israelites at Sinai.

We, however, cannot be certain of what in the Torah was revealed at Sinai and what was revealed on various other, later occasions. First, the Torah does not represent the revelation itself, but, as we have discussed, a later record of Israel's interpretation of the revelation. Second, the record of Israel's interpretation of the revelation appears to have undergone a process of transmission in which generations passed on the record according to their own understanding or interpretation of it.

But third, and most importantly, we cannot accept the Israelite tradition that all the mitzvot in the Torah were revealed at Sinai or during the career of Moses for historical reasons. Modern Bible scholars are more or less agreed that various laws contained in the Torah entered Israelite tradition in different periods and under diverse historical circumstances. The Bible itself contains a good deal of evidence that indicates that this was so. For example, the book of Numbers presents a law concerning how to divide the spoils of war (31:25 ff.). The law states that soldiers who do battle in the front lines must share the spoils equally with any soldiers who remain behind to watch the gear. Now although the Torah accredits this ruling to Moses, according to 1 Samuel it was King David who first introduced this law (30:21–25), about 300 years after Moses.

Another example concerns the laws for observing the Pesaḥ ritual. According to Exod. 12:1–14, each family was to slaughter and consume the Pesaḥ lamb offering in its own locality. According to Deut. 16:1–8, however, each household was to bring the Pesaḥ offering to one central site, where all the Israelites would celebrate the *ḥag* together. We learn from 2 Kings 22–23 that the practice of all Israel observing the Pesaḥ at one site was not adopted until the reign of King Josiah, around 622 B.C.E. Thus, within the Torah we find laws that appear to have been introduced earlier in Israel's history and laws that appear to have been introduced somewhat later.

There is no reason to think that after Sinai there were no revelations between God and Israel. The Bible reports numerous revelations, among the prophets and others. There were, it seems, certain periods in which revelation was more or less common than in others (compare 1 Sam. 3:1). But Sinai was only the first event in a history of revelation experiences for Israel. Sinai, being the first and the model for all later experiences of Israel, was the greatest revelation event. The content of every subsequent revelation had to be evaluated against the fundamental principles revealed at Sinai, somewhat as the Supreme Court measures all U.S. legislation against the Constitution. No later revelation could be accepted as valid unless it was in line with the Sinai *brit*.

But throughout the course of its history, Israel developed forms of religious observance that were additional to the laws already existing or that differed in their interpretation or understanding from the laws of earlier periods. Those observances that the Israelites accepted as revealed were included within the sacred traditions of Israel and were then represented in the laws of the Torah.

The traditions of the Torah, then, encompass the records of revelation experiences from many periods of Israel's growth. But the biblical tradition "telescoped" the accumulated revelations of Israel into one great revelation, beginning at Sinai and continuing through the career of our greatest teacher-leader, Moses. "Telescoping" is a common technique used in passing on traditions. Many events occurring over a long period of time are viewed as occurring at one, prime moment, usually the first great moment in the tradition. It is a natural function of the mind. In this case, Israel's responses to God's presence in later generations were telescoped into the Mosaic age as though, as in the midrash cited above, they had existed from the first meeting of God and Israel at Sinai. Israelites of later times could not imagine a relationship between God and themselves without the components of the *brit* it as it existed in their own time.

Once Israel accepted a tradition as revealed truth, it was understood to have existed from time immemorial. Compare a rule book for a game such as baseball. A book of baseball rules includes the current rules of the game. It might appear, to someone unfamiliar with the history of the game, that the current rules of baseball had always existed in their present form, more or less like the rules of chess. But actually, the various rules of baseball have been introduced at different times in the relatively brief history of the game. The basic structure and principal rules were there from the start. But various other aspects of the game developed later in response to changing historical circumstances (night games were introduced after adequate lighting was devised, designated hitters were introduced when fans became bored with the poor hitting of pitchers, etc.). These later rules were sometimes added; but some replaced earlier ones and are found alongside the earlier, unmodified rules in the books. Thus, a baseball book of rules comprises the accumulated regulations of all periods of the game's history.

The Torah is similar, except that it contains traditions deriving from different periods without allowing for older laws, which may even have been replaced, to be omitted. The rules of baseball are produced by people and can, therefore, be changed and replaced at human discretion. But the content of Israel's revelations is sacred and divine and not subject to change by human initiative. Thus, the traditions of Israel, being revealed, were preserved in the Torah regardless of whether or not various traditions might duplicate or contradict one another. The Torah does not only tell us where we are going. It tells us where we have been.

We shall return later on to the matter of laws within the Torah that are inconsistent or that contradict each other and in what ways Jewish tradition has interpreted them.

❐ CAN WE IDENTIFY GOD'S CONTRIBUTION?

At this point we shall confront one of the questions that must inevitably arise from our view of the mitzvot as a combination of God's revelation and Israel's response: Is there any way of telling which aspects of the mitzvot result from God's presence in history and which derive from Israel's own cultural conditions as they existed prior to the experience of revelation? In other words, what in the mitzvot seems to have been Israelite practice even without revelation, and what may be attributed to revelation? What difference did revelation make?

At the outset, let us reiterate a point that we already stressed. We regard revelation as a process, an interaction in which we cannot draw a rigid distinction between the contributions of the "sender" of the revelation (God) and the "receiver" of the revelation (Israel). Nevertheless, we can provide some illustrations that identify both a revealed and a human component in those of the mitzvot that lend themselves to such an analysis. As we shall see, modern studies of the various cultures of the ancient Near East furnish much material that is helpful to our investigation.

One kind of example:

The Torah (the latter part of Exodus in particular) contains laws that govern the construction of the tabernacle (*mishkan*, "dwelling-place of the Lord") in the wilderness. The first book of Kings describes the design and building of the Temple. Both texts represent the idea and the design for such a building as God-given or at least God-approved. Now archeological excavation throughout the Middle East has unearthed the remains of numerous temples and altars as well as several texts describing those religious buildings. Comparisons between the architectural design of the Israelite sanctuaries and those of other ancient near eastern peoples clearly show that the Israelites were using common ancient Near Eastern building practices and materials in the construction of their own altars and temples. The laws in the Torah, therefore, incorporate a good deal that was common among pagan peoples, too. This conclusion, incidentally, was already reached in the early fourteenth century by the Medieval Jewish philosopher and commentator, Rabbi Levi Ben Gershon (Gersonides), who recognized that the specific designs of the mishkan were products of the ancient Israelites' own cultural milieu.

We may say, then, that the physical design and construction of the mishkan (and the Temple) form part of the Israelites' own contribution to the mitzvot concerning the construction of the mishkan. God's contribution to these mitzvot may be seen in the events of the Exodus and the Sinai covenant,in which Israel recognized God's presence among them and undertook to identify God's presence and worship God through the mishkan and its rituals. That is, it was YHWH ("Adonai") who was to be recognized as the true God, the God responsible for the deliverance of the Israelites from Egypt, and it was YHWH alone who was to be worshipped. God's revelation to Israel involved an obligation for the Israelites to "house" God's presence in their midst. But the architectural designs for making such a "house" were adapted by the Israelites from their cultural environment. The mitzvot, then, comprise both the revelation experience (God's involvement in Israelite history) and Israel's response to that experience (an adaptation of sanctuary building technology to the worship of YHWH).

Another kind of example:

All peoples of the ancient Near East, the Israelites among them, owned slaves. Both biblical and other ancient Near Eastern law codes contain statutes governing the treatment of slaves. But there is a significant difference between the laws of slavery among the Israelites and those among other peoples of the ancient Near East. Elsewhere slaves were simply the permanent property of their owners. If a slave ran away, it was the obligation of any citizen who found the slave to return him to his owner. According to biblical law, however—particularly as it is formulated in Deuteronomy—a slave was a person who had to be released after a fixed period of service (six years). Upon release, the owner was to provide the slave with some belongings so that he might begin life as a freeman. If an owner injured his slave, he would have to free him. If a slave ran away, it was illegal to return him to his owner. The assumption is that if the master had treated the slave properly, the slave would not have fled his master's household.

Our comparison of biblical laws concerning slavery with other laws about slaves produces the following impressions. Both Israel and other peoples of the ancient Near East had slaves. Slavery and perhaps some of the practices involved in the purchase and deployment of slaves were part of Israel's contributions to the mitzvot regarding slavery. But Israel's uniquely enlightened laws concerning the humane treatment of slaves may be held to be the revealed aspect of the mitzvot. In their deliverance from Egyptian bondage the Israelites recognized God's presence in their history and perceived that freedom and the individual worth of the person are values ordained by God. The Torah calls upon the Israelites to show compassion for the underprivileged in remembrance of the fact that they themselves had been slaves in Egypt. We may surmise, then, that the revelations Israel experienced in the Exodus and Sinai events (and confirmed in subsequent Israelite history) contributed to the differences between Israel's laws on slavery and those of other ancient near eastern peoples.

Many of the mitzvot that reflect high spiritual or ethical values are found not only in the Bible but also in other ancient Near Eastern literatures, some of which precede the Israelites by centuries. Among these are such laws as maintaining fair weights and measures and leaving a margin of the field for the poor to gather produce. In what sense are these mitzvot revealed? There are at least two ways to approach this issue, and the two need *not* be mutually exclusive.

On the other hand one may say that God "spoke" to Hammurapi (the famous Babylonian king of the eighteenth century B.C.E.) and to other ancient Near Eastern lawmakers just as God "spoke" to Moses and other Israelites. To believe in the special revelation experience between God and the Israelites during the Exodus and at Sinai does not require us to deny that God might have revealed himself and his ways to others who lived before Israel and in other places. The Bible itself reports dialogues between God and early Mesopotamian men and women (Adam and Eve, Noah, etc.) and revelations of God to non-Israelites (Pharaoh, Abimelech, Balaam, etc.). Many of the mitzvot, then, may have been revealed prior to the formation of the people Israel and were later "reiterated" in the various revelation experiences of the Israelites.

On the other hand one may say that the Israelites, in their own revelation experiences, were enabled to recognize the merit of certain laws and practices among their neighbors and adopt those laws and practices as their own. The insights that grew out of the revelation enabled the Israelites to *select* from among the existing laws and practices those that were fitting (such as those concerning economic damages); to reject those that were not fitting (such as those that permitted the acceptance of a monetary fine from a murderer); and to modify those that could be reformed for Israelite use (such as the laws of slavery).

(Yet another way to approach this issue is to employ another understanding of revelation. In accord with the thinking of Medieval Jewish philosophers such as Maimonides and Gersonides, one may take revelation to be a natural process of the human mind. God, the creator, implanted in the human mind the capacity to discover the eternal truths that are present in the world and available to human comprehension. When a person makes such a discovery, or has such an insight, we may view this as the actual source of revelation. The revelation is not entirely human but also divine since it is God who created the conditions in the world and in the mind for such a discovery of truths or God's will to take place. Using this understanding of revelation, we may say that Hammurapi and others—prior to Moses or even Abraham—took advantage of their God-given capacity to see the truth and perceived "revealed" laws, which they imposed upon their subjects.)

To return to our central point, we have seen that the mitzvot embody the result of a revelation process that includes both divine and human dimensions. For some of the mitzvot it is even possible to put our finger on what is divine and what is human.

❒ THE GROWTH OF HALAKHAH

For the person who is interested only in understanding what we mean by saying that God revealed the mitzvot in the Torah, the discussion above may have addressed most of the key questions that such a person would ask (What do we mean by "God"? What do we mean by revelation? What in the Torah is revealed? In what sense are the mitzvot in the Torah revealed?). But for the concerned and practicing Jew we have not carried our discussion far enough.

We know that traditional Jewish observance is not confined to those mitzvot that are *explicitly* ordained by the five books of the Torah. We know that we are obliged to perform many practices and observe many rituals that are not specifically—or even generally—mentioned by the Torah. The Torah, as it is recorded in the biblical text, does not discuss daily prayer and the order of the siddur. It does not require the kindling of the Shabbat candles nor even refer to Hanukkah. It does not spell out the details of such rituals as Shabbat observance and marriage ceremonies. Nevertheless, the practicing Jew regards these observances as what God requires of him or her.

The practicing Jew seeks to shape his or her behavior according to the Torah, the way ordained by God. Such a Jew attains to a life of religious behavior through following Jewish law according to a much broader formulation than that which the written Torah (*torah shebikhtav*) itself presents. This large body of Jewish law is called the halakhah, and it is incumbent upon us to describe more precisely what we mean by halakhah and then to deal with certain questions that must inevitably arise: Now that we have discussed in what sense we take the mitzvot in the Torah to be revealed, in what way, if any, is the halakhah revealed? How is the halakhah determined? What authority stands behind the halakhah? Where does that authority stem from?

For the time being we shall speak of the halakhah as the law that governs Jewish behavior, in all areas of life, in an authoritative way. Our understanding will become broader—and we hope deeper—as we discuss the origins of the halakhah and the nature of its authority.

According to rabbinic tradition, the halakhah is embodied within what is called the "Oral Torah" (*torah shebe'al peh*).* For the ancient rabbis (and for many moderns, too) the Oral Torah is a necessary companion to the written Torah (the five books of the Humash), serving to explain it and apply it to any conceivable situation. The source of the Oral Torah is the same as that of the written Torah, according to this tradition. That is, together with the Written Torah "Moses received the [Oral] Torah at Sinai. He passed it on to Joshua, and Joshua to the Elders, and the Elders to the Prophets; and the Prophets passed it on to the Men of the Great Assembly." From there the earliest rabbis received the Oral Torah and passed it among themselves (Pirkei Avot 1:1 and following).

---

* We shall avoid the term "Oral Law" and employ instead "Oral Torah" since we have in these pages been leaving the term "Torah" untranslated and because in any case *torah* means "Instruction" and not "Law."

By this assertion the rabbis of the early Roman period claim that they possess the God-given, and therefore authoritative, application of the Torah to all aspects of Jewish life. Their teaching of the law, the halakhah, is revealed, as is the Written Torah: by God to Moses at Sinai.

But just as we do not accept the tradition's belief that the entire five books of the Written Torah were spoken word-for-word by God to Moses (see above), we do not share, on the whole, the tradition's understanding of the origins of the halakhah. And just as we presented a much more complex understanding of the Sinai revelation than that of the Talmud, so must we suggest a more complex explanation of the growth of the halakhah, its revealed nature, and the source of its authority.

Our model for understanding the revealed character of the halakhah will be similar to the model by which we understood the revealed character of the (Written) Torah. In that model, we explained the content of the (Written) Torah as the result of interactions between God's involvement in history and the people Israel's perceptions of and responses to God's presence. We understand the halakhah, too, as the result of interaction. But in this case we must build another component into the model: that of the Written Torah. That is, whereas the Written Torah emerged from a revelation process between God and Israel, the halakhah emerged—and continues to emerge—from revelation processes between God, the Jewish people, *and* the written Torah, as the following simplified diagram illustrates:

In fact, we understand the halakhah to have developed not very differently from the Written Torah—with the addition of the Written Torah component. But in order to explain our model of the origins of the halakhah, it will be necessary to examine, at least in its general contours, the history of the Jews' adoption of the Written Torah and the development of the authoritative halakhah.

We cannot be certain about when, precisely, the entire five books of the Written Torah were combined into one book, a single large scroll. But the late "historical" books of the Bible (Chronicles, Ezra, Nehemiah) indicate that in the fifth century B.C.E. the Torah-book had been accepted by the Jews as the revealed law of God, transmitted through the prophet Moses: "The rest of the people, the priests, the Levites, the gatekeepers, the singers, the temple servants, and all who have separated themselves from the peoples of the lands to the law of God, their wives, their sons, their daughters, all who have knowledge and understanding, join with their brethren, their nobles, and enter into a curse and an oath [i.e., a covenant] to walk in God's law which was given by Moses the servant of God, and to observe and do all the commandments of the Lord our Lord and his ordinances and his statutes" (Neh. 10:29–30, translation of the RSV).

The Torah-book was read out before the Jewish public (Neh. 8:11 ff) as the authoritative source of God's will. But as we have said, the Torah as written often fails to provide explicit instructions concerning what exactly God would want of us for certain observances and in various situations. The written Torah was adopted as the "Constitution" of the new Judean community, but the specific applications to everyday life and even ritual performance were not clearly defined. Consequently, it was necessary to interpret the written Torah; that is, to draw out the application of the written Torah to a given situation, to make the law live in practice.

The newly derived law forms part of the halakhah. It is important to recognize that the Written Torah by itself was never a complete system of law, but rather a sourcebook of God-given guidelines—some extensive and detailed, others sketchy and general—that by its nature required explanation and exemplification by a teacher. Thus, in the very period in which Nehemiah led the Jews in accepting the Written Torah as their authority, Ezra the "Bookman" began to teach, explain, and interpret the Written Torah so that it could be addressed to the lives of the people: "For Ezra set his mind to interpret [*lidrosh*] the Torah of the Lord, and to perform and teach law and statute in Israel" (Ezra 7:10).

The verb that is used in this verse to describe the process of drawing out an implication or application from the Written Torah is *darash*, "to seek, to inquire." The use of this verb is more significant than it might at first appear. In earlier times, when the Israelites wanted to know God's will, they would approach a known prophet and inquire (*darash*) of God's word through the medium of the prophet (see, e.g., Jer. 21:1–2; Ezek. 14:1–2). The purpose of the inquiry was no less than to receive a revelation. The source of God's will prior to and during the periods of the First Temple and the Exile was revelation that was mediated between God and Israel through the person of a prophet. Thus, although all Israel is said to have experienced the Sinai revelation as a community, the laws of the Sinai covenant were formalized by the prophet Moses.

But from the time of the Second Temple, the Jews no longer relied on—nor even accepted as authoritative—revelation through prophecy. According to rabbinic tradition, "When the last prophets, Haggai, Zechariah, and Malachi, died, the Holy Spirit (i.e., the source of prophecy) was removed from Israel" (Sanhedrin 11a). Instead, in the period of Ezra and Nehemiah, the Jews adopted a new form of revelation: *midrash*. In the place of the prophet stood the written text of the Torah and the other holy books. In order to learn or to verify a teaching or a practice, a Jew would turn not to a prophet but to a holy book—or to a teacher-interpreter of the book, a "book man" (*sofer*). The Written Torah would not be read strictly according to the plain meaning of its text. It would be read not only for what it says explicitly but for whatever meaning might be drawn out of it through official interpretation (*meforash*, Neh. 8:1–8).

The text becomes standardized and fixed. The words, the letters, become unchanging for generations, centuries. But people change, times change, places change, life changes. Each change in history requires a new adaptation of the Torah. Each change in human understanding, in the human spirit, leads to a reinterpretation, seeing the written Torah in a new way, with new eyes. Such reinterpretations of the Torah are, in our view, not human modifications of the Torah's revelation. They are, rather, *revelation itself*, and not so different in kind from the revelation at Sinai and subsequent revelations in the history of ancient Israel.

We spoke of biblical revelation above as an experience in which people became keenly aware of God's presence in their history, moving them to respond to God by developing new ways of behaving in accordance with God's will, as it is manifested in human events and in nature. We explained revelation as a new way of seeing our religious responsibilities in the light of God's behavior. The course of human events is understood by the religious person (at least in biblical religion, Judaism, and its so-called "daughter" religions) not as an arbitrary series of chance occurrences but as a reflection of God's will. The religious person seeks to make sense of the "message" delivered by significant phenomena. The Israelites read their miraculous deliverance from Egypt as a "message" from God, leading to the establishment of the covenant between God and

Appendix — Understanding the Sinai Revelation

Israel. This was not by any means the last significant event in the history of the Israelites or the Jewish people.

We are all familiar with the story of the Maccabees—their miraculous triumph over the Hellenizers and their restoration of the Jerusalem Temple to the proper service of the Lord. The event is recorded nowhere in the books of the Jewish Bible but in the Apocrypha, the books that the Jews would not include among their sacred writings. Nevertheless, the Jewish people saw God's hand in the Maccabean achievements and responded not only by rededicating the Temple to its former, pure state but also by establishing the Festival of Hanukkah to commemorate God's favors toward the Maccabees and the Jewish people. The Rabbis understood the institution of Hanukkah as a mitzvah, an observance that represents God's will, and they formulated the blessing over the kindling of the Hanukkah lights as follows:

> Blessed are you, Lord our God, king of the Universe, who has sanctified us with his commandments *and has commanded us* to kindle the Hanukkah lamp.

A new revelation bred a new practice within the laws of Jewish observance, the halakhah.

It must be admitted that few halakhot stem from a revelation experience as dramatic as the Maccabean war and its aftermath. But the point I am trying to make is nonetheless firm: The halakhah is not simply a reading out of interpretations from the written Torah. It is, like the revelation at Sinai, the product of an interaction between God's behavior toward the world and the Jewish people's responses to it. The major difference between biblical revelation and later revelation (as embodied in the halakhah and haggadah) is that later revelation must find a basis in the written Torah—a point we shall be returning to below.

Now we said just above that the halakhah changes when historical circumstances and human understanding change. For example, when the Jerusalem Temple was destroyed by the Romans, major changes in Jewish worship had to be adopted. Prayer and the synagogue service, though in existence to some degree already, had to take on new importance. When the Jews lived among Gentiles who regarded the wearing of a headcovering to be an essential sign of piety, Jews, who certainly would not want to seem impious, adopted as halakhah the practice of wearing a hat or skullcap. The fact that the particulars of the halakhah arise out of specific historical circumstances is nowhere more evident than in the fact that different Jewish communities, living apart, developed different halakhot. Thus, Ashkenazic Jews prohibit the eating of rice on Pesaḥ, regarding it as *hametz*, while Sephardic Jews permit rice, not considering it to be *hametz*.

The halakhah also changes when human attitudes change, whether as a result of new scientific knowledge (as in the Rabbinical Assembly's decision to permit the use of electricity on Shabbat) or as a result of new views of morality (as in the medieval prohibition against polygamy).

This means, of course, that the halakhah is not simply an explanation of the Written Torah. It is frequently a revision of the plain sense of the Torah text in the light of changing human understanding. And since these new perspectives result from a new seeing of what is right through a new understanding of the world and our relation to it, we may say that our new views result from revelation. For we have explained revelation as a new seeing based on experiencing God's presence in the world, in human events.

In fact, it appears that many laws in the Written Torah itself grew out of a revision of the older laws in the Torah through a new seeing, through subsequent revelation. Certain laws in Leviticus and Deuteronomy, for example, seem to be intended as modifications of earlier laws, such as those found in Exodus 20–23. For instance, according to Exod. 21:2–4 a female slave is not emancipated after six years, as is a male slave. But according to Deut. 15:12, both male and female slaves must be set free after six years of service. Unfortunately, the Bible does not furnish us with a complete cultural history of the ancient Israelites, and, consequently, we do not know for certain what historical factors led to the new attitude toward women (and human beings in general) that one finds in the book of Deuteronomy. But there is sufficient evidence in the case of other biblical ordinances to establish that there were changing historical circumstances and new ethical perspectives that led to the adoption of new biblical laws.

As an illustration, one may point to the law in Deut. 17:2–4 that prohibits the worship of the astral deities—"the sun, the moon, or the entire host of the heavens. "Although idolatry is forbidden in other books of the Torah, too, only Deuteronomy specifically outlaws this cult. Apparently, the need to single out this abomination in particular arose from the fact that only in the middle of the seventh century B.C.E. did a Judean king, Manasseh, introduce this idolatrous practice into the Jerusalem Temple (2 Kings 21:1 ff.). A new historical event demanded a new injunction in biblical law. In a similar vein, King David's contemporary sense of fairness led to his formulation of a new biblical law regarding sharing the spoils of war, as we discussed above.

Therefore, we have reason to assume that changes in biblical law from one book to another emerged from an interaction between the written (already established) law, the Israelites, and their new understanding of what God demanded of them by experiencing God's presence in their history. That is, the model that we have proposed for explaining the development of halakhah may also be applied toward understanding the growth of biblical law. The source of the revealed character of the Written Torah and of the Oral Torah is, therefore, quite similar.

(In this regard we agree with the rabbinic tradition that in some sense the Written Torah and the Oral Torah were revealed in the same manner. But whereas the Rabbis telescoped all written and Oral Torah into a single revelation event at Sinai, we understand both Written and Oral Torah to have been adopted by the Jewish people by stages in the course of history.)

What this means, then, is that, in our view, as long as there is history—and as long as there are religiously sensitive people, people who see the world and what happens in it in terms of God—there will be revelation. As long as there is revelation, there will be new contributions to the Oral Torah, new halakhah. To raise a case in point: The establishment and continued survival of the State of Israel is considered in many quarters to constitute a divine act. With this act we may perceive a revelation: God cares for the State of Israel, and Jews around the world should support it however they can. The founding of the State of Israel is now commemorated, somewhat like Ḥanukkah, with a day of celebration—*Yom Ha'atzma'ut*—in religious schools, synagogues, and in other Jewish institutions. *Yom Ha'atzma'ut* seems to be growing into an observance ordained by the halakhah, as contemporary Jews discuss such issues as: Should the *Hallel* prayer be recited on *Yom Ha'atzma'ut* as it is on other festivals? The halakhah is not a fixed text, like the Written Torah. It is a growing code of Jewish conduct that is transformed through history, as Jews change.

❐ HOW IS HALAKHAH DERIVED?

But if new historical circumstances lead to the adoption of new halakhah, or at least halakhah that is not communicated in explicit terms by the Written Torah, then in what sense do we say that the halakhah emerges from the interaction of God's presence in history, the Jewish people, *and* the Written Torah? What relation does the halakhah bear to the written text of the Ḥumash?

There are different sorts of halakhot, and these different types relate to the Written Torah in various ways. Some halakhot follow directly from ordinances that are expressly stated in some form in the Ḥumash. In such cases the halakhah spells out the particular applications of specific biblical laws. As a simple illustration, the book of Exodus prohibits in very general terms the kindling of fire on the Shabbat (35:3). Rabbinic literature goes on to discuss in detail the prohibition of fire and the ways in which fire *may* be used during the Shabbat (say, to warm food) as long as the fire was ignited earlier (see, e.g., Mishnah Shabbat chapter 3).

Other halakhot do not issue directly from the written text. For example, the Mishnah (Shabbat 7:2) prohibits on the Shabbat such acts as tanning leather and sewing, although nowhere does the Written Torah expressly forbid them. From early biblical times until the codification of the Mishnah (around 215 C.E.) the specific aspects of Shabbat observance developed historically along with the Jewish people. The institution of Shabbat as a holy day is certainly one of the major elements of the Sinai covenant, dating from the time when Israel first became a people. But as the nature of Israel's life and its understanding of the meaning of Shabbat evolved, so did the particular practices that were prohibited and required for the proper observance of Shabbat.

Thus, although Jews came to adopt specific laws of Shabbat as essential for fulfilling the mitzvot of the written Torah to keep the Shabbat, there was no explicit basis for many Shabbat observances—various prohibitions, lighting candles, etc.—in the text of the Ḥumash.

Nevertheless, the Rabbis were able to relate these particulars of the halakhah to the Written Torah because they believed in the following fundamental assumptions: (1) all of the Oral Torah is contained within the Written Torah; (2) it is possible to find the basis for the halakhah in the Written Torah if one employs the proper methods of interpretation.

The Written Torah, for the Rabbis, was no ordinary text. It was literally the word of God. Now since God wants us to know what we are supposed to be doing, and since God did not make many aspects of the halakhah explicit in the written text of the Torah, it would follow, they reasoned, that God must have concealed the rest of the halakhah within the text, leaving it to human beings to disclose its hidden meaning. In this the Rabbis shared the view of many peoples in the ancient world that sacred texts, like dreams, possessed crucial information from God that needed to be decoded.

The means for seeking the concealed meanings of the text, breaking the code, are the procedures of the *midrash*. The text of the Written Torah itself provides clues for the seeker. Passages are arranged in a curious sequence; words are spelled in an unusual or inconsistent manner; peculiar wording is employed; verses seem to contradict each other, language suggests it is being used symbolically. The midrash regards these and other peculiarities of the text as significant, beckoning interpretation.

The Rabbis, accordingly, adopted certain techniques of midrash (the *middot*, or canons of interpretation) by which they could either draw out a new meaning from the text or find a proof text for a known halakhah in the Written Torah. Many of these techniques seem to have been widely used in the ancient world for the interpretation of dreams (which were often taken to be revelations from God) and sacred or legal texts. The Rabbis believed that the procedures of the midrash were themselves part of the Oral Torah and, consequently, revealed. The fact that these procedures would so often manage to relate the halakhah to the Written Torah successfully must have further corroborated the Rabbis' confidence in them.

Here are a number of illustrations of certain of the midrashic procedures.

As we saw above, the Written Torah does not spell out all the various categories of work that the Oral Torah prohibits on Shabbat. But the Rabbis found a basis for grounding the thirty-nine categories of the Mishnah (Shabbat 7:2) in the Ḥumash by following up a clue presented by the book of Exodus. In the course of describing the plans for the construction of the tabernacle (miskhan) in the wilderness, the narrative is twice interrupted by passages that call for the observance of Shabbat (Exod. 31:12–17, 35:1–3). The Rabbis were drawn by this curious arrangement of passages (*semikhut parashiyot*) and induced that there must be a significant relationship between the building of the tabernacle and the observance of Shabbat. it was, to wit, that the types of labor that are forbidden on Shabbat are those that were necessary for constructing the tabernacle.

Another item. Three times the Written Torah prohibits "boiling a kid in its mother's milk." This threefold repetition and, perhaps, its precise and graphic nature led the Rabbis to take this law to imply something more than its limited, literal meaning. From this the

Rabbis developed the entire system of regulations for separating dairy dishes (food and utensils) from meat dishes.

Contradictions within the Written Torah suggest to the modern scholar that the conflicting statements originate from different sources. But for the purposes of midrash the conflicting statements point to some meaning beyond the plain sense of either one of them. For instance, Exod. 12:15 (compare 34:18) commands us to eat matzot for seven days during the Festival of Matzot. But Deut. 16:8 soys that we are to eat matzot for only six days. Both verses agree on the six days, but there appears to be a contradiction concerning the seventh day. One source says that we must eat matzot on that day, and the other implies that we need not. Here the Rabbis applied a midrashic technique (the eighth *middah* of Rabbi Yishmael, which is included near the beginning of the morning service in the siddur) that holds that if a verse comes to make exception to part of another verse, the exception applies not only to the part in question but to the entire verse. In our case, the second verse contradicts the first by excepting the seventh day from the commandment to eat matzot. The principle of midrash holds that if an exception is made for the seventh day, then it applies to the six preceding days as well. That is, according to the halakhah, we need not eat matzot during the full seven days of the festival (although we may if we want to). We are obliged to eat matzot only on the seder night(s), which is derived from another verse (Exod. 12:8), over which there is no conflict.

As these examples, especially the last, demonstrate, the halakhah is in reality not so much a reading out of the meaning of the Written Torah as a code of Jewish conduct that emerges from the experience of the Jewish people as much as, if not more than, from the interpretation of the Written Torah. The halakhah may be said to emerge *ultimately* from the Written Torah because it was the Sinai covenant that established the foundations of the halakhah in the first place. The Jewish people has adopted halakhah in order to fulfill the basic principles of the Written Torah, as it has been understood, and we have always evaluated the halakhah by measuring its particulars against those basic general principles—much as the United States Supreme Court measures particular legislation according to its understanding of the Constitution.

The halakhah is, for the most part, not a mere invention of the Rabbis. As we said above, the Written Torah does not include laws to regulate many aspects of life; it often describes observances in very general ways, leaving details unmentioned. Yet we know that the ancient Israelites had already observed many regulations of the halakhah that the Written Torah does not explain. For example, we may gather from the words of Amos (8:4–5) and Jeremiah (17:19–27) that engaging in business was a violation of Shabbat in biblical times, even though the Ḥumash does not forbid it explicitly.

The point is that specific halakhic practices grew up alongside the Written Torah. They had been accepted as ordinances of the Oral Torah for ages before they had become codified in the Mishnah or another rabbinic document. But because the rabbis believed that the Oral Torah is contained within the Written Torah, and because they had to defend their own version of the halakhah against opposing versions (of the Sadducees, the Essenes, the early Christians, etc.), the rabbis employed midrash in order to find a connection between the halakhah and the written text. In other words, the rabbis often knew and agreed upon the halakhah, but they did not always have at hand a basis for the halakhah in the Written Torah. For this they would have to seek—*lidrosh*—via midrash of the text.

That the halakhah would often exist alongside the Written Torah and not necessarily emerge directly from it is evident from the fact that the rabbis could often agree on the halakhah but not on the midrashic procedure for drawing the halakhah out of the biblical text. For example, the Rabbis of the Talmud all accepted the thirty-nine categories of work that are prohibited on the Shabbat. But at times they could not agree on how to relate a specific category of work to the construction of the tabernacle. Or, they would disagree on explaining the basis in the Written Torah for counting the number of work categories as thirty-nine. Some rabbis—after the fact, it must be admitted—reasoned that it would require precisely these thirty-nine categories of labor to build the tabernacle. Others argued that the number of categories derives from the number of times the word "work" (מְלָאכָה) appears in the Ḥumash (Shabbat 49b).

We have seen, then, that the midrash of the Written Torah serves at least two basic functions: (1) to draw out new halakhah from the biblical text; and (2) to find a basis in the text for already existing halakhah. Returning to our triangular model for describing the origins of the halakhah, we would understand the revealed aspect of the halakhah to reside chiefly in different parts of the model depending on whether the midrash serves function #1 or function #2. For convenience, our model is reproduced at the top of the following page.

For function #1 the Written Torah itself plays an important role. The text itself is revealed, in the manner we have discussed at length above. It, in turn, serves as a major source of revelation when the Jewish people come to study it and draw meaning from it. On the other hand, the function of God's presence in history is not absent

because the Jewish people's awareness of this factor often provides the stimulus to seek meaning in the written Torah. Perhaps we can diagram function #1 in the following way in order to throw emphasis on the more important factors:

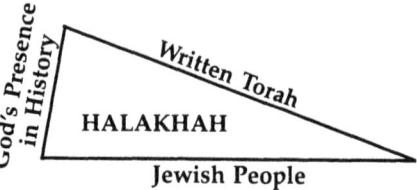

For function #2 the halakhah emerges out of the Jewish life experiences without a constant awareness of the rootedness of the halakhah in the Written Torah. On the other hand, as we have said above, the Written Torah may be viewed as the ultimate stimulus to develop halakhah. Thus, perhaps the following diagram can describe the relative importance of the factors involved in carrying out function #2:

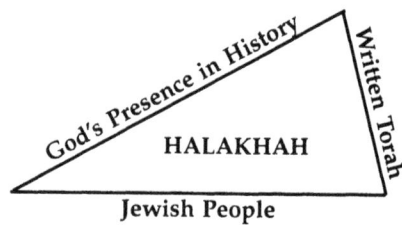

These two processes of midrash, however, do not comprise the sole sources of halakhah. This is because both these processes involve somehow grounding the content of the halakhah in the written Torah. But some halakhah is not grounded directly in the biblical text. For example, the observance of Hanukkah or Tish'ah B'Av does not stem from the Written Torah. The source of such observances, which we have seen are regarded as God-given mitzvot, is in the teachings of the rabbis. Through midrash the Oral Torah itself confers authority upon the rabbis to determine halakhah that does not possess a distinct basis in the Written Torah. This conferral of authority is, however, rooted in the text of the Humash in such verses as Deut. 17:11:

> You shall act in accordance with the instructions given you and the ruling handed down to you [by the magistrates]; you must not deviate from the verdict that they announce to you either to the right or to the left. (New JPS translation)

Or, in a midrashic reading of Deut. 32:7:

> Ask your father, he will inform you,
> Your elders, they will tell you.
> (New JPS translation)

The Rabbis identify their role in the Jewish community with that of the ancient magistrate or elder. As one rabbi put it, "From the time that the Temple was destroyed, Torah was taken away from the prophets and given to the Sages" (Bava Batra 12a).

❐ WHO DECIDES HALAKHAH?

This brings us to the question of who decides—then and now—what the correct halakhah is. What authority determines the halakhah? Who is in charge of defining what is the revealed will of God and what is not?

The halakhic process begins with a question in the mind of some member of the Jewish community, be it a lay person or a rabbi. The person who wants to know the halakhah addresses a formal question (*she'elah*) to an authority, awaiting a response (*teshuvah*). If the response is not readily at hand, where does the authority turn? Since ancient times the sources have changed.

The triangular model of the origins of the halakhah that I have proposed may describe the development of the halakhah in early rabbinic times, near the turn of the Common Era. But it does not apply to the development in later or modern times—at least not within the Conservative Movement. In former times, the Rabbis believed that the way to derive and legitimate the halakhah is through the procedures of midrash. They applied techniques of interpretation that to our mind are methods of the ancient world which we ourselves would not employ for the purpose of deriving halakhah. A modern authority would not examine the text of the Ḥumash to derive laws based on the presence or absence of a letter, etc.

Just as the Jewish people in ancient times studied the Torah in the manner that was considered then to be appropriate, so we moderns derive halakhah in the manner that seems fitting to us. Just as the halakhah, Jewish conduct, changes, the methods of determining the halakhah—which are part and parcel of the halakhah itself—change.

Today the halakhic authority stands not before the Written Torah but before the Oral Torah as it has been formulated in its classical sources (especially the Mishnah and the Babylonian Talmud), the commentaries and opinions of the medieval rabbinic scholars, and the codes of Jewish law and rabbinic opinions from Medieval to modern times. He or she places importance not only on the particulars of the traditional halakhah but on its principles and ideals as well. He or she studies contemporary Jewish experience and its insights—its scientific and ethical beliefs—and evaluates the degree to which the halakhah embodies these insights. When there arises a necessary conflict between the contemporary Jewish experience and its insights and the traditional halakhah, the modern authority seeks a means within the traditional framework of the halakhah to revise the halakhah so that it conforms to contemporary Jewish life. This may be accomplished by reinterpreting a principle of halakhah, by reordering the hierarchy of competing principles of halakhah, through a technical legal device, by showing that the halakhah does not apply to new historical conditions, or by some other means. (For examples of the development of Conservative Jewish halakhah, see Mordecai Waxman, ed., *Tradition and Change;* and Seymour Siegel, ed., *Conservative Judaism and Jewish Law.* For a code of Conservative Jewish law, see Isaac Klein, *A Guide to Jewish Religious Practice.*)

We should not be led to believe that such modern manipulations of the traditional halakhah fly in the face of revealed authority. On the contrary, the impetus to reconsider and adapt the existing halakhah, when it is performed responsibly, comes from a new reading of the message of Jewish history, of the relation between the Jewish people and the world. That is, it derives from an attempt to interpret the meaning of God's presence in most recent history.

If so, then why are there today so many different adaptations of the halakhah, so many varieties of Orthodox and Conservative teaching? This question returns us to the issue of what authority determines the halakhah and the source from which that authority derives its power.

In reality the issues of authority and power are combined. An authority is an authority not only by virtue of his or her—or its (in the case of a book, say)—learning, skills, experience, insight, and character. Authority derives from the recognition of some or all of these qualities by some community or group. The group trusts the authority's knowledge or opinion, follows its instructions or advice, gives it the power to exert some sort of control over the group. Ultimately, then, the source of the power of an authority on halakhah is the Jewish people.

In early biblical times the law was presented to the Israelites by a prophetic leader (such as Moses or Samuel) as a covenant with God. The authority of the law lay in the people's acceptance of the covenant relationship. The people accepted the covenant as the result of their understanding of God's involvement in their history and its meaning for them (see above). Thus, the prophetic leader was given the power of authority because he was recognized as representing the correct interpretation of the covenant and its obligations.

In the late Hellenistic and Roman periods, just preceding and following the turn of the Common Era, the Jewish people were not a single community. Different groups—the Pharisees, the Sadducees, the Essenes, and others about whom we know very little—competed for authority among the Jews. Eventually the Pharisees established their influence over most Jews, and Jewish tradition continues to follow the interpretation of the halakhah of the Pharisaic group, the Rabbis. The Rabbis resolved to determine the particulars of the halakhah through decision by a majority of their number, basing themselves on Exod. 23:2 (see Bava Metzia 59b).

The Jews were no longer a homogeneous group sharing a history or culture common to all. The meaning of revelation, of reading God's presence in history, was different for disparate groups or communities of Jews. The halakhah of the Palestinian Talmud is not always the halakhah of the Babylonian Talmud since the life experiences and cultural outlooks of the Jews in Eretz Israel were different from those of the Jews of Babylonia. Each community respected its own halakhic authorities.

To be sure, there were periods in which the Jews sought to transcend the geographic and cultural gulfs between them by consenting to abide by a single authority—an individual rabbi (or *gaon*), a certain school, or a particular code. Such, for example, occurred toward the end of the seventeenth century when European Jewish authorities adopted the *Shulḥan Arukh* as a binding code in order to impose order upon the chaos that ensued following the Chmielnitzki massacres of 1648 and the aborted messianic campaign of Shabbetai Zvi. But inevitably in the course of time and growing apart, diverse communities of Jews would develop somewhat different adaptations of the halakhah.

Today, too, we Jews are fragmented into religious communities, with each one entrusting the power to decide on issues of halakhah to a different authority. Within the Conservative Movement, the most widely recognized authority is probably the Committee on Law and Standards of the Rabbinical Assembly, although individual Jews and communities may turn to a particular rabbi or some other source, such as a written guide or the decision of an entire group, for halakhic teaching. In a sense, we will choose as our halakhic guide the person(s) who read(s) the meaning of contemporary revelation as we ourselves see it.

❐ SELECTED BIBLIOGRAPHY

REVELATION

John Baillie, *The Idea of Revelation in Recent Thought* (New York, 1956). A Christian discussion.

Bernard J. Bamberger, "Torah as God's Revelation to Israel," in Abraham E. Millgram, ed., *Great Jewish Ideas* (New York, 1964), pp. 63–79.

David R. Blumenthal, "Revelation: A Modern Dilemma," *Conservative Judaism* 31/2 (1977), pp. 64–69.

Elliot N. Dorff, "Revelation," *Conservative Judaism* 31/1–2 (1976–77), pp. 58–64.

Avery Dulles, *Models of Revelation* (New York, 1983). A Catholic view.

Emil L. Fackenheim, *God's Presence in History* (New York, 1970). Important contribution, at least to the formulation of some of the ideas in the present essay.

———. "Martin Buber's Concept of Revelation," in Paul A. Schilpp and M. Friedman, Ed., *The Philosophy of Martin Buber* (Lasalle, IL, 1967), pp. 273–96.

Jacques Guillet, *A God Who Speaks* (New York, 1979). Geared to contemporary Christian Bible study.

Will Herberg, *Judaism and Modern Man* (New York, 1970), pp.243–61. Modern Jewish statement.

Abraham J. Herschel, *God in Search of Man* (New York, 1955), pp. 191–99.

Louis Jacobs, *A Jewish Theology* (New York, 1973), pp. 199–210. Best summary.

Mordecai M. Kaplan, *The Greater Judaism in the Making* (New York, 1960), pp. 502–3. One of the Reconstructionist's statements.

Steven T. Katz, *Jewish Ideas and Concepts* (New York, 1977), pp. 170–82. Fine historical surveys.

H. Richard Niehbuhr, *The Meaning of Revelation* (New York, 1960). A major statement by a Protestant theologian.

Emanuel Rackman, "Israel and God: Reflections on Their Encounter," *Judaism* 11/3 (1962), pp. 233–41. A modern Orthodox perspective.

Franz Rosenzweig. *On Jewish Learning* (New York, 1965), pp. 119–24. Deals with divine and human contributions to revelation.

Gershom Scholem, "Reflections on Jewish Theology," *On Jews and Judaism in Crisis* (New York, 1976), pp. 261–97. Important thinking.

———. *On the Kabbalah and Its Symbolism* (New York, 1965), pp. 5–86. Torah and authority in Jewish mysticism.

Arnold J. Wolf, ed., *Rediscovering Judaism* (Chicago, 1965). The essays by Emil Fackenheim and Jacob J. Petuchowski are particularly relevant to the various Jewish concepts of revelation.

MODELS

Ian G. Barbour, *Myths, Models and Paradigms* (New York, 1974).

BIBLICAL STORM-GOD IMAGE

Leonard Greenspoon, "The Warrior God, or God, the Divine Warrior," in Peter H. Merkl and I. Smart, Ed., *Religion and Politics in the Modern World* (New York, 1983), pp. 205–31.

ORAL TRANSMISSION OF BIBLICAL TRADITION

William F. Albright, *From the Stone Age to Christianity*, 2nd ed. (New York, 1957), pp. 64–76.

Robert Alter, *The Art of Biblical Narrative* (New York, 1981), especially pp. 47–62.

Robert C. Culley, "Oral Tradition and Historicity," in John W. Wevers and D. B. Redford, Ed., *Studies on the Ancient Palestinian World* (Toronto, 1972), pp. 102–16.

MIDRASH AND THE DEVELOPMENT OF HALAKHAH

Louis Ginzberg, *On Jewish Law and Lore* (New York, 1955), pp. 77–184. On the historical origins of Jewish tradition.

Judas Goldin, "From Text to Interpretation and from Experience to the Interpreted Text," *Prooftexts* 3 (1983), pp. 131–55. A scholarly yet introductory essay on Midrash.

Robert Gordis, "A Dynamic Halakhah: Principles and Procedures," *Judaism* 28 (1979), pp. 263–82. One of this important Conservative rabbi's formulations.

R. Traverse Herford, *The Pharisees* (Boston, 1962). especially pp. 53–87. The Rabbis' method and thinking.

Isaac Klein, *A Guide to Jewish Religious Practice* (New York, 1979). A code of Conservative Jewish law.

James L. Kugel, "Two Introductions to Midrash," *Prooftexts* 3 (1983), pp. 131–55. From the Bible to Rabbinic literature.

Ruth Link-Salinger, ed., *Jewish Law in Our Time* (Denver, 1982). Includes essays on Bible, Rabbinic law, and contemporary halakhah.

Jacob Neusner, *Midrash in Context* (Philadelphia, 1983). The historical origins of Midrash.

Fritz A. Rothschild, "Truth and Metaphor in the Bible: An Essay on Interpretation," in Ruth Zielenziger, *Genesis: A New Teacher's*

Guide, 3rd ed. (New York, 1991), pp. 335–56. Fine survey of the development of Jewish Bible interpretation.

Howard Schwartz, "Reimagining the Bible," *Response* no. 44 (Spring 1983), pp. 35–46. Popular, but a good place to begin.

Seymour Siegel, ed., *Conservative Judaism and Jewish Law* (New York, 1977). On the development of Conservative Jewish halakhah.

Philip Sigal, *New Dimensions in Judaism: Creative Analysis of Rabbinic Concepts* (Hicksville, N.Y., 1972). A liberal Conservative Jewish perspective.

Geza Vermes, "Bible and Midrash: Early Old Testament Exegesis," in Peter R. Ackroyd and C. F. Evans, ed., *The Cambridge History of the Bible*, vol. 1 (Cambridge, 1970), pp. 199–231. Fine scholarly analysis of early midrash.

Mordecai Waxman, ed., *Tradition and Change* (New York, 1958). On the development of Conservative Jewish halakhah.

❐ ACKNOWLEDGMENT

Many people have shared their reactions to an earlier draft of this essay over a period of about six years. I express special thanks to Dr. Elaine Morris, who commissioned the essay for the Melton Research Center, and for their guidance to Profs. Ruth Zielenziger, Fritz Rothschild, Joseph Schwab, and David W. Silverman.

www.ingramcontent.com/pod-product-compliance
Ingram Content Group UK Ltd.
Pitfield, Milton Keynes, MK11 3LW, UK
UKHW021314180426
11947UKWH00015B/1227